C-4551   CAREER EXAMINATION SERIES

This is your
PASSBOOK for...

Associate Housing Development Specialist

Test Preparation Study Guide
Questions & Answers

COPYRIGHT NOTICE

This book is SOLELY intended for, is sold ONLY to, and its use is RESTRICTED to individual, bona fide applicants or candidates who qualify by virtue of having seriously filed applications for appropriate license, certificate, professional and/or promotional advancement, higher school matriculation, scholarship, or other legitimate requirements of education and/or governmental authorities.

This book is NOT intended for use, class instruction, tutoring, training, duplication, copying, reprinting, excerption, or adaptation, etc., by:

1) Other publishers
2) Proprietors and/or Instructors of "Coaching" and/or Preparatory Courses
3) Personnel and/or Training Divisions of commercial, industrial, and governmental organizations
4) Schools, colleges, or universities and/or their departments and staffs, including teachers and other personnel
5) Testing Agencies or Bureaus
6) Study groups which seek by the purchase of a single volume to copy and/or duplicate and/or adapt this material for use by the group as a whole without having purchased individual volumes for each of the members of the group
7) Et al.

Such persons would be in violation of appropriate Federal and State statutes.

PROVISION OF LICENSING AGREEMENTS – Recognized educational, commercial, industrial, and governmental institutions and organizations, and others legitimately engaged in educational pursuits, including training, testing, and measurement activities, may address request for a licensing agreement to the copyright owners, who will determine whether, and under what conditions, including fees and charges, the materials in this book may be used them. In other words, a licensing facility exists for the legitimate use of the material in this book on other than an individual basis. However, it is asseverated and affirmed here that the material in this book CANNOT be used without the receipt of the express permission of such a licensing agreement from the Publishers. Inquiries re licensing should be addressed to the company, attention rights and permissions department.

All rights reserved, including the right of reproduction in whole or in part, in any form or by any means, electronic or mechanical, including photocopying, recording, or by any information storage and retrieval system, without permission in writing from the Publisher.

Copyright © 2024 by
National Learning Corporation

212 Michael Drive, Syosset, NY 11791
(516) 921-8888 • www.passbooks.com
E-mail: info@passbooks.com

PUBLISHED IN THE UNITED STATES OF AMERICA

PASSBOOK® SERIES

THE *PASSBOOK® SERIES* has been created to prepare applicants and candidates for the ultimate academic battlefield – the examination room.

At some time in our lives, each and every one of us may be required to take an examination – for validation, matriculation, admission, qualification, registration, certification, or licensure.

Based on the assumption that every applicant or candidate has met the basic formal educational standards, has taken the required number of courses, and read the necessary texts, the *PASSBOOK® SERIES* furnishes the one special preparation which may assure passing with confidence, instead of failing with insecurity. Examination questions – together with answers – are furnished as the basic vehicle for study so that the mysteries of the examination and its compounding difficulties may be eliminated or diminished by a sure method.

This book is meant to help you pass your examination provided that you qualify and are serious in your objective.

The entire field is reviewed through the huge store of content information which is succinctly presented through a provocative and challenging approach – the question-and-answer method.

A climate of success is established by furnishing the correct answers at the end of each test.

You soon learn to recognize types of questions, forms of questions, and patterns of questioning. You may even begin to anticipate expected outcomes.

You perceive that many questions are repeated or adapted so that you can gain acute insights, which may enable you to score many sure points.

You learn how to confront new questions, or types of questions, and to attack them confidently and work out the correct answers.

You note objectives and emphases, and recognize pitfalls and dangers, so that you may make positive educational adjustments.

Moreover, you are kept fully informed in relation to new concepts, methods, practices, and directions in the field.

You discover that you are actually taking the examination all the time: you are preparing for the examination by "taking" an examination, not by reading extraneous and/or supererogatory textbooks.

In short, this PASSBOOK®, used directedly, should be an important factor in helping you to pass your test.

ASSOCIATE HOUSING DEVELOPMENT SPECIALIST

DUTIES

Under direction, Associate Housing Development Specialists perform very complex and responsible analytical or coordination work related to the development, and/or implementation of housing programs designed to preserve and upgrade neighborhoods, or to improve urban renewal areas or public and private housing; may supervise subordinate staff. May perform the duties of subordinate personnel; may perform the duties of the supervisor in his/her absence. All Associate Housing Development Specialists perform related work.

Some of the physical activities which may be performed by Associate Housing Development Specialists and environmental conditions experienced include walking to, from and within buildings and neighborhoods; visiting neighborhoods with a high incidence of crime and buildings having hazardous conditions; climbing and descending stairs; and working outdoors in all kinds of weather.

HOW TO TAKE A TEST

I. YOU MUST PASS AN EXAMINATION

A. WHAT EVERY CANDIDATE SHOULD KNOW

Examination applicants often ask us for help in preparing for the written test. What can I study in advance? What kinds of questions will be asked? How will the test be given? How will the papers be graded?

As an applicant for a civil service examination, you may be wondering about some of these things. Our purpose here is to suggest effective methods of advance study and to describe civil service examinations.

Your chances for success on this examination can be increased if you know how to prepare. Those "pre-examination jitters" can be reduced if you know what to expect. You can even experience an adventure in good citizenship if you know why civil service exams are given.

B. WHY ARE CIVIL SERVICE EXAMINATIONS GIVEN?

Civil service examinations are important to you in two ways. As a citizen, you want public jobs filled by employees who know how to do their work. As a job seeker, you want a fair chance to compete for that job on an equal footing with other candidates. The best-known means of accomplishing this two-fold goal is the competitive examination.

Exams are widely publicized throughout the nation. They may be administered for jobs in federal, state, city, municipal, town or village governments or agencies.

Any citizen may apply, with some limitations, such as the age or residence of applicants. Your experience and education may be reviewed to see whether you meet the requirements for the particular examination. When these requirements exist, they are reasonable and applied consistently to all applicants. Thus, a competitive examination may cause you some uneasiness now, but it is your privilege and safeguard.

C. HOW ARE CIVIL SERVICE EXAMS DEVELOPED?

Examinations are carefully written by trained technicians who are specialists in the field known as "psychological measurement," in consultation with recognized authorities in the field of work that the test will cover. These experts recommend the subject matter areas or skills to be tested; only those knowledges or skills important to your success on the job are included. The most reliable books and source materials available are used as references. Together, the experts and technicians judge the difficulty level of the questions.

Test technicians know how to phrase questions so that the problem is clearly stated. Their ethics do not permit "trick" or "catch" questions. Questions may have been tried out on sample groups, or subjected to statistical analysis, to determine their usefulness.

Written tests are often used in combination with performance tests, ratings of training and experience, and oral interviews. All of these measures combine to form the best-known means of finding the right person for the right job.

II. HOW TO PASS THE WRITTEN TEST

A. NATURE OF THE EXAMINATION

To prepare intelligently for civil service examinations, you should know how they differ from school examinations you have taken. In school you were assigned certain definite pages to read or subjects to cover. The examination questions were quite detailed and usually emphasized memory. Civil service exams, on the other hand, try to discover your present ability to perform the duties of a position, plus your potentiality to learn these duties. In other words, a civil service exam attempts to predict how successful you will be. Questions cover such a broad area that they cannot be as minute and detailed as school exam questions.

In the public service similar kinds of work, or positions, are grouped together in one "class." This process is known as *position-classification*. All the positions in a class are paid according to the salary range for that class. One class title covers all of these positions, and they are all tested by the same examination.

B. FOUR BASIC STEPS

1) Study the announcement

How, then, can you know what subjects to study? Our best answer is: "Learn as much as possible about the class of positions for which you've applied." The exam will test the knowledge, skills and abilities needed to do the work.

Your most valuable source of information about the position you want is the official exam announcement. This announcement lists the training and experience qualifications. Check these standards and apply only if you come reasonably close to meeting them.

The brief description of the position in the examination announcement offers some clues to the subjects which will be tested. Think about the job itself. Review the duties in your mind. Can you perform them, or are there some in which you are rusty? Fill in the blank spots in your preparation.

Many jurisdictions preview the written test in the exam announcement by including a section called "Knowledge and Abilities Required," "Scope of the Examination," or some similar heading. Here you will find out specifically what fields will be tested.

2) Review your own background

Once you learn in general what the position is all about, and what you need to know to do the work, ask yourself which subjects you already know fairly well and which need improvement. You may wonder whether to concentrate on improving your strong areas or on building some background in your fields of weakness. When the announcement has specified "some knowledge" or "considerable knowledge," or has used adjectives like "beginning principles of…" or "advanced … methods," you can get a clue as to the number and difficulty of questions to be asked in any given field. More questions, and hence broader coverage, would be included for those subjects which are more important in the work. Now weigh your strengths and weaknesses against the job requirements and prepare accordingly.

3) Determine the level of the position

Another way to tell how intensively you should prepare is to understand the level of the job for which you are applying. Is it the entering level? In other words, is this the position in which beginners in a field of work are hired? Or is it an intermediate or advanced level? Sometimes this is indicated by such words as "Junior" or "Senior" in the class title. Other jurisdictions use Roman numerals to designate the level – Clerk I, Clerk II, for example. The word "Supervisor" sometimes appears in the title. If the level is not indicated by the title, check the description of duties. Will you be working under very close supervision, or will you have responsibility for independent decisions in this work?

4) Choose appropriate study materials

Now that you know the subjects to be examined and the relative amount of each subject to be covered, you can choose suitable study materials. For beginning level jobs, or even advanced ones, if you have a pronounced weakness in some aspect of your training, read a modern, standard textbook in that field. Be sure it is up to date and has general coverage. Such books are normally available at your library, and the librarian will be glad to help you locate one. For entry-level positions, questions of appropriate difficulty are chosen – neither highly advanced questions, nor those too simple. Such questions require careful thought but not advanced training.

If the position for which you are applying is technical or advanced, you will read more advanced, specialized material. If you are already familiar with the basic principles of your field, elementary textbooks would waste your time. Concentrate on advanced textbooks and technical periodicals. Think through the concepts and review difficult problems in your field.

These are all general sources. You can get more ideas on your own initiative, following these leads. For example, training manuals and publications of the government agency which employs workers in your field can be useful, particularly for technical and professional positions. A letter or visit to the government department involved may result in more specific study suggestions, and certainly will provide you with a more definite idea of the exact nature of the position you are seeking.

III. KINDS OF TESTS

Tests are used for purposes other than measuring knowledge and ability to perform specified duties. For some positions, it is equally important to test ability to make adjustments to new situations or to profit from training. In others, basic mental abilities not dependent on information are essential. Questions which test these things may not appear as pertinent to the duties of the position as those which test for knowledge and information. Yet they are often highly important parts of a fair examination. For very general questions, it is almost impossible to help you direct your study efforts. What we can do is to point out some of the more common of these general abilities needed in public service positions and describe some typical questions.

1) General information

Broad, general information has been found useful for predicting job success in some kinds of work. This is tested in a variety of ways, from vocabulary lists to questions about current events. Basic background in some field of work, such as sociology or economics, may be sampled in a group of questions. Often these are principles which have become familiar to most persons through exposure rather than through formal training. It is difficult to advise you how to study for these questions; being alert to the world around you is our best suggestion.

2) Verbal ability

An example of an ability needed in many positions is verbal or language ability. Verbal ability is, in brief, the ability to use and understand words. Vocabulary and grammar tests are typical measures of this ability. Reading comprehension or paragraph interpretation questions are common in many kinds of civil service tests. You are given a paragraph of written material and asked to find its central meaning.

3) Numerical ability

Number skills can be tested by the familiar arithmetic problem, by checking paired lists of numbers to see which are alike and which are different, or by interpreting charts and graphs. In the latter test, a graph may be printed in the test booklet which you are asked to use as the basis for answering questions.

4) Observation

A popular test for law-enforcement positions is the observation test. A picture is shown to you for several minutes, then taken away. Questions about the picture test your ability to observe both details and larger elements.

5) Following directions

In many positions in the public service, the employee must be able to carry out written instructions dependably and accurately. You may be given a chart with several columns, each column listing a variety of information. The questions require you to carry out directions involving the information given in the chart.

6) Skills and aptitudes

Performance tests effectively measure some manual skills and aptitudes. When the skill is one in which you are trained, such as typing or shorthand, you can practice. These tests are often very much like those given in business school or high school courses. For many of the other skills and aptitudes, however, no short-time preparation can be made. Skills and abilities natural to you or that you have developed throughout your lifetime are being tested.

Many of the general questions just described provide all the data needed to answer the questions and ask you to use your reasoning ability to find the answers. Your best preparation for these tests, as well as for tests of facts and ideas, is to be at your physical and mental best. You, no doubt, have your own methods of getting into an exam-taking mood and keeping "in shape." The next section lists some ideas on this subject.

IV. KINDS OF QUESTIONS

Only rarely is the "essay" question, which you answer in narrative form, used in civil service tests. Civil service tests are usually of the short-answer type. Full instructions for answering these questions will be given to you at the examination. But in case this is your first experience with short-answer questions and separate answer sheets, here is what you need to know:

1) Multiple-choice Questions

Most popular of the short-answer questions is the "multiple choice" or "best answer" question. It can be used, for example, to test for factual knowledge, ability to solve problems or judgment in meeting situations found at work.

A multiple-choice question is normally one of three types—
- It can begin with an incomplete statement followed by several possible endings. You are to find the one ending which *best* completes the statement, although some of the others may not be entirely wrong.
- It can also be a complete statement in the form of a question which is answered by choosing one of the statements listed.

- It can be in the form of a problem – again you select the best answer.

Here is an example of a multiple-choice question with a discussion which should give you some clues as to the method for choosing the right answer:

When an employee has a complaint about his assignment, the action which will *best* help him overcome his difficulty is to
- A. discuss his difficulty with his coworkers
- B. take the problem to the head of the organization
- C. take the problem to the person who gave him the assignment
- D. say nothing to anyone about his complaint

In answering this question, you should study each of the choices to find which is best. Consider choice "A" – Certainly an employee may discuss his complaint with fellow employees, but no change or improvement can result, and the complaint remains unresolved. Choice "B" is a poor choice since the head of the organization probably does not know what assignment you have been given, and taking your problem to him is known as "going over the head" of the supervisor. The supervisor, or person who made the assignment, is the person who can clarify it or correct any injustice. Choice "C" is, therefore, correct. To say nothing, as in choice "D," is unwise. Supervisors have and interest in knowing the problems employees are facing, and the employee is seeking a solution to his problem.

2) True/False Questions

The "true/false" or "right/wrong" form of question is sometimes used. Here a complete statement is given. Your job is to decide whether the statement is right or wrong.

SAMPLE: A roaming cell-phone call to a nearby city costs less than a non-roaming call to a distant city.

This statement is wrong, or false, since roaming calls are more expensive.

This is not a complete list of all possible question forms, although most of the others are variations of these common types. You will always get complete directions for answering questions. Be sure you understand *how* to mark your answers – ask questions until you do.

V. RECORDING YOUR ANSWERS

Computer terminals are used more and more today for many different kinds of exams.
For an examination with very few applicants, you may be told to record your answers in the test booklet itself. Separate answer sheets are much more common. If this separate answer sheet is to be scored by machine – and this is often the case – it is highly important that you mark your answers correctly in order to get credit.

An electronic scoring machine is often used in civil service offices because of the speed with which papers can be scored. Machine-scored answer sheets must be marked with a pencil, which will be given to you. This pencil has a high graphite content which responds to the electronic scoring machine. As a matter of fact, stray dots may register as answers, so do not let your pencil rest on the answer sheet while you are pondering the correct answer. Also, if your pencil lead breaks or is otherwise defective, ask for another.

Since the answer sheet will be dropped in a slot in the scoring machine, be careful not to bend the corners or get the paper crumpled.

The answer sheet normally has five vertical columns of numbers, with 30 numbers to a column. These numbers correspond to the question numbers in your test booklet. After each number, going across the page are four or five pairs of dotted lines. These short dotted lines have small letters or numbers above them. The first two pairs may also have a "T" or "F" above the letters. This indicates that the first two pairs only are to be used if the questions are of the true-false type. If the questions are multiple choice, disregard the "T" and "F" and pay attention only to the small letters or numbers.

Answer your questions in the manner of the sample that follows:

32. The largest city in the United States is
   A. Washington, D.C.
   B. New York City
   C. Chicago
   D. Detroit
   E. San Francisco

1) Choose the answer you think is best. (New York City is the largest, so "B" is correct.)
2) Find the row of dotted lines numbered the same as the question you are answering. (Find row number 32)
3) Find the pair of dotted lines corresponding to the answer. (Find the pair of lines under the mark "B.")
4) Make a solid black mark between the dotted lines.

VI. BEFORE THE TEST

Common sense will help you find procedures to follow to get ready for an examination. Too many of us, however, overlook these sensible measures. Indeed, nervousness and fatigue have been found to be the most serious reasons why applicants fail to do their best on civil service tests. Here is a list of reminders:

- Begin your preparation early – Don't wait until the last minute to go scurrying around for books and materials or to find out what the position is all about.
- Prepare continuously – An hour a night for a week is better than an all-night cram session. This has been definitely established. What is more, a night a week for a month will return better dividends than crowding your study into a shorter period of time.
- Locate the place of the exam – You have been sent a notice telling you when and where to report for the examination. If the location is in a different town or otherwise unfamiliar to you, it would be well to inquire the best route and learn something about the building.
- Relax the night before the test – Allow your mind to rest. Do not study at all that night. Plan some mild recreation or diversion; then go to bed early and get a good night's sleep.
- Get up early enough to make a leisurely trip to the place for the test – This way unforeseen events, traffic snarls, unfamiliar buildings, etc. will not upset you.
- Dress comfortably – A written test is not a fashion show. You will be known by number and not by name, so wear something comfortable.

- Leave excess paraphernalia at home – Shopping bags and odd bundles will get in your way. You need bring only the items mentioned in the official notice you received; usually everything you need is provided. Do not bring reference books to the exam. They will only confuse those last minutes and be taken away from you when in the test room.
- Arrive somewhat ahead of time – If because of transportation schedules you must get there very early, bring a newspaper or magazine to take your mind off yourself while waiting.
- Locate the examination room – When you have found the proper room, you will be directed to the seat or part of the room where you will sit. Sometimes you are given a sheet of instructions to read while you are waiting. Do not fill out any forms until you are told to do so; just read them and be prepared.
- Relax and prepare to listen to the instructions
- If you have any physical problem that may keep you from doing your best, be sure to tell the test administrator. If you are sick or in poor health, you really cannot do your best on the exam. You can come back and take the test some other time.

VII. AT THE TEST

The day of the test is here and you have the test booklet in your hand. The temptation to get going is very strong. Caution! There is more to success than knowing the right answers. You must know how to identify your papers and understand variations in the type of short-answer question used in this particular examination. Follow these suggestions for maximum results from your efforts:

1) Cooperate with the monitor
The test administrator has a duty to create a situation in which you can be as much at ease as possible. He will give instructions, tell you when to begin, check to see that you are marking your answer sheet correctly, and so on. He is not there to guard you, although he will see that your competitors do not take unfair advantage. He wants to help you do your best.

2) Listen to all instructions
Don't jump the gun! Wait until you understand all directions. In most civil service tests you get more time than you need to answer the questions. So don't be in a hurry. Read each word of instructions until you clearly understand the meaning. Study the examples, listen to all announcements and follow directions. Ask questions if you do not understand what to do.

3) Identify your papers
Civil service exams are usually identified by number only. You will be assigned a number; you must not put your name on your test papers. Be sure to copy your number correctly. Since more than one exam may be given, copy your exact examination title.

4) Plan your time
Unless you are told that a test is a "speed" or "rate of work" test, speed itself is usually not important. Time enough to answer all the questions will be provided, but this does not mean that you have all day. An overall time limit has been set. Divide the total time (in minutes) by the number of questions to determine the approximate time you have for each question.

5) Do not linger over difficult questions

If you come across a difficult question, mark it with a paper clip (useful to have along) and come back to it when you have been through the booklet. One caution if you do this – be sure to skip a number on your answer sheet as well. Check often to be sure that you have not lost your place and that you are marking in the row numbered the same as the question you are answering.

6) Read the questions

Be sure you know what the question asks! Many capable people are unsuccessful because they failed to *read* the questions correctly.

7) Answer all questions

Unless you have been instructed that a penalty will be deducted for incorrect answers, it is better to guess than to omit a question.

8) Speed tests

It is often better NOT to guess on speed tests. It has been found that on timed tests people are tempted to spend the last few seconds before time is called in marking answers at random – without even reading them – in the hope of picking up a few extra points. To discourage this practice, the instructions may warn you that your score will be "corrected" for guessing. That is, a penalty will be applied. The incorrect answers will be deducted from the correct ones, or some other penalty formula will be used.

9) Review your answers

If you finish before time is called, go back to the questions you guessed or omitted to give them further thought. Review other answers if you have time.

10) Return your test materials

If you are ready to leave before others have finished or time is called, take ALL your materials to the monitor and leave quietly. Never take any test material with you. The monitor can discover whose papers are not complete, and taking a test booklet may be grounds for disqualification.

VIII. EXAMINATION TECHNIQUES

1) Read the general instructions carefully. These are usually printed on the first page of the exam booklet. As a rule, these instructions refer to the timing of the examination; the fact that you should not start work until the signal and must stop work at a signal, etc. If there are any *special* instructions, such as a choice of questions to be answered, make sure that you note this instruction carefully.

2) When you are ready to start work on the examination, that is as soon as the signal has been given, read the instructions to each question booklet, underline any key words or phrases, such as *least, best, outline, describe* and the like. In this way you will tend to answer as requested rather than discover on reviewing your paper that you *listed without describing*, that you selected the *worst* choice rather than the *best* choice, etc.

3) If the examination is of the objective or multiple-choice type – that is, each question will also give a series of possible answers: A, B, C or D, and you are called upon to select the best answer and write the letter next to that answer on your answer paper – it is advisable to start answering each question in turn. There may be anywhere from 50 to 100 such questions in the three or four hours allotted and you can see how much time would be taken if you read through all the questions before beginning to answer any. Furthermore, if you come across a question or group of questions which you know would be difficult to answer, it would undoubtedly affect your handling of all the other questions.

4) If the examination is of the essay type and contains but a few questions, it is a moot point as to whether you should read all the questions before starting to answer any one. Of course, if you are given a choice – say five out of seven and the like – then it is essential to read all the questions so you can eliminate the two that are most difficult. If, however, you are asked to answer all the questions, there may be danger in trying to answer the easiest one first because you may find that you will spend too much time on it. The best technique is to answer the first question, then proceed to the second, etc.

5) Time your answers. Before the exam begins, write down the time it started, then add the time allowed for the examination and write down the time it must be completed, then divide the time available somewhat as follows:
    - If 3-1/2 hours are allowed, that would be 210 minutes. If you have 80 objective-type questions, that would be an average of 2-1/2 minutes per question. Allow yourself no more than 2 minutes per question, or a total of 160 minutes, which will permit about 50 minutes to review.
    - If for the time allotment of 210 minutes there are 7 essay questions to answer, that would average about 30 minutes a question. Give yourself only 25 minutes per question so that you have about 35 minutes to review.

6) The most important instruction is to *read each question* and make sure you know what is wanted. The second most important instruction is to *time yourself properly* so that you answer every question. The third most important instruction is to *answer every question*. Guess if you have to but include something for each question. Remember that you will receive no credit for a blank and will probably receive some credit if you write something in answer to an essay question. If you guess a letter – say "B" for a multiple-choice question – you may have guessed right. If you leave a blank as an answer to a multiple-choice question, the examiners may respect your feelings but it will not add a point to your score. Some exams may penalize you for wrong answers, so in such cases *only*, you may not want to guess unless you have some basis for your answer.

7) Suggestions
    a. Objective-type questions
        1. Examine the question booklet for proper sequence of pages and questions
        2. Read all instructions carefully
        3. Skip any question which seems too difficult; return to it after all other questions have been answered
        4. Apportion your time properly; do not spend too much time on any single question or group of questions

5. Note and underline key words – *all, most, fewest, least, best, worst, same, opposite,* etc.
6. Pay particular attention to negatives
7. Note unusual option, e.g., unduly long, short, complex, different or similar in content to the body of the question
8. Observe the use of "hedging" words – *probably, may, most likely,* etc.
9. Make sure that your answer is put next to the same number as the question
10. Do not second-guess unless you have good reason to believe the second answer is definitely more correct
11. Cross out original answer if you decide another answer is more accurate; do not erase until you are ready to hand your paper in
12. Answer all questions; guess unless instructed otherwise
13. Leave time for review

b. Essay questions
   1. Read each question carefully
   2. Determine exactly what is wanted. Underline key words or phrases.
   3. Decide on outline or paragraph answer
   4. Include many different points and elements unless asked to develop any one or two points or elements
   5. Show impartiality by giving pros and cons unless directed to select one side only
   6. Make and write down any assumptions you find necessary to answer the questions
   7. Watch your English, grammar, punctuation and choice of words
   8. Time your answers; don't crowd material

8) Answering the essay question

Most essay questions can be answered by framing the specific response around several key words or ideas. Here are a few such key words or ideas:

M's: manpower, materials, methods, money, management
P's: purpose, program, policy, plan, procedure, practice, problems, pitfalls, personnel, public relations

   a. Six basic steps in handling problems:
      1. Preliminary plan and background development
      2. Collect information, data and facts
      3. Analyze and interpret information, data and facts
      4. Analyze and develop solutions as well as make recommendations
      5. Prepare report and sell recommendations
      6. Install recommendations and follow up effectiveness

   b. Pitfalls to avoid
      1. *Taking things for granted* – A statement of the situation does not necessarily imply that each of the elements is necessarily true; for example, a complaint may be invalid and biased so that all that can be taken for granted is that a complaint has been registered

2. *Considering only one side of a situation* – Wherever possible, indicate several alternatives and then point out the reasons you selected the best one
3. *Failing to indicate follow up* – Whenever your answer indicates action on your part, make certain that you will take proper follow-up action to see how successful your recommendations, procedures or actions turn out to be
4. *Taking too long in answering any single question* – Remember to time your answers properly

IX. AFTER THE TEST

Scoring procedures differ in detail among civil service jurisdictions although the general principles are the same. Whether the papers are hand-scored or graded by machine we have described, they are nearly always graded by number. That is, the person who marks the paper knows only the number – never the name – of the applicant. Not until all the papers have been graded will they be matched with names. If other tests, such as training and experience or oral interview ratings have been given, scores will be combined. Different parts of the examination usually have different weights. For example, the written test might count 60 percent of the final grade, and a rating of training and experience 40 percent. In many jurisdictions, veterans will have a certain number of points added to their grades.

After the final grade has been determined, the names are placed in grade order and an eligible list is established. There are various methods for resolving ties between those who get the same final grade – probably the most common is to place first the name of the person whose application was received first. Job offers are made from the eligible list in the order the names appear on it. You will be notified of your grade and your rank as soon as all these computations have been made. This will be done as rapidly as possible.

People who are found to meet the requirements in the announcement are called "eligibles." Their names are put on a list of eligible candidates. An eligible's chances of getting a job depend on how high he stands on this list and how fast agencies are filling jobs from the list.

When a job is to be filled from a list of eligibles, the agency asks for the names of people on the list of eligibles for that job. When the civil service commission receives this request, it sends to the agency the names of the three people highest on this list. Or, if the job to be filled has specialized requirements, the office sends the agency the names of the top three persons who meet these requirements from the general list.

The appointing officer makes a choice from among the three people whose names were sent to him. If the selected person accepts the appointment, the names of the others are put back on the list to be considered for future openings.

That is the rule in hiring from all kinds of eligible lists, whether they are for typist, carpenter, chemist, or something else. For every vacancy, the appointing officer has his choice of any one of the top three eligibles on the list. This explains why the person whose name is on top of the list sometimes does not get an appointment when some of the persons lower on the list do. If the appointing officer chooses the second or third eligible, the No. 1 eligible does not get a job at once, but stays on the list until he is appointed or the list is terminated.

X. HOW TO PASS THE INTERVIEW TEST

The examination for which you applied requires an oral interview test. You have already taken the written test and you are now being called for the interview test – the final part of the formal examination.

You may think that it is not possible to prepare for an interview test and that there are no procedures to follow during an interview. Our purpose is to point out some things you can do in advance that will help you and some good rules to follow and pitfalls to avoid while you are being interviewed.

What is an interview supposed to test?

The written examination is designed to test the technical knowledge and competence of the candidate; the oral is designed to evaluate intangible qualities, not readily measured otherwise, and to establish a list showing the relative fitness of each candidate – as measured against his competitors – for the position sought. Scoring is not on the basis of "right" and "wrong," but on a sliding scale of values ranging from "not passable" to "outstanding." As a matter of fact, it is possible to achieve a relatively low score without a single "incorrect" answer because of evident weakness in the qualities being measured.

Occasionally, an examination may consist entirely of an oral test – either an individual or a group oral. In such cases, information is sought concerning the technical knowledges and abilities of the candidate, since there has been no written examination for this purpose. More commonly, however, an oral test is used to supplement a written examination.

Who conducts interviews?

The composition of oral boards varies among different jurisdictions. In nearly all, a representative of the personnel department serves as chairman. One of the members of the board may be a representative of the department in which the candidate would work. In some cases, "outside experts" are used, and, frequently, a businessman or some other representative of the general public is asked to serve. Labor and management or other special groups may be represented. The aim is to secure the services of experts in the appropriate field.

However the board is composed, it is a good idea (and not at all improper or unethical) to ascertain in advance of the interview who the members are and what groups they represent. When you are introduced to them, you will have some idea of their backgrounds and interests, and at least you will not stutter and stammer over their names.

What should be done before the interview?

While knowledge about the board members is useful and takes some of the surprise element out of the interview, there is other preparation which is more substantive. It *is* possible to prepare for an oral interview – in several ways:

1) Keep a copy of your application and review it carefully before the interview

This may be the only document before the oral board, and the starting point of the interview. Know what education and experience you have listed there, and the sequence and dates of all of it. Sometimes the board will ask you to review the highlights of your experience for them; you should not have to hem and haw doing it.

2) Study the class specification and the examination announcement

Usually, the oral board has one or both of these to guide them. The qualities, characteristics or knowledges required by the position sought are stated in these documents. They offer valuable clues as to the nature of the oral interview. For example, if the job involves supervisory responsibilities, the announcement will usually indicate that knowledge of modern supervisory methods and the qualifications of the candidate as a supervisor will be tested. If so, you can expect such questions, frequently in the form of a hypothetical situation which you are expected to solve. NEVER go into an oral without knowledge of the duties and responsibilities of the job you seek.

3) Think through each qualification required

Try to visualize the kind of questions you would ask if you were a board member. How well could you answer them? Try especially to appraise your own knowledge and background in each area, *measured against the job sought*, and identify any areas in which you are weak. Be critical and realistic – do not flatter yourself.

4) Do some general reading in areas in which you feel you may be weak

For example, if the job involves supervision and your past experience has NOT, some general reading in supervisory methods and practices, particularly in the field of human relations, might be useful. Do NOT study agency procedures or detailed manuals. The oral board will be testing your understanding and capacity, not your memory.

5) Get a good night's sleep and watch your general health and mental attitude

You will want a clear head at the interview. Take care of a cold or any other minor ailment, and of course, no hangovers.

What should be done on the day of the interview?

Now comes the day of the interview itself. Give yourself plenty of time to get there. Plan to arrive somewhat ahead of the scheduled time, particularly if your appointment is in the fore part of the day. If a previous candidate fails to appear, the board might be ready for you a bit early. By early afternoon an oral board is almost invariably behind schedule if there are many candidates, and you may have to wait. Take along a book or magazine to read, or your application to review, but leave any extraneous material in the waiting room when you go in for your interview. In any event, relax and compose yourself.

The matter of dress is important. The board is forming impressions about you – from your experience, your mannors, your attitude, and your appearance. Give your personal appearance careful attention. Dress your best, but not your flashiest. Choose conservative, appropriate clothing, and be sure it is immaculate. This is a business interview, and your appearance should indicate that you regard it as such. Besides, being well groomed and properly dressed will help boost your confidence.

Sooner or later, someone will call your name and escort you into the interview room. *This is it.* From here on you are on your own. It is too late for any more preparation. But remember, you asked for this opportunity to prove your fitness, and you are here because your request was granted.

What happens when you go in?

The usual sequence of events will be as follows: The clerk (who is often the board stenographer) will introduce you to the chairman of the oral board, who will introduce you to the other members of the board. Acknowledge the introductions before you sit down. Do not be surprised if you find a microphone facing you or a stenotypist sitting by. Oral interviews are usually recorded in the event of an appeal or other review.

Usually the chairman of the board will open the interview by reviewing the highlights of your education and work experience from your application – primarily for the benefit of the other members of the board, as well as to get the material into the record. Do not interrupt or comment unless there is an error or significant misinterpretation; if that is the case, do not hesitate. But do not quibble about insignificant matters. Also, he will usually ask you some question about your education, experience or your present job – partly to get you to start talking and to establish the interviewing "rapport." He may start the actual questioning, or turn it over to one of the other members. Frequently, each member undertakes the questioning on a particular area, one in which he is perhaps most competent, so you can expect each member to participate in the examination. Because time is limited, you may also expect some rather abrupt switches in the direction the questioning takes, so do not be upset by it. Normally, a board member will not pursue a single line of questioning unless he discovers a particular strength or weakness.

After each member has participated, the chairman will usually ask whether any member has any further questions, then will ask you if you have anything you wish to add. Unless you are expecting this question, it may floor you. Worse, it may start you off on an extended, extemporaneous speech. The board is not usually seeking more information. The question is principally to offer you a last opportunity to present further qualifications or to indicate that you have nothing to add. So, if you feel that a significant qualification or characteristic has been overlooked, it is proper to point it out in a sentence or so. Do not compliment the board on the thoroughness of their examination – they have been sketchy, and you know it. If you wish, merely say, "No thank you, I have nothing further to add." This is a point where you can "talk yourself out" of a good impression or fail to present an important bit of information. Remember, *you close the interview yourself.*

The chairman will then say, "That is all, Mr. _____, thank you." Do not be startled; the interview is over, and quicker than you think. Thank him, gather your belongings and take your leave. Save your sigh of relief for the other side of the door.

How to put your best foot forward
Throughout this entire process, you may feel that the board individually and collectively is trying to pierce your defenses, seek out your hidden weaknesses and embarrass and confuse you. Actually, this is not true. They are obliged to make an appraisal of your qualifications for the job you are seeking, and they want to see you in your best light. Remember, they must interview all candidates and a non-cooperative candidate may become a failure in spite of their best efforts to bring out his qualifications. Here are 15 suggestions that will help you:

1) Be natural – Keep your attitude confident, not cocky

If you are not confident that you can do the job, do not expect the board to be. Do not apologize for your weaknesses, try to bring out your strong points. The board is interested in a positive, not negative, presentation. Cockiness will antagonize any board member and make him wonder if you are covering up a weakness by a false show of strength.

2) Get comfortable, but don't lounge or sprawl

Sit erectly but not stiffly. A careless posture may lead the board to conclude that you are careless in other things, or at least that you are not impressed by the importance of the occasion. Either conclusion is natural, even if incorrect. Do not fuss with your clothing, a pencil or an ashtray. Your hands may occasionally be useful to emphasize a point; do not let them become a point of distraction.

3) Do not wisecrack or make small talk

This is a serious situation, and your attitude should show that you consider it as such. Further, the time of the board is limited – they do not want to waste it, and neither should you.

4) Do not exaggerate your experience or abilities

In the first place, from information in the application or other interviews and sources, the board may know more about you than you think. Secondly, you probably will not get away with it. An experienced board is rather adept at spotting such a situation, so do not take the chance.

5) If you know a board member, do not make a point of it, yet do not hide it

Certainly you are not fooling him, and probably not the other members of the board. Do not try to take advantage of your acquaintanceship – it will probably do you little good.

6) Do not dominate the interview

Let the board do that. They will give you the clues – do not assume that you have to do all the talking. Realize that the board has a number of questions to ask you, and do not try to take up all the interview time by showing off your extensive knowledge of the answer to the first one.

7) Be attentive

You only have 20 minutes or so, and you should keep your attention at its sharpest throughout. When a member is addressing a problem or question to you, give him your undivided attention. Address your reply principally to him, but do not exclude the other board members.

8) Do not interrupt

A board member may be stating a problem for you to analyze. He will ask you a question when the time comes. Let him state the problem, and wait for the question.

9) Make sure you understand the question

Do not try to answer until you are sure what the question is. If it is not clear, restate it in your own words or ask the board member to clarify it for you. However, do not haggle about minor elements.

10) Reply promptly but not hastily

A common entry on oral board rating sheets is "candidate responded readily," or "candidate hesitated in replies." Respond as promptly and quickly as you can, but do not jump to a hasty, ill-considered answer.

11) Do not be peremptory in your answers

A brief answer is proper – but do not fire your answer back. That is a losing game from your point of view. The board member can probably ask questions much faster than you can answer them.

12) Do not try to create the answer you think the board member wants

He is interested in what kind of mind you have and how it works – not in playing games. Furthermore, he can usually spot this practice and will actually grade you down on it.

13) Do not switch sides in your reply merely to agree with a board member

Frequently, a member will take a contrary position merely to draw you out and to see if you are willing and able to defend your point of view. Do not start a debate, yet do not surrender a good position. If a position is worth taking, it is worth defending.

14) Do not be afraid to admit an error in judgment if you are shown to be wrong

The board knows that you are forced to reply without any opportunity for careful consideration. Your answer may be demonstrably wrong. If so, admit it and get on with the interview.

15) Do not dwell at length on your present job

The opening question may relate to your present assignment. Answer the question but do not go into an extended discussion. You are being examined for a *new* job, not your present one. As a matter of fact, try to phrase ALL your answers in terms of the job for which you are being examined.

Basis of Rating

Probably you will forget most of these "do's" and "don'ts" when you walk into the oral interview room. Even remembering them all will not ensure you a passing grade. Perhaps you did not have the qualifications in the first place. But remembering them will help you to put your best foot forward, without treading on the toes of the board members.

Rumor and popular opinion to the contrary notwithstanding, an oral board wants you to make the best appearance possible. They know you are under pressure – but they also want to see how you respond to it as a guide to what your reaction would be under the pressures of the job you seek. They will be influenced by the degree of poise you display, the personal traits you show and the manner in which you respond.

ABOUT THIS BOOK

This book contains tests divided into Examination Sections. Go through each test, answering every question in the margin. We have also attached a sample answer sheet at the back of the book that can be removed and used. At the end of each test look at the answer key and check your answers. On the ones you got wrong, look at the right answer choice and learn. Do not fill in the answers first. Do not memorize the questions and answers, but understand the answer and principles involved. On your test, the questions will likely be different from the samples. Questions are changed and new ones added. If you understand these past questions you should have success with any changes that arise. Tests may consist of several types of questions. We have additional books on each subject should more study be advisable or necessary for you. Finally, the more you study, the better prepared you will be. This book is intended to be the last thing you study before you walk into the examination room. Prior study of relevant texts is also recommended. NLC publishes some of these in our Fundamental Series. Knowledge and good sense are important factors in passing your exam. Good luck also helps. So now study this Passbook, absorb the material contained within and take that knowledge into the examination. Then do your best to pass that exam.

EXAMINATION SECTION

EXAMINATION SECTION
TEST 1

DIRECTIONS: Each question or incomplete statement is followed by several suggested answers or completions. Select the one that BEST answers the question or completes the statement. *PRINT THE LETTER OF THE CORRECT ANSWER IN THE SPACE AT THE RIGHT.*

1. Of the following, an important goal of the reorganization of a human services agency is to

    A. strengthen the centralization of services at agency headquarters
    B. provide services within the neighborhoods according to local needs
    C. equalize the distribution of responsibilities between headquarters and neighborhood offices
    D. give more authority and responsibility to neighborhood offices than to headquarters

    1.____

2. The one of the following which is NOT a purpose of the movement toward decentralization of city government is to

    A. reduce citizen alienation
    B. bolster city services
    C. respond to local needs
    D. discourage the local power structure

    2.____

3. Of the following, the MOST desirable way to strengthen the capacity of communities to contribute to the solution of their own problems is to

    A. encourage participation of local residents in service planning and delivery
    B. establish city-wide job training programs
    C. reduce technical assistance to local small business so that they will learn by experience
    D. make local residents accountable to government agencies for funds and services provided

    3.____

4. In organizing the residents of a disadvantaged neighborhood to develop projects for community improvement, the MOST effective of the following approaches is to

    A. concentrate on the group with most members
    B. devote more attention to groups which have vested interests
    C. try to include all groups
    D. give special consideration to official groups

    4.____

5. The one of the following which has been the MOST common problem which occurs when attempts are made to obtain community participation in a project such as a neighborhood improvement program is

    A. domination by an aggressive but unrepresentative group
    B. public opposition by representatives of government agencies
    C. fragmentation and disruption of community services
    D. serious deterioration in the quality of services

    5.____

6. Of the following, the MOST important aim of the community organizer in his early contacts with a community group should be to

    A. build a core of common interests
    B. establish himself as a forceful leader who can make decisions
    C. inform the group of its legal rights
    D. curb discussion of opposing viewpoints in order to develop harmonious relations

7. The one of the following which is the BEST method of encouraging neighborhood people to attend a community meeting is to

    A. send out notices at least a week in advance
    B. set up an agenda that deals with issues of serious local concern
    C. invite a prominent public figure to address the meeting
    D. send invitations to community people with similar viewpoints on the problem to be discussed

8. A basic difference between pure experimental research and action research is that experimental research is primarily concerned with the analysis of data for scientific or technological generalization, while action research is

    A. based on the results of trial and error
    B. designed to effect improvement in an on-going process
    C. intuitive rather than scientific in nature
    D. primarily concerned with the analysis of data for universal generalization

9. Assume that a community worker is assigned to organize a client group to participate in planning for services they particularly need.
    Of the following, it would be LEAST important for the organizer to become familiar with the

    A. local store owners
    B. neighborhood resources
    C. potential leaders
    D. informal leaders

10. Of the following, the factor which is MOST important in encouraging a high level of local participation in community projects is the

    A. degree of sophistication of the local people
    B. attitudes of the community development workers towards the local people
    C. amount of money available for training
    D. amount of time available for stimulation of community interest

11. Assume that you are the discussion leader of a meeting of a group of residents of a poverty area, many of whom are against a proposal to locate a methadone maintenance treatment center in the neighborhood.
    The BEST way for you to assist the group is to help them FIRST to

    A. get to know each other on an informal basis
    B. understand the overall background of the drug problem and the need for such a facility in the community
    C. concentrate on all the issues until they iron out conflicting viewpoints
    D. discuss the pros and cons briefly, take a vote, and accept the decision of the majority

12. Of the following, the MOST important aim of the community development process is primarily to strengthen the

    A. long-established social and political pattern of relationships
    B. influence of dominant ethnic and religious groups
    C. long-standing power of traditional central government
    D. positive impulses of people working toward a common goal

13. One method of influencing human behavior is based upon an optimistic belief in human potential for development and betterment.
    Workers in the human services who apply this method expect that it will

    A. awaken initiative in clients
    B. demand a pre-chosen response from clients
    C. give clients a spirit of competition
    D. get clients to accept new ideas

14. The community development process is MOST effective when

    A. final decisions are made solely by the community development expediters
    B. a firm plan is made after a project gets under way
    C. decisions are left in the hands of community people
    D. militant factions are permitted to take a firm stand

15. Of the following, the MOST significant indication that an organizer of a community group has done an effective job would be a situation where the group

    A. continues to grow in size and strength after the organizer has departed
    B. disperses after the organizer has departed because it has fulfilled its purpose
    C. attains its goals only under the organizer's guidance
    D. has a warm and friendly relationship with the organizer

16. The MAIN purpose of group discussion of community issues by local residents is to

    A. present a predetermined point of view
    B. provide an outlet for release of the participants' aggressions
    C. consider and work through common problems
    D. improve relationships among participants

17. Of the following, the MOST important reason why the community development worker in a disadvantaged community of a major metropolis should seek to understand the motivations of the local residents is that he will be more capable of assisting them in developing

    A. self-help activities
    B. projects which will get publicity
    C. an overall master plan
    D. projects which do not require technical assistance

18. At certain times, there is a tendency for community groups to disregard democratic procedures in making decisions, particularly in a situation where   18.___

    A. action depends on availability of community services
    B. the executive board makes the decision
    C. there is need for speedy action
    D. there is no sound basis for the decision

19. The employment of residents of poverty areas with little or no educational qualifications to assist professional staff members in working with clients of human services agencies is GENERALLY considered   19.___

    A. *advisable,* mainly because local paraprofessionals can be expected to bridge the gap between the middle class professional worker and lower class recipients of service
    B. *inadvisable,* mainly because the employment of workers who are not professionals will lower the professional standards of the agency's staff
    C. *advisable,* mainly because employment of paraprofes–sional local residents will save agency funds
    D. *inadvisable,* mainly because clients will receive services of poorer quality than services provided by professional workers

20. The social work activist who was a leader in the movement to achieve welfare reform by organizing welfare clients and encouraging the poor to demand their legal rights to public assistance is (was)   20.___

    A. Saul Alinsky   B. Richard Cloward
    C. Bertram Beck   D. Jesse Gray

Questions 21–26.

DIRECTIONS: Questions 21 through 26 are to be answered SOLELY on the basis of the following passage.

Too often in the past, society has accepted the existing social welfare programs, preferring to tinker with refinements when fundamental reform was in order. It has been a *demeaning*, degrading welfare system in which the instrument of government was wrongfully and *ineptly* used. It has been a system which has only alienated those forced to benefit from it and demoralized those who had to administer it at the level where the pain was clearly visible.

There is a need to put this nation on a course in which cash benefits, providing a basic level or support, are conferred in such a way as to intrude as little as possible into privacy and self–respect. It is difficult to define a basic level of support, no matter how high or low it might be set. In the end, however, the decision is not determined so much by how much is truly adequate for a family to meet all of its needs, but by the resources available to carry out the promise. That may be a harsh fact of life but it is also just that—a fact of life.

21. Of the following, the MOST suitable title for the above passage would be 21._____
    A. THE NEED FOR GOVERNMENT CONTROL OF WELFARE
    B. DETERMINING THE BASIC LEVEL OF SUPPORT
    C. THE NEED FOR WELFARE REFORM
    D. THE ELIMINATION OF WELFARE PROGRAMS

22. In this passage, the author's GREATEST criticism of the welfare system is that it is too 22._____
    A. disrespectful of recipients
    B. expensive to administer
    C. limited by regulations
    D. widespread in application

23. According to the passage, the basic level of support is ACTUALLY determined by 23._____
    A. how much is required for a family to meet all of its needs
    B. the age of the recipients
    C. how difficult it is to administer the program
    D. the economic resources of the nation

24. In this passage, the author does NOT argue for 24._____
    A. a work Incentive system   B. a basic level of support
    C. cash benefits   D. the privacy of recipients

25. As used in the above passage, the italicized word *demeaning* means MOST NEARLY 25._____
    A. ineffective   B. expensive
    C. overburdened   D. humiliating

26. As used in the above passage, the italicized word *ineptly* means MOST NEARLY 26._____
    A. foolishly   B. unsuccessfully
    C. unskillfully   D. unhappily

Questions 27–30.

DIRECTIONS: Questions 27 through 30 are to be answered SOLELY on the basis of the following paragraph.

The unemployment rate, which counts those unemployed in the sense that they are actively looking for work and unable to find it, gives a relatively *superficial* index of economic conditions in a community. A better index is the subemployment rate which includes the unemployment rate and also includes those working part–time while they are trying to get full–time work; those heads of households under 65 years of age who earn less than $240 per week working full–time, and those individuals under 65 who are not heads of households and earn less than $220 per week in a full–time job; and an estimate of the males *not counted*, which is a very real concern in ghetto areas.

27. Of the following, the MOST suitable title for the above paragraph would be

    A. EMPLOYMENT IN THE UNITED STATES
    B. PART-TIME WORKERS AND THE ECONOMY
    C. THE LABOR MARKET AND THE COMMUNITY
    D. TWO INDICATORS OF ECONOMIC CONDITIONS

28. On the basis of the paragraph, which of the following statements is CORRECT? The

    A. unemployment rate includes everyone who is not fully employed
    B. subemployment rate is higher than the unemployment rate
    C. unemployment rate gives a more complex picture of the economic situation than the subemployment rate
    D. subemployment rate indicates how many part-time workers are dissatisfied with the number of hours they work per week

29. As used in the above paragraph, the italicized word *superficial* means MOST NEARLY

    A. exaggerated   B. official
    C. surface   D. current

30. According to the paragraph, which of the following is included in the subemployment rate?

    A. Everyone who is unemployed
    B. All part-time workers
    C. Everyone under 65 who earns less than $224 per week in a full-time job
    D. All heads of households who earn less than $240 per week in a full-time job

KEY (CORRECT ANSWERS)

1. B	11. B	21. C
2. D	12. D	22. A
3. A	13. A	23. D
4. C	14. C	24. A
5. A	15. A	25. D
6. A	16. C	26. C
7. B	17. A	27. D
8. B	18. C	28. B
9. A	19. A	29. C
10. B	20. B	30. C

TEST 2

DIRECTIONS: Each question or incomplete statement is followed by several suggested answers or completions. Select the one that BEST answers the question or completes the statement. *PRINT THE LETTER OF THE CORRECT ANSWER IN THE SPACE AT THE RIGHT.*

1. The one of the following which accounts for the LARGEST portion of the budget of the Human Resources Administration is   1.____

    A. personnel and support services
    B. public assistance and medicaid
    C. services to children and youth
    D. community organization and development

2. According to the latest statistics published by the U. S. Department of Health, Education and Welfare, the state which spent the LARGEST amount of money per person for public assistance is   2.____

    A. California
    B. Massachusetts
    C. Pennsylvania
    D. New York

3. According to the MOST recent U.S. Census Bureau Report, the group living in New York City which has the lowest income level is the   3.____

    A. Blacks
    B. Puerto Ricans
    C. Dominicans
    D. Haitians

4. The group that contains the LARGEST number of individuals receiving public assistance is   4.____

    A. children under working age
    B. unemployed heads of families
    C. the aged, disabled, and blind
    D. unemployed single persons

5. A MAJOR difficulty faced by new arrivals to cities since 1970 which did not exist for earlier European immigrants is the fact that the majority of present–day arrivals   5.____

    A. must forfeit their native culture patterns
    B. have an obviously darker skin color than most longtime residents
    C. have little education
    D. have few occupational skills

6. Generally speaking, low–income persons do not make maximum use of opportunities and services available to them MAINLY because   6.____

    A. most paraprofessional workers, while sincere in the desire to serve, are unable to reach the hard core
    B. much of the routine paperwork in public assistance programs is now assigned to paraprofessional workers
    C. they have become increasingly self-reliant and prefer to cope with their problems without help
    D. they lack the confidence and know-how necessary to make their needs known to the proper persons or agencies

7. The one of the following problems which has once again become a serious concern of youth services agencies is the

   A. increasing high school drop-out rate
   B. resurgence of fighting youth gangs
   C. spread of youth narcotics addiction
   D. lack of recreation programs

8. Of the following, the MOST recent development with regard to welfare recipients is

   A. introduction of the declaration of need instead of an investigation of eligibility
   B. a major emphasis on employment programs
   C. increased use of casework therapy and psychiatric counseling
   D. acceptance of narcotics addicts for home relief

9. According to a recent decision by a federal court, regular reporting at state employment service offices to pick up checks or accept work can NO LONGER be required of recipients of

   A. Aid to the Disabled
   B. Home Relief
   C. Aid to Dependent Children
   D. Medicaid

10. A BASIC objective of the proposal for revenue sharing under consideration by the U.S. Congress is to provide

    A. state and local governments with new sources of revenue from the federal government and greater control over how this revenue is spent
    B. the federal government with greater control over spending of certain federally-raised tax revenues
    C. safeguards against improper allocation of funds by state and local officials and incentives to states for reporting violations by local government
    D. a method of sharing federal revenue with the states and localities in accordance with their required expenditures for public assistance and social welfare services

11. The component of the human services agency which sets policy for the administration, coordination, and allocation of funds for community action programs is the

    A. Community Development Agency
    B. Department of Social Services
    C. Council on Poverty
    D. Manpower and Career Development Agency

12. The policies of the Council Against Poverty are carried out by the

    A. Community Development Agency
    B. Manpower and Career Development Agency
    C. Department of Social Services
    D. Neighborhood Manpower Service Centers

13. The reorganization of the human services agency has established the unit of organization for provisions of services at the neighborhood level as the

    A. designated poverty area
    B. human resources district
    C. catchment area
    D. census tract

14. The Child Development Commission established by the Agency for Child Development can BEST be described as a group comprised of

    A. professionals in child psychology and early childhood education who will consult with Agency staff members on policy and programs
    B. parents, community organizations, and concerned citizens who will help the Agency determine, review, and modify policies and guidelines for childcare services
    C. child–care experts who will provide technical assistance to private groups that want to develop early childhood centers
    D. professionals who will offer health and nutrition consultation and a variety of support and referral services for children and parents

15. The BASIC purpose of the office of Community Social Services in the Department of Social Services is to

    A. help local community leaders establish liaison with private social service agencies in their communities
    B. determine the social service needs of each community and provide services in accordance with these needs
    C. provide information and referral to all HRA services existing in a particular community and to services provided by other city agencies and private organizations
    D. assume responsibility for a variety of social services mandated by federal and state regulations

16. The Social Service Exchange is CORRECTLY described as a

    A. recruitment center for the training and placement of volunteers for social and health agencies
    B. center which maintains a central index of case records of families and individuals known to social and health agencies
    C. center which provides information about and makes referrals to social and health agencies and proprietary nursing homes
    D. confidential advisory service to help potential contributors evaluate local voluntary health and welfare agencies

17. Which one of the following is an IMPORTANT purpose of the formation of the Office of Special Services for Children in the Department of Social Services?

    A. Greater programmatic integration of the protective and supportive services to children who are abused, neglected, dependent, delinquent, or in need of services
    B. More professional attention to child abuse cases and prompt court action to penalize parents of abused or neglected children
    C. Separation of programs and facilities for children adjudged to be delinquent from special services for other dependent, abused, or neglected children
    D. Increased attention to home–finding and foster care and adoption services rather than institutional care for dependent children

18. The one of the following which is provided by the Department of Social Services for current, former, and potential public assistance recipients ONLY is _____ services.

    A. information
    B. child welfare
    C. referral
    D. homemaker

19. A MAJOR goal of the Department of Social Services which is part of the reorganization and the separation of income maintenance from social services is to

    A. limit the provision of public social services to those persons who are eligible for public assistance
    B. make public social services available to all persons, whether or not they require financial assistance
    C. refer clients who require social services to private agencies wherever possible
    D. emphasize casework treatment and referral of clients for psychiatric services rather than programs to effect environmental change

20. Of the following, the MAIN functions of the Manpower and Career Development Agency (MCDA) of a human services agency are to

    A. train the unskilled, upgrade existing skills, develop job opportunities, and place newly-trained people in jobs
    B. operate manpower, recruitment, and testing centers under contract with private organizations
    C. provide remedial education and follow-up for dis-advantaged potential college students and vocational testing and counseling for veterans and ex-addicts
    D. provide job development, interviewing and placement, and manpower research services

Questions 21-25.

DIRECTIONS: Questions 21 through 25 are to be answered SOLELY on the diagram presented below.

HOW THE INNER-CITY FAMILY IN URBANVILLE SPENDS ITS MONEY

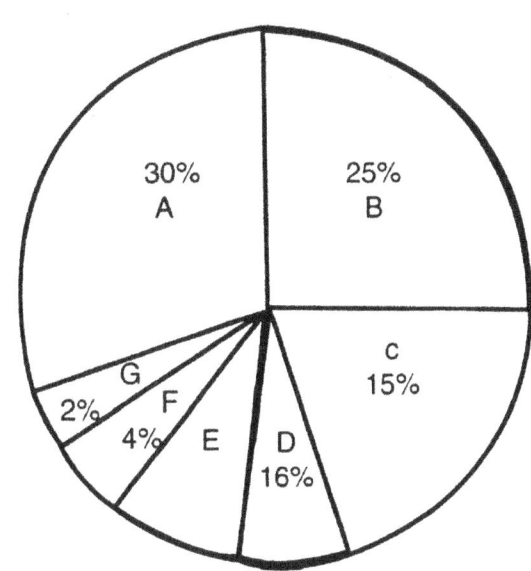

A. Food
B. Shelter
C. Clothing
D. Household Operation
E. Medical Care
F. Transportation
G. Miscellaneous

21. According to the above diagram, the percentage spent on medical care is   21.____

    A. 7%   B. 8%   C. 16%   D. 18%

22. According to the above diagram, the total percentage spent on food, shelter, and clothing is   22.____

    A. 55%   B. 60%   C. 70%   D. 75%

23. In a typical period, if the family spent $60 on transportation, how much did it spend on household operation?   23.____

    A. $240   B. $384   C. $600   D. $960

24. If the family income is $250 a week, how much does it spend on transportation each year?   24.____

    A. $120   B. $520   C. $1,200   D. $5,200

25. Assume that the annual income of a family was $10,800 for several years. Last year, the income went up 5%, and the family then tripled the typical percentage for household operation.
    The amount spent on this item last year was MOST NEARLY   25.____

    A. $1,782   B. $2,268   C. $2,592   D. $5,442

Questions 26–30.

DIRECTIONS: Questions 26 through 30 are to be answered SOLELY on the basis of the table presented below.

AFDC FAMILY MEMBERS IN URBANVILLE
Referred to and Enrolled in WIN Program, 2001-2002

Family Member	Referred		Enrolled	
	2001	2002	2001	2002
Mother	1,091	1,306	730	877
Father	743	950	520	731
Child, age 16 and over	170	222	150	184

26. According to the above table, how many AFDC family members were referred to WIN in 2002?

    A. 1,792   B. 2,004   C. 2,388   D. 2,478

27. According to the above table, the number of AFDC children 16 and over who were enrolled in WIN in 2002 was GREATER than the number enrolled in 2001 by

    A. 12   B. 34   C. 38   D. 52

28. According to the above table, the number of AFDC mothers who were enrolled in 2002 INCREASED over the number enrolled in 2001 MOST NEARLY by

    A. 20%   B. 32%   C. 54%   D. 83%

29. In 2003, if the number of AFDC mothers referred to WIN increases 5% over 2002, the number of fathers referred increases 8% over 2002, and the number of children referred increases 5% over 2002, the TOTAL number of AFDC family members that will be referred in 2003 is MOST NEARLY

    A. 1,424   B. 1,524   C. 3,130   D. 3,990

30. According to the above table, the percentage of AFDC fathers NOT enrolled in WIN in 2002 of the number referred that year is MOST NEARLY

    A. 23%   B. 25%   C. 71%   D. 77%

KEY (CORRECT ANSWERS)

1. B	11. C	21. B
2. D	12. A	22. C
3. D	13. B	23. A
4. A	14. B	24. B
5. B	15. B	25. D
6. D	16. B	26. D
7. B	17. A	27. B
8. B	18. D	28. A
9. C	19. B	29. C
10. A	20. A	30. A

EXAMINATION SECTION
TEST 1

DIRECTIONS: Each question or incomplete statement is followed by several suggested answers or completions. Select the one that BEST answers the question or completes the statement. *PRINT THE LETTER OF THE CORRECT ANSWER IN THE SPACE AT THE RIGHT.*

1. The type of open space plaza built in conjunction with high rise buildings, now encouraged by city zoning laws, was first installed in the city of

   A. Lever House
   B. United Nations Headquarters
   C. Rockefeller Center
   D. Lincoln Center

2. Of the following, *open space* in a residential site development is BEST insured by

   A. cluster design
   B. gridiron layout
   C. mixed building types
   D. density zoning

3. Of the following statements concerning cast iron fronts built in the 19th century in the city, the one that is CORRECT is that they are

   A. still structurally sound
   B. being condemned for structural reasons
   C. not complex enough for preservation even though basically sound
   D. easily duplicated in the modern town houses.

4. Of the following, the BEST example of the use of *eminent domain* is a

   A. planning board's reversal of a contested land use
   B. sale of public land for private development
   C. mayor authorizing the implementation of a zoning change
   D. tract of private land taken by the government for public purposes.

5. Of the following measures of central tendency, the value of the variable which occurs MOST frequently is called the

   A. arithmetic mean
   B. harmonic mean
   C. median
   D. mode

6. A MAJOR reason that industrial plants have been moving out of the city to the suburbs is that

   A. a cheap labor force is available
   B. union influence is eliminated
   C. plants can expand horizontally
   D. they will be closer to their market area

7. The total floor area of a building divided by the lot area is called the

   A. net defensible space
   B. floor-area ratio
   C. rentable ratio
   D. open-space factor

8. The State Multiple Dwelling Law defines a multiple dwelling as one that has _____ dwelling units.

   A. two or more
   B. three or more
   C. five or more
   D. over ten

9. Most zoning ordinances are NOT concerned with

   A. bulk regulations
   B. setbacks
   C. parking
   D. building materials

10. The site plan included in a set of drawings for a housing project will include all of the following EXCEPT

    A. existing structures
    B. easements and rights of way
    C. a plan of a typical floor
    D. boundary lines and distances

11. *Good* neighborhood planning should provide for

    A. the use of loop roads
    B. the use of cul-de-sacs
    C. a combination of loop roads and cul-de-sacs for ease of auto travel
    D. the separation of pedestrians and vehicles

12. An origin-destination survey is PRIMARILY made by

    A. educational planners
    B. market analysis expert
    C. transportation planners
    D. utility planners

13. Of the following, the concept of linear growth in urban areas refers PRIMARILY to growth of

    A. one type of dwelling only in each specific urban area
    B. the urban area along a major highway
    C. one-industry towns in a specific urban area
    D. urban areas in an orderly plan as opposed to haphazard development

14. In urban areas, it is BEST to locate mass transit facilities

    A. underground
    B. water's edge
    C. along major avenues
    D. so as to inter-connect high rise buildings

15. Of the following, the MAJOR contributing factor to the poor air quality in the city is

    A. smokestack emissions
    B. incinerators
    C. industrial waste
    D. auto exhaust emissions

16. The Municipal Loan Program was established to provide funds for

    A. new one-family housing
    B. low-cost housing in built-up areas
    C. altering and renovating old apartment buildings
    D. local planning boards

17. The towns of Radburn and Reston are *similar* to the extent that each　　　　17.____

　　A. has a man-made lake
　　B. has a high rise housing building
　　C. depends almost entirely on a cul-de-sac road system
　　D. has mostly one-and two-story housing.

18. Of the following characteristics, the one MOST applicable to *zoning* is that zoning　　　　18.____

　　A. requires a sub-division layout for houses
　　B. permits planned unit development in selected cases
　　C. represents an attempt by local authorities to legally regulate use of land
　　D. requires a typical topographic survey before enactment

19. Zoning laws are generally NOT concerned with　　　　19.____

　　A. architectural style　　　　B. building heights
　　C. land use　　　　　　　　　 D. population density

20. In an average urban community, the percentage of land *usually* devoted to the street system is MOST NEARLY　　　　20.____

　　A. 5%　　　　B. 15%　　　　C. 35%　　　　D. 50%

21. The *railroad flat* obtained its name because it　　　　21.____

　　A. had all rooms in a straight line
　　B. contained efficiency units
　　C. was built with dimensions similar to Pullman train roomettes
　　D. was originally built for railroad workers

22. A cul-de-sac is a　　　　22.____

　　A. circular driveway　　　　B. dead-end road
　　C. highway interchange　　 D. vehicular turning radius

23. MOST zoning ordinances prescribe minimum setbacks in order to provide　　　　23.____

　　A. adequate parking space
　　B. maximum fire safety
　　C. space for landscaping
　　D. sufficient access, light, and air

24. The Critical Path Method　　　　24.____

　　A. is a form of scheduling operations against time periods and resources
　　B. deals with program evaluation and actual costs
　　C. concerns least cost estimating and scheduling
　　D. is a tool to assure management that operations will proceed readily

25. According to the Building Code, every habitable room must be provided with natural light from windows. The sum of the areas of these windows must be at least equal to what minimum percentage of floor area of the room?　　　　25.____

　　A. 5%　　　　B. 10%　　　　C. 20%　　　　D. 25%

KEY (CORRECT ANSWERS)

1.	C	11.	D
2.	A	12.	C
3.	A	13.	B
4.	D	14.	A
5.	D	15.	D
6.	C	16.	C
7.	B	17.	D
8.	B	18.	C
9.	D	19.	A
10.	C	20.	C

21. A
22. B
23. D
24. A
25. B

TEST 2

DIRECTIONS: Each question or incomplete statement is followed by several suggested answers or completions. Select the one that BEST answers the question or completes the statement. *PRINT THE LETTER OF THE CORRECT ANSWER IN THE SPACE AT THE RIGHT.*

1. *Seed* money as it pertains to a new housing development is intended to　　1.____

    A. broaden its scope
    B. restrict and channel the budget of the development
    C. encourage flexibilities and alternatives in the construction of development
    D. get it started

2. Incentive zoning is intended to compensate builders for　　2.____

    A. inclusion of special projects in their proposal
    B. increasing the assessed valuation of property
    C. diversifying land use constraints
    D. addition of open space

3. A *performance bond* guarantees that　　3.____

    A. a contractor will execute the terms of the contract
    B. the architect will oversee the completion of the contract
    C. the owner will pay the contractor upon the completion of his work
    D. the labor unions will enforce the proper completion of the contract

4. For buildings, the Zoning Resolution controls　　4.____

    A. use, types, and bulk
    B. structure, materials, and egress
    C. heating, garbage, and superintendence
    D. landmark preservation, urban esthetics, and pollution

5. Of the following, the one that would contribute MOST toward reducing air pollution in an urban area is　　5.____

    A. an increase in the number of parking garages
    B. the reduction of the number of cylinders in automobiles
    C. use of lower octane gasoline in automobiles
    D. an effective rapid transit system

6. PUD design refers to　　6.____

    A. high rise housing
    B. housing spaced closely to net more open space
    C. less detached houses, more twinned and row houses
    D. roads around groups of houses

7. The one of the following that is the MOST common characteristic of an *educational park* in the United States is　　7.____

    A. vertical high schools in large landscaped areas
    B. buildings for various levels of education in a related complex

C. various coeducational facilities at the high school level
D. high schools related to commerce and industry all on one site

8. An advantage of the *gridiron* system of urban layout is that it

   A. is most easily saleable by real estate brokers
   B. provides the most air and sunlight
   C. is easily adapted by surveyors
   D. makes use of normal topography

9. When parking is required in urban areas, the one of the following that is the MOST important benefit of creating this parking underground is

   A. the cost of the parking project is reduced
   B. air pollution in the area is reduced
   C. the land above may be used for other purposes
   D. cars are then hidden from sight

10. The MAJOR advantage of the use of the *superblock* is that it

    A. improves separation of vehicular and pedestrian circulation
    B. lends itself to modular expansion
    C. affords space to zone residential from industrial areas
    D. lends itself to flexible multi-zoning principles

11. The phrase *public right-of-way* refers to

    A. civil rights of individuals
    B. an easement
    C. a city street
    D. a public parking garage

12. A city-approved schedule of long-range construction projects extending over approximately a 6-year period is known as a(n)

    A. capital improvement program
    B. expense budget
    C. master plan
    D. flow chart

13. *Urban renewal* is the federal program PRIMARILY concerned with

    A. urban design
    B. advocate planning
    C. construction of new housing
    D. construction of new highways

14. As used in city planning, the number of persons per acre is referred to as the

    A. density   B. use-ratio
    C. space-factor   D. census

15. Of the following, the MOST efficient type of sanitary sewage disposal system is a 15._____

    A. cesspool B. public sewer
    C. septic tank D. storm drain

16. Full ownership of a dwelling unit and common ownership of community facilities is known as a 16._____

    A. cooperative B. rental unit
    C. condominium D. high rise development

17. The number of square feet in one acre of land is 17._____

    A. 22,100 B. 40,280 C. 43,560 D. 96,000

18. The MAIN function of a *collector street* is to 18._____

    A. conduct traffic from local streets to arterials
    B. provide access to abutting property
    C. provide open space between buildings
    D. carry heavy traffic

19. The *distinguishing* characteristic of a topographic map is its 19._____

    A. high and low water lines
    B. representation of terrestrial relief
    C. indications of the different types of soils
    D. illustrations of drainage areas

20. The *input-output* technique for urban economic analysis was originally designed for which one of the following economies? 20._____

    A. Municipal B. National C. State D. Regional

21. The *cohort survival model* is one method of determining 21._____

    A. population B. death rate
    C. migration D. birth rate

22. Which one of the following items is DIRECTLY related to an urban land use survey? 22._____

    A. The classification system
    B. Physiographic features
    C. Flood area data
    D. The economic base

23. According to the requirements of the zoning ordinance, the basis of granting a variance is MOST often 23._____

    A. an economic loss B. physical hardship
    C. greater density D. change of use

24. Restrictive covenants or deed restrictions are MOST often considered to be 24._____

    A. local government regulations
    B. supplementary public controls
    C. subdivision plot requirements
    D. private contracts by property owners.

25. In the U.S. as a whole, when land is to be developed, the determination of street alignments would MOST frequently be made by which one of the following regulations? 25.___

   A. Zoning Ordinances
   B. Subdivision Regulations
   C. Health Department Rules
   D. Highway Department specifications

KEY (CORRECT ANSWERS)

1.	D	11.	C
2.	A	12.	A
3.	A	13.	C
4.	A	14.	A
5.	D	15.	B
6.	B	16.	C
7.	B	17.	C
8.	C	18.	A
9.	C	19.	B
10.	A	20.	B

21. A
22. D
23. B
24. D
25. B

EXAMINATION SECTION
TEST 1

DIRECTIONS: Each question or incomplete statement is followed by several suggested answers or completions. Select the one that BEST answers the question or completes the statement. *PRINT THE LETTER OF THE CORRECT ANSWER IN THE SPACE AT THE RIGHT.*

1. The type of open space plaza built in conjunction with high rise buildings, now encouraged by city zoning laws, was first installed in the city of   1.____

   A. Lever House
   B. United Nations Headquarters
   C. Rockefeller Center
   D. Lincoln Center

2. Of the following, *open space* in a residential site development is BEST insured by   2.____

   A. cluster design   B. gridiron layout
   C. mixed building types   D. density zoning

3. Of the following statements concerning cast iron fronts built in the 19th century in the city, the one that is CORRECT is that they are   3.____

   A. still structurally sound
   B. being condemned for structural reasons
   C. not complex enough for preservation even though basically sound
   D. easily duplicated in the modern town houses.

4. Of the following, the BEST example of the use of *eminent domain* is a   4.____

   A. planning board's reversal of a contested land use
   B. sale of public land for private development
   C. mayor authorizing the implementation of a zoning change
   D. tract of private land taken by the government for public purposes.

5. Of the following measures of central tendency, the value of the variable which occurs MOST frequently is called the   5.____

   A. arithmetic mean   B. harmonic mean
   C. median   D. mode

6. A MAJOR reason that industrial plants have been moving out of the city to the suburbs is that   6.____

   A. a cheap labor force is available
   B. union influence is eliminated
   C. plants can expand horizontally
   D. they will be closer to their market area

7. The total floor area of a building divided by the lot area is called the   7.____

   A. net defensible space   B. floor-area ratio
   C. rentable ratio   D. open-space factor

8. The State Multiple Dwelling Law defines a multiple dwelling as one that has _____ dwelling units.

   A. two or more
   B. three or more
   C. five or more
   D. over ten

9. Most zoning ordinances are NOT concerned with

   A. bulk regulations
   B. setbacks
   C. parking
   D. building materials

10. The site plan included in a set of drawings for a housing project will include all of the following EXCEPT

    A. existing structures
    B. easements and rights of way
    C. a plan of a typical floor
    D. boundary lines and distances

11. *Good* neighborhood planning should provide for

    A. the use of loop roads
    B. the use of cul-de-sacs
    C. a combination of loop roads and cul-de-sacs for ease of auto travel
    D. the separation of pedestrians and vehicles

12. An origin-destination survey is PRIMARILY made by

    A. educational planners
    B. market analysis expert
    C. transportation planners
    D. utility planners

13. Of the following, the concept of linear growth in urban areas refers PRIMARILY to growth of

    A. one type of dwelling only in each specific urban area
    B. the urban area along a major highway
    C. one-industry towns in a specific urban area
    D. urban areas in an orderly plan as opposed to haphazard development

14. In urban areas, it is BEST to locate mass transit facilities

    A. underground
    B. water's edge
    C. along major avenues
    D. so as to inter-connect high rise buildings

15. Of the following, the MAJOR contributing factor to the poor air quality in the city is

    A. smokestack emissions
    B. incinerators
    C. industrial waste
    D. auto exhaust emissions

16. The Municipal Loan Program was established to provide funds for

    A. new one-family housing
    B. low-cost housing in built-up areas
    C. altering and renovating old apartment buildings
    D. local planning boards

17. The towns of Radburn and Reston are *similar* to the extent that each

    A. has a man-made lake
    B. has a high rise housing building
    C. depends almost entirely on a cul-de-sac road system
    D. has mostly one-and two-story housing.

18. Of the following characteristics, the one MOST applicable to *zoning* is that zoning

    A. requires a sub-division layout for houses
    B. permits planned unit development in selected cases
    C. represents an attempt by local authorities to legally regulate use of land
    D. requires a typical topographic survey before enactment

19. Zoning laws are generally NOT concerned with

    A. architectural style   B. building heights
    C. land use   D. population density

20. In an average urban community, the percentage of land *usually* devoted to the street system is MOST NEARLY

    A. 5%   B. 15%   C. 35%   D. 50%

21. The *railroad flat* obtained its name because it

    A. had all rooms in a straight line
    B. contained efficiency units
    C. was built with dimensions similar to Pullman train roomettes
    D. was originally built for railroad workers

22. A cul-de-sac is a

    A. circular driveway   B. dead-end road
    C. highway interchange   D. vehicular turning radius

23. MOST zoning ordinances prescribe minimum setbacks in order to provide

    A. adequate parking space
    B. maximum fire safety
    C. space for landscaping
    D. sufficient access, light, and air

24. The Critical Path Method

    A. is a form of scheduling operations against time periods and resources
    B. deals with program evaluation and actual costs
    C. concerns least cost estimating and scheduling
    D. is a tool to assure management that operations will proceed readily

25. According to the Building Code, every habitable room must be provided with natural light from windows. The sum of the areas of these windows must be at least equal to what minimum percentage of floor area of the room?

    A. 5%   B. 10%   C. 20%   D. 25%

KEY (CORRECT ANSWERS)

1. C
2. A
3. A
4. D
5. D

6. C
7. B
8. B
9. D
10. C

11. D
12. C
13. B
14. A
15. D

16. C
17. D
18. C
19. A
20. C

21. A
22. B
23. D
24. A
25. B

TEST 2

DIRECTIONS: Each question or incomplete statement is followed by several suggested answers or completions. Select the one that BEST answers the question or completes the statement. *PRINT THE LETTER OF THE CORRECT ANSWER IN THE SPACE AT THE RIGHT.*

1. *Seed* money as it pertains to a new housing development is intended to 1.____

    A. broaden its scope
    B. restrict and channel the budget of the development
    C. encourage flexibilities and alternatives in the construction of development
    D. get it started

2. Incentive zoning is intended to compensate builders for 2.____

    A. inclusion of special projects in their proposal
    B. increasing the assessed valuation of property
    C. diversifying land use constraints
    D. addition of open space

3. A *performance bond* guarantees that 3.____

    A. a contractor will execute the terms of the contract
    B. the architect will oversee the completion of the contract
    C. the owner will pay the contractor upon the completion of his work
    D. the labor unions will enforce the proper completion of the contract

4. For buildings, the Zoning Resolution controls 4.____

    A. use, types, and bulk
    B. structure, materials, and egress
    C. heating, garbage, and superintendence
    D. landmark preservation, urban esthetics, and pollution

5. Of the following, the one that would contribute MOST toward reducing air pollution in an urban area is 5.____

    A. an increase in the number of parking garages
    B. the reduction of the number of cylinders in automobiles
    C. use of lower octane gasoline in automobiles
    D. an effective rapid transit system

6. PUD design refers to 6.____

    A. high rise housing
    B. housing spaced closely to net more open space
    C. less detached houses, more twinned and row houses
    D. roads around groups of houses

7. The one of the following that is the MOST common characteristic of an *educational park* in the United States is 7.____

    A. vertical high schools in large landscaped areas
    B. buildings for various levels of education in a related complex

C. various coeducational facilities at the high school level
D. high schools related to commerce and industry all on one site

8. An advantage of the *gridiron* system of urban layout is that it

   A. is most easily saleable by real estate brokers
   B. provides the most air and sunlight
   C. is easily adapted by surveyors
   D. makes use of normal topography

9. When parking is required in urban areas, the one of the following that is the MOST important benefit of creating this parking underground is

   A. the cost of the parking project is reduced
   B. air pollution in the area is reduced
   C. the land above may be used for other purposes
   D. cars are then hidden from sight

10. The MAJOR advantage of the use of the *superblock* is that it

    A. improves separation of vehicular and pedestrian circulation
    B. lends itself to modular expansion
    C. affords space to zone residential from industrial areas
    D. lends itself to flexible multi-zoning principles

11. The phrase *public right-of-way* refers to

    A. civil rights of individuals
    B. an easement
    C. a city street
    D. a public parking garage

12. A city-approved schedule of long-range construction projects extending over approximately a 6-year period is known as a(n)

    A. capital improvement program
    B. expense budget
    C. master plan
    D. flow chart

13. *Urban renewal* is the federal program PRIMARILY concerned with

    A. urban design
    B. advocate planning
    C. construction of new housing
    D. construction of new highways

14. As used in city planning, the number of persons per acre is referred to as the

    A. density   B. use-ratio
    C. space-factor   D. census

15. Of the following, the MOST efficient type of sanitary sewage disposal system is a

    A. cesspool
    B. public sewer
    C. septic tank
    D. storm drain

16. Full ownership of a dwelling unit and common ownership of community facilities is known as a

    A. cooperative
    B. rental unit
    C. condominium
    D. high rise development

17. The number of square feet in one acre of land is

    A. 22,100   B. 40,280   C. 43,560   D. 96,000

18. The MAIN function of a *collector street* is to

    A. conduct traffic from local streets to arterials
    B. provide access to abutting property
    C. provide open space between buildings
    D. carry heavy traffic

19. The *distinguishing* characteristic of a topographic map is its

    A. high and low water lines
    B. representation of terrestrial relief
    C. indications of the different types of soils
    D. illustrations of drainage areas

20. The *input-output* technique for urban economic analysis was originally designed for which one of the following economies?

    A. Municipal   B. National   C. State   D. Regional

21. The *cohort survival model* is one method of determining

    A. population
    B. death rate
    C. migration
    D. birth rate

22. Which one of the following items is DIRECTLY related to an urban land use survey?

    A. The classification system
    B. Physiographic features
    C. Flood area data
    D. The economic base

23. According to the requirements of the zoning ordinance, the basis of granting a variance is MOST often

    A. an economic loss
    B. physical hardship
    C. greater density
    D. change of use

24. Restrictive covenants or deed restrictions are MOST often considered to be

    A. local government regulations
    B. supplementary public controls
    C. subdivision plot requirements
    D. private contracts by property owners.

25. In the U.S. as a whole, when land is to be developed, the determination of street alignments would MOST frequently be made by which one of the following regulations?   25.___

    A. Zoning Ordinances
    B. Subdivision Regulations
    C. Health Department Rules
    D. Highway Department specifications

KEY (CORRECT ANSWERS)

1.	D	11.	C
2.	A	12.	A
3.	A	13.	C
4.	A	14.	A
5.	D	15.	B
6.	B	16.	C
7.	B	17.	C
8.	C	18.	A
9.	C	19.	B
10.	A	20.	B

21. A
22. D
23. B
24. D
25. B

EXAMINATION SECTION
TEST 1

DIRECTIONS: Each question or incomplete statement is followed by several suggested, answers or completions. Select the one that BEST answers the question or completes the statement. *PRINT THE LETTER OF THE CORRECT ANSWER IN THE SPACE AT THE RIGHT.*

1. The authority to establish zoning ordinances by a community comes from

    A. the police power of the state
    B. local determination
    C. the federal government
    D. implied powers of the community

2. On a land use map, the standard color used to designate residential use is

    A. green B. blue C. purple D. yellow

3. In population analysis, a population pyramid indicates

    A. male and female age groupings
    B. total population projections
    C. fertility ratios
    D. educational achievements

4. The determination of a standard metropolitan statistical area is established by

    A. local considerations B. regional agencies
    C. the U.S. Census Bureau D. state agencies

5. The population census of the United States is taken every _____ years.

    A. 2 B. 4 C. 5 D. 10

6. There are strong indications that planning agencies are developing a new approach to the traditional methods of city planning.
This new approach is called

    A. advocacy planning
    B. long-range physical planning
    C. community development
    D. policies planning

7. A key element of a comprehensive plan for a community is the

    A. zoning ordinance B. land use plan
    C. official map D. subdivision regulation

8. The official map of a community is a document that

    A. shows population projections and educational trends
    B. pinpoints the location of future streets and other public facilities
    C. identifies capital improvements and budgets
    D. indicates all community facilities

9. During the past decade, planning programs generally have become increasingly concerned with which one of the following?

   A. Long-range physical design
   B. Highway locations
   C. Social welfare
   D. Natural resources

10. The city planning process encompasses several basic phases. Which one of the following phases would NOT be considered typical?

    A. Cost-benefit analysis
    B. Goal formulation
    C. Data collection and research
    D. Plan preparation and programming

11. The MOST common use of easements in new housing subdivisions is for

    A. air rights   B. utilities
    C. open space   D. absorption fields

12. The phrase *non-complying use* relates to which one of the following regulations?

    A. Zoning Ordinance   B. Building Code
    C. Subdivision regulations   D. Health Code

13. Performance standards are generally associated with which one of the following types of zoning districts?

    A. Residential   B. Commercial
    C. Manufacturing   D. Flood plain

14. The PRIMARY goal of cluster-type development is to

    A. increase population density
    B. insure open space
    C. discourage rapid development
    D. bypass zoning requirements

15. Which of the following is MOST closely related to the land-use intensity standards developed by the Federal Housing Administration?

    A. Quality of housing   B. Planned unit development
    C. Low-cost housing   D. Land management policy

16. If the density of a residential subdivision is 8 dwelling units per acre, then the average size lot should be APPROXIMATELY

    A. 25 ft. x 100 ft.   B. 55 ft. x 100 ft.
    C. 100 ft. x 100 ft.   D. 200 ft. x 200 ft.

17. In planning the open parking area for community facilities, the amount of space allocated per care should be APPROXIMATELY _____ sq.ft.

    A. 150   B. 300   C. 600   D. 800

18. Which of the following facilities would be MOST appropriate on the roof of a building? 18.____

    A. Stolport   B. Heliport
    C. Airport   D. Cargo port

19. Sanitary landfill is a method of 19.____

    A. sewage disposal   B. composting
    C. incineration   D. refuse disposal

20. Which of the following is NOT considered to be an air pollutant by the Environmental Protection Agency? 20.____

    A. Nitrates   B. Sulfur oxides
    C. Carbon monoxide   D. Hydrocarbons

21. Which of the following recreation facilities is NOT considered a typical neighborhood facility? 21.____

    A. Tot lot   B. Playground
    C. Wading pool   D. Playfield

22. Which of the following methods would be the MOST accurate in making a population projection for a small community? 22.____

    A. Migration and natural increase
    B. Apportionment and voting records
    C. School enrollment and housing starts
    D. Geometric extrapolation

23. When a planning map is to be reproduced to different sizes, the map scale should be expressed 23.____

    A. mathematically   B. in graphic form
    C. in feet and inches D. by metes and bounds

24. The one of the following characteristics which is NOT typical of new industrial parks is 24.____

    A. off-street loading   B. extensive landscaping
    C. employee parking   D. 2-story structures

25. A greenbelt surrounding a community can be used for many activities. The one of the following activities LEAST appropriate for greenbelt use is 25.____

    A. farming   B. recreation
    C. local shopping   D. flood plain control

KEY (CORRECT ANSWERS)

1.	A	11.	B
2.	D	12.	A
3.	A	13.	C
4.	C	14.	B
5.	D	15.	B
6.	D	16.	B
7.	B	17.	B
8.	B	18.	B
9.	C	19.	D
10.	A	20.	A

21. D
22. A
23. B
24. D
25. C

TEST 2

DIRECTIONS: Each question or incomplete statement is followed by several suggested answers or completions. Select the one that BEST answers the question or completes the statement. *PRINT THE LETTER OF THE CORRECT ANSWER IN THE SPACE AT THE RIGHT.*

1. The *neighborhood unit* concept does NOT provide for

    A. elementary schools
    B. playgrounds
    C. local shopping
    D. industrial development

    1.____

2. Which of the following areas is LEAST likely to be considered part of social welfare planning?

    A. Urban design
    B. Education
    C. Health
    D. Anti-poverty

    2.____

3. Both the census of business and the census of manufacturing compiled by the U.S. Bureau of the Census are made every _____ years.

    A. three   B. five   C. seven   D. ten

    3.____

4. The MOST frequently used governmental source for topographical maps is the U.S.

    A. Department of Agriculture
    B. Geological Survey
    C. Department of Housing and Urban Development
    D. Coast Guard

    4.____

5. The importance of assessed valuation of land and buildings to a community is to

    A. establish school taxes
    B. establish property taxes
    C. determine tax exemptions
    D. determine land uses

    5.____

6. Of the following countries, the MOST extensive progress in establishing new towns during the 20th century has taken place in

    A. the United States
    B. France
    C. Italy
    D. England

    6.____

7. A street classification system is PRIMARILY used for street

    A. naming
    B. construction
    C. differentiation
    D. location

    7.____

8. The *Greenbelt* towns were a product of the

    A. city beautiful movement
    B. garden city movement
    C. atomic energy commission
    D. resettlement administration

    8.____

33

9. The apportionment method of population projection is concerned PRIMARILY with

    A. migration
    B. natural increase
    C. large geographic areas
    D. birth rate

10. Under ideal conditions, which type of parking arrangement should yield the MOST parking spaces?

    A. Parallel   B. 45°   C. 60°   D. 90°

11. A MAJOR disadvantage of a depressed highway through a built-up area as compared to a highway on grade is its

    A. poor appearance
    B. inadequate width of right-of-way
    C. lack of access
    D. noise generation

12. The customary test made to determine the ability of a soil to drain off liquids, such as those discharged by a cesspool, is known as the _____ test.

    A. percolation
    B. absorption
    C. drainage
    D. sump

13. The Mitchell-Lama Housing Law was originally intended to assist the construction of

    A. low-income housing
    B. middle-income housing
    C. suburban residential projects
    D. housing for mixed racial communities

14. A community will MOST frequently acquire the development rights of existing farm land in order to

    A. protect land values
    B. provide sites for public projects
    C. insure open space
    D. develop a land bank

15. In recent years, local participation in the city planning process has *substantially* increased because of the

    A. establishment of local school boards
    B. high crime rate in the streets
    C. emergence of private citizen organizations
    D. establishment of community planning boards

16. A unique feature of the State Urban Development Corporation when first established was that it

    A. was an autonomous organization
    B. was not required to conform to local zoning regulations
    C. could only build housing when invited by local communities
    D. used only private funds for its projects

17. The concept of *defensible space* has recently emerged to help fight crime in urban areas. 17.____
 The principle of *defensible space* is that public areas should be

    A. completely enclosed
    B. eliminated
    C. placed adjacent to areas of activity
    D. patroled by volunteer citizen groups

18. Of the following, the MAJOR planning implication of a 3-bedroom dwelling unit as compared to a 1-bedroom dwelling unit is that 18.____

    A. the family with the larger dwelling unit has more income
    B. with larger dwelling units there will be fewer municipal services necessary
    C. more children will be enrolled in school
    D. smaller dwelling units are cheaper to build than larger units

19. A landscaped buffer strip is MOST appropriately placed between which of the following land uses? 19.____

    A. Light and heavy manufacturing
    B. Residential and commercial
    C. Commercial and manufacturing
    D. Residential of low density and residential of high density

20. The employment trend in the city over the past 20 years has shown that 20.____

    A. *both* white collar and blue collar jobs have increased
    B. *both* white collar and blue collar jobs have decreased
    C. *only* white collar jobs have decreased
    D. *only* blue collar jobs have decreased

21. For traffic safety, the BEST angle between two intersecting streets is 21.____

    A. 15   B. 30   C. 45   D. 90

22. In the city, the system used by the tax department to identify property is by 22.____

    A. house numbers   B. zoning maps
    C. block and lot numbers   D. the official city map

23. The name of the report by which the U.S. Environmental Protection Agency establishes the effect of a proposed project on the environment is called the 23.____

    A. input-output analysis   B. economic base study
    C. ambient air study   D. impact statement

24. Planners recommend that utility lines be located underground because utility lines built this way are 24.____

    A. cheaper to construct
    B. not required to follow street alignments
    C. aesthetically more attractive
    D. more efficient

25. *Scatter-site* housing means that the housing will be
   - A. located in all use districts
   - B. built with large areas of recreation space between buildings
   - C. of different heights on each site
   - D. built on small, by-passed sites in built-up areas

KEY (CORRECT ANSWERS)

1.	D	11.	C
2.	A	12.	A
3.	B	13.	B
4.	B	14.	C
5.	B	15.	D
6.	D	16.	B
7.	C	17.	C
8.	D	18.	C
9.	C	19.	B
10.	D	20.	D

21. D
22. C
23. D
24. C
25. D

EXAMINATION SECTION
TEST 1

DIRECTIONS: Each question or incomplete statement is followed by several suggested answers or completions. Select the one that BEST answers the question or completes the statement. *PRINT THE LETTER OF THE CORRECT ANSWER IN THE SPACE AT THE RIGHT.*

1. The Model Cities program, which was authorized by the *Demonstration Cities and Metropolitan Development Act* was designed to

    A. help selected areas plan, administer, and carry out coordinated physical and social programs to improve the environment
    B. aid non-profit organizations to develop and demonstrate new ways of providing housing for low-income families
    C. encourage architects and builders to devise new large-scale construction techniques
    D. offer an alternative to usual urban renewal procedures through funding specific renewal activities on a yearly basis

2. The MAJOR purpose of the capital budgeting process in local government is to

    A. provide operating funds for the various departments
    B. centralize budget decision power in the executive branch
    C. centralize budget decision power in the Council
    D. establish a rational system of priorities for construction

3. The economic base of a community is

    A. the number of wealthy people with annual earnings in excess of $100,000 per year as a ratio to the total population
    B. the percentage of factory employed residents as a ratio of the total work force
    C. the productive industries located within the boundaries of a community
    D. those activities which provide the basic employment and income on which the rest of the local economy depends

4. One of the reasons for the creation of *superagencies* within city government was to

    A. create agencies that would serve as liaisons between the mayor's office and the community
    B. decentralize some of the functions for which the old agencies formerly had responsibility
    C. make each agency autonomous
    D. eliminate duplication of activities among different agencies

5. The word *autonomy* means

    A. automatic
    B. disregard of externals
    C. unlimited power or authority
    D. independent, self-governing

6. De facto, as in de facto segregation, means

   A. by right, in accordance with law
   B. actual
   C. disguised
   D. unintentional

7. American cities gain their legal powers from

   A. the Federal government
   B. the State government
   C. the United States Constitution
   D. common law

8. In an average urban area, the one of the following land uses that would account for the LARGEST percentage of land is

   A. residences
   B. streets
   C. business and industry
   D. public and semi-public uses

9. A cul-de-sac street is a

   A. dead-end street terminating in a circular turn-around
   B. loop street branching off from a collector street
   C. narrow street which has become congested as the result of commercial development
   D. gridiron street on which through traffic is prohibited

10. In the city, the capital budget is initially prepared by the

    A. city council
    B. comptroller
    C. city planning commission
    D. budget director

11. Reasonably well-to-do residential communities have joined the search for non-residential taxpayers but have shown LEAST inclination to plan for

    A. the necessary public utilities
    B. adequate access to the sites
    C. housing the workers
    D. the Budget Director

12. The GREATEST percentage of the daytime population of the business center of the city arrives by

    A. railroad
    B. subway
    C. bus
    D. passenger car

13. The LARGEST single public expenditure in most cities and suburbs in the State is for

    A. schools and education
    B. highways
    C. hospitals and health facilities
    D. police protection

14. The legal basis of zoning is 14.____

    A. the police power
    B. the power to levy taxes
    C. the Federal Constitution
    D. a special act of Congress

15. A drug used in addiction programs as a substitute for heroin is 15.____

    A. benzedrine   B. librium
    C. methadone   D. methanimine

16. The STOLcraft is a(n) 16.____

    A. high speed hydrofoil proposed as an alternative to the use of the ferry
    B. vehicle which travels just above the surface of either land or water on a cushion of air
    C. airplane intended for short distance trips between city centers
    D. cargo ship for containerized freight

Questions 17-21.

DIRECTIONS: Questions 17 through 21 are to be answered on the basis of the following information.

FLOOR AREA

Floor area is the sum of the gross areas of the several floors of a building or buildings, measured from the exterior faces of exterior walls or from the center lines of walls separating two buildings.

FLOOR AREA RATIO

Floor area ratio is the total floor area on a zoning lot, divided by the lot area of that zoning lot. (For example, a building containing 20,000 square feet of floor area on a zoning lot of 10,000 square feet has a floor area ratio of 2.0.) Expressed as a formula:

$$FAR = \frac{Floor\ Area}{Lot\ Area}$$

OPEN SPACE RATIO

The *open space ratio* of a zoning lot is the number of square feet of open space on the zoning lot, expressed as a percentage of the floor area on that zoning lot. (For example, if for a particular building an open space ratio of 20 is required, 20,000 square feet of floor area in the building would necessitate 4,000 square feet of open space on the zoning lot upon which the building stands, or, if 6,000 square feet of lot area were in open space, 30,000 square feet of floor area could be in the building on that zoning lot.) Each square foot of open space per 100 square feet of floor area is referred to as one point.

Expressed as a formula:

$$OSR = \frac{100 \times open\ space}{Floor\ Area}$$

17. If a building can be built with a maximum floor area ratio (FAR) of 10.0, this means 17.___
    A. the building can have a maximum of ten stories
    B. the maximum ratio of gross square feet of floor area to area of the first floor is 10:1
    C. that open space on the zoning lot must be provided in an amount equal to ten percent of the total floor area of the building
    D. the maximum ratio of gross square feet of floor area to lot area is 10:1

18. If the open space ratio of a particular building is 18.5 and the actual amount of open space is 13,550 square feet, the floor area of the building must be MOST NEARLY 18.___
    A. 250,675   B. 73,243   C. 28,170   D. 79,027

19. Given: A housing site of 43,560 square feet. 19.___
    At an FAR of 3.33, the allowable total floor area of a proposed building would be MOST NEARLY
    A. 30,736   B. 484,482   C. 48,448   D. 145,055

20. Given: A housing site of 43,560 square feet. 20.___
    At an FAR of 2.94 and an open space ratio of 24.0, how much open space must be provided?
    A. 30,736   B. 10,454   C. 14,816   D. 18,150

21. Given: A housing site of 43,560 square feet. 21.___
    If a proposed building on this site were to have 122,839 gross square feet of floor space, what would the FAR be?
    A. 10.0
    B. 25.5
    C. 2.82
    D. Cannot be determined from data given

Questions 22-24.

DIRECTIONS: Questions 22 through 24 are to be answered on the basis of the following table.

The age characteristics of the total population in a certain neighborhood are as follows:

Age	Number of People
3	2
5	4
12	3
18	3
20	1
21	3
22	4
50	2
56	1
72	2

22. The mean age of the population in the neighborhood described above is MOST NEARLY 22.____

A. 15 B. 19 C. 23 D. 27

23. The median age of the population in the neighborhood described above is MOST NEARLY 23.____

A. 15 B. 20 C. 25 D. 30

24. The percentage of the population over age 65 in the neighborhood described above is MOST NEARLY 24.____

A. 2 B. 4 C. 6 D. 8

25. 25.____

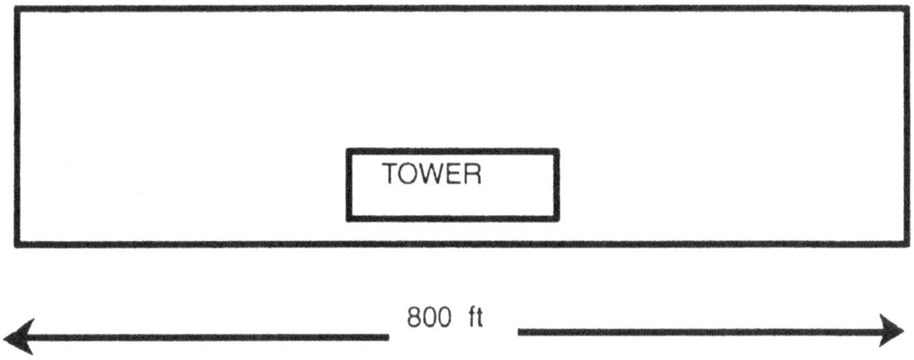

Assume that the above drawing has been made to scale. The total gross floor area of the 20-story tower is, in square feet, MOST NEARLY

A. 200,000 B. 100,000 C. 1,000 D. 50,000

KEY (CORRECT ANSWERS)

1.	A	11.	C
2.	D	12.	B
3.	D	13.	A
4.	D	14.	A
5.	D	15.	C
6.	B	16.	C
7.	B	17.	D
8.	A	18.	B
9.	A	19.	D
10.	C	20.	A

21. C
22. C
23. B
24. D
25. A

TEST 2

DIRECTIONS: Each question or incomplete statement is followed by several suggested answers or completions. Select the one that BEST answers the question or completes the statement. *PRINT THE LETTER OF THE CORRECT ANSWER IN THE SPACE AT THE RIGHT.*

1. In the city, the body that is responsible for choosing the specific location of sites for public improvement is the

    A. city planning commission
    B. department of public works
    C. site selection board
    D. fine arts commission

    1._____

2. Publicly-sponsored Early Childhood programs in the city do NOT include

    A. Family Day Care
    B. Headstart Program
    C. playschools for 2- and 3-year olds
    D. pre-kindergarten in elementary schools

    2._____

3. The one of the following that is NOT a current method of controlling pollution is the

    A. requirement that incinerators in the city be upgraded
    B. project for recycling waste paper and aluminum goods for re-use
    C. sale of non-leaded gasoline for automobiles
    D. conversion of all combined sewers in the city to separate sanitary and storm sewers

    3._____

4. In general, the MOST accurate 5-year projection of population can be made for the

    A. nation   B. metropolitan area
    C. inner city   D. neighborhood

    4._____

5. The type of area in which the GREATEST percentage increase in population occurred between 1960 and 1980 was in the

    A. central cities   B. suburban rings
    C. rural non-farm areas D. rural farm areas

    5._____

6. The one of the following that should NOT be included in a community planning study undertaken by a city planning department is

    A. a survey of how land is used in the area
    B. compilation of data on school utilization
    C. determination of rent levels in the area
    D. renovation of an old building at rents suitable for low-income people

    6._____

7. The one of the following men who had a role in laying out cities along the formal lines of the *City Beautiful* movement was

    A. Rexford Tugwell   B. Daniel Burnham
    C. Clarence Stein   D. Frank Lloyd Wright

    7._____

8. A key factor leading to the development of suburban growth in recent decades is

   A. a series of regional government compacts
   B. the large increase in automobile ownership
   C. the drying up of immigration
   D. the gradual shifting of some shopping and employment from the center of the city to the outskirts

9. A controlled aerial mosaic photograph would be LEAST useful in which of the following types of planning work?

   A. Land use study of undeveloped land
   B. Review of subdivision plats
   C. Study of proposed highway locations
   D. Building condition study of CBD

10. The MAJOR function of the city community planning boards is

    A. to prepare capital and expense budgets for community planning districts
    B. to advise the county executives and city agencies on planning issues
    C. as an umbrella organization for local poverty groups
    D. to provide technical planning help to local community groups

11. Special revenue sharing is intended to

    A. be available only for cities of over 1 million population
    B. be available for general purpose use, to be determined by the cities
    C. replace money previously distributed to cities for categorical grants
    D. in all instances be passed from the state to the city

12. The city's water pollution control plants are being upgraded to _____ treatment which removes _____.

    A. primary; "approximately" 65% of pollutants
    B. secondary; approximately 90% of pollutants
    C. tertiary; approximately 99% of pollutants
    D. desalination; all the mineral matter

13. *Turnkey* housing refers to

    A. a method of housing construction whereby a private developer finances and constructs the housing to the city's standards and the housing is then purchased by the city
    B. the conversion of old-law housing to co-op housing in moderate rent areas, including rent subsidies for low-income families
    C. brownstone renovation with no public subsidy in historic districts where the design must be approved by the landmarks commission
    D. a form of mixing housing with commercial or industrial space, as in the incentive zoning amendment

14. The Planned-Unit Development is a provision of the city zoning resolution which 14.____

    A. provides for industrial development on the outskirts of the city
    B. requires the building of schools, community centers, and shopping facilities as part of a large residential development
    C. permits housing to be built close together in clusters, leaving substantial land areas in their natural state as common open spaces
    D. provides a means of constructing off-street parking facilities in high density residential neighborhoods

15. The official map differs from the master plan in that it 15.____

    A. deals only with proposed streets as they relate to existing streets
    B. includes a detailed engineering design for the existing and proposed street system
    C. is an accurate description of the location of public improvements existing and proposed
    D. is tied directly to the Capital Budget and Improvement Program

16. According to the zoning resolution, a legal non-conforming use in zoning is one established 16.____

    A. prior to the adoption of the ordinance provision prohibiting it
    B. by a special exception permit issued by the planning commission
    C. by a variance issued by the board of standards and appeals
    D. for many years despite the prohibition in the ordinance and which had not been proceeded against

17. The formula for financing interstate highways under state and Federal law provides that the government of the city shall pay what percent of the cost of highway construction? 17.____

    A. 100%   B. 90%   C. 40%   D. 0%

18. The one of the following statements that MOST NEARLY expresses the city's long-term program in regard to arterial highways is to 18.____

    A. provide many routes throughout the city in order to minimize travel time from all points
    B. provide quick vehicular access from the business center to the suburbs
    C. build up bypass routes to discourage traffic from entering the business center
    D. build up the highway network in the outer boroughs and to landbank land in the business center for future through routes

19. The city planning commission 19.____

    A. consists of lifetime members, who annually elect a chairman
    B. administers the zoning resolution and hears appeals for variances
    C. prepares the annual 5-year capital improvement plan
    D. prepares the architectural designs for all public buildings, except schools

20. The feature of the city zoning resolution before 1961 which gave the city's skyscrapers their MOST distinctive architectural character was its 20.____
    A. height bonus for added setbacks
    B. rear yard provisions
    C. off-street parking and loading requirements
    D. density restrictions

KEY (CORRECT ANSWERS)

1.	C	11.	C
2.	C	12.	B
3.	D	13.	A
4.	A	14.	C
5.	B	15.	A
6.	D	16.	A
7.	B	17.	D
8.	B	18.	C
9.	D	19.	C
10.	B	20.	A

TEST 3

DIRECTIONS: Each question or incomplete statement is followed by several suggested answers or completions. Select the one that BEST answers the question or completes the statement. *PRINT THE LETTER OF THE CORRECT ANSWER IN THE SPACE AT THE RIGHT.*

Questions 1-3.

DIRECTIONS: Questions 1 through 3, inclusive, are to be answered in accordance with the following paragraphs.

Into the nine square miles that make up Manhattan's business districts, about two million people travel each weekday to go to work — the equivalent of the combined populations of Boston, Baltimore, and Cincinnati. Some 140,000 drive there in cars, 200,000 take buses, and 100,000 ride the commuter railroads. The great majority, however, go by subway — approximately 1.4 million people.

It is some ride. The last major improvement in the subway system was completed in 1935. The subways are dirty and noisy. Many local lines operate well beneath capacity; but many express lines are strained way beyond capacity in particular, the lines to Manhattan, now overloaded by 39,000 passengers during peak hours.

But for all its discomforts, the subway system is inherently a far more efficient way of moving people than automobiles and highways. Making this system faster, more convenient, and more comfortable for people must be the core of the city's transportation effort.

1. The CENTRAL point of the above text is that
    A. the equivalent of the combined populations of Boston, Baltimore, and Cincinnati commute into Manhattan's business district each weekday
    B. the improvement of the subway system is the key to the solution of moving people efficiently in and out of Manhattan's business district
    C. the subways are dirty and noisy, resulting in a terrible ride
    D. we should increase the ability of people to get in and out of Manhattan by cars, subways, and commuter railroads in order to ease the load from the subways

2. In accordance with the above paragraphs, 1.4 million people commute by subway and _____ by other mass transportation means.
    A. 200,000   B. 100,000   C. 440,000   D. 300,000

3. From the information given in the above paragraphs, one could logically conclude that, next to the subways, the transportation system that carries the LARGEST number of passengers is (the)
    A. railroads   B. cars
    C. buses   D. local lines

Questions 4-6.

DIRECTIONS: Questions 4 through 6, inclusive, are to be answered in accordance with the following paragraphs.

Incentive zoning is an affirmative tool that has widespread applications. The Zoning Resolution which became effective in 1981 substantially reduced the amount of floor space that a developer could put up on a given size lot and increased the light and air. In the Chrysler Building, which was built under the old legislation, the floor space is 27 times the size of the lot. The maximum ratio allowed for buildings now without a special permit is 18.

The newer zoning ordinance provided incentives to developers to devote part of the plot to public plazas or arcades. This space is needed to supplement the sidewalks, which in many cases are as narrow as they were when the midtown area was lined with brownstone or brickfront houses.

While the newer zoning has produced plazas, it has not of itself proved to be a sufficient development control. Stretches of Third Avenue and the Avenue of the Americas, for example, have been almost completely redeveloped in the last few years. This massive private investment has produced several fine individual buildings. The total environment produced, however, has been disappointing in a number of respects, and there is nowhere near the amenity that there could have been.

4. According to the paragraphs above, the use of incentive zoning has not been entirely successful because it has

    A. discouraged redevelopment
    B. encouraged massive private development along Third Avenue
    C. been ineffective in controlling overall redevelopment
    D. not significantly increased the number of parks and plazas being built

5. According to the above paragraphs, one might conclude that before the new Zoning Resolution was passed,

    A. buildings on a given site were required to have greater setbacks
    B. the amount of private investment in development was significantly smaller than it is today
    C. no controls on development existed
    D. the provision of parks and plazas was less frequent

6. In the context of the above paragraphs, the word *amenity* means

    A. compliance with regulations
    B. correction of undesirable environmental aspects
    C. responsiveness to guidelines and incentives
    D. pleasant or desirable features

Questions 7-8.

DIRECTIONS: Questions 7 and 8 are to be answered in accordance with the following paragraphs.

We must also find better ways to handle the relocation of people uprooted by projects. In the past, many renewal plans have foundered on this problem, and it is still the most difficult part of community development. Large-scale replacement of low-income residents – many ineligible for public housing – has contributed to deterioration of surrounding communities, as in Manhattan's West Side, Coney Island, and Arverne. Recently, thanks to changes in Housing Authority procedures, relocation has been accomplished in a far more satisfactory fashion. The step-by-step community development projects we advocate in this plan should bring further improvement.

But additional measures will be necessary. There are going to be more people to be moved; and, with the current shortage of apartments, large ones especially, it is going to be tougher to find places to move them to. The city should have more freedom to buy or lease housing that comes on the market because of normal turnover and make it available to relocatees.

7. According to the above paragraphs, one of the reasons a neighborhood may deteriorate is that 7._____

   A. there is a scarcity of large apartments
   B. step-by-step community development projects have failed
   C. people in the given neighborhood are uprooted from their homes
   D. a nearby renewal project has an inadequate relocation plan

8. From the above paragraphs, one might conclude that the relocation phase of community renewal has been improved 8._____

   A. by changes in Housing Authority procedures
   B. by development of step-by-step community development projects
   C. through expanded city powers to buy housing for relocation
   D. through the Housing Authority Leasing Program

Questions 9-10.

DIRECTIONS: Questions 9 and 10 are to be answered in accordance with the following paragraphs.

Provision of decent housing for the lower half of the population (by income) was thus taken on as a public responsibility. Public housing was to assist the poorest quarter of urban families while the 221(d)(3) Housing Program would assist the next quarter. But limited funds meant that the supply of subsidized housing could not stretch nearly far enough to help this half of the population. Who were to be left out in the rationing process which was accomplished by the sifting of applicants for housing on the part of public and private authorities?

Discrimination on the grounds of race or color is not allowed under Federal law. In all sections of the country, encouragingly, housing programs are found which allow this law to the letter. Yet, housing programs in some cities still suffer from the residue of racial segregation policies and attitudes that for years were condoned or even encouraged.

Some sifting in the 221(d)(3) Housing Program follows the practice of many public housing authorities, the imposition of requirements with respect to character. This is a delicate matter. To fill a project overwhelmingly with broken families, alcoholics, criminals, delinquents, and other problem tenants would hardly make it a wholesome environment. Yet the total exclusion of such families is hardly an acceptable alternative. To the extent this exclusion is practiced, the very people whose lives are described in order to persuade lawmakers and the public to instigate new programs find the door shut in their faces when such programs come into being. The proper balance is difficult to achieve, but society's neediest families surely should not be totally denied the opportunities for rejuvenation in subsidized housing.

9. From the above paragraphs, it can be assumed that the 221(d)(3) Housing Program

    A. served a population earning more than the median income
    B. served a less affluent population than is served by public housing
    C. excludes all problem families from its projects
    D. is a subsidized housing program

10. According to the above paragraphs, the provision of housing for the poor

    A. has not been completely accomplished with public monies
    B. is never influenced by segregationist policies
    C. is limited to providing housing for only the neediest families
    D. is primarily the responsibility of the Federal government

Questions 11-12.

DIRECTIONS: Questions 11 and 12 are to be answered in accordance with the following paragraph.

Though the recent trend toward apartment construction may appear to be the region's response to large-lot zoning and centralized industry, it really is not. It is mainly a function of the age of the population (coupled with a rush to build apartments in the city between the passage of the newer zoning ordinance and its enforcement in December 1981). Most of the apartments are occupied by one- and two-person families — young people out of school but without a family of their own and older people whose children have grown. Both groups have been increasing in number; and, in this region, they characteristically live in apartments. It is this increased demand for apartments and the simultaneous decrease in demand for one-family houses that dramatically raised the percentage of building permits issued for multi-family housing units from 36 percent in 1977 to 67 percent in 1981. The fact that three-fourths of the apartments were built in the Core between 1977 and 1981 at the same time as the Core was losing population underscores the failure of the apartment boom to slow the outward spread of the population.

11. According to the above paragraph, one of the reasons for the increase in the number of building permits issued for multi-family construction in the city metropolitan region is

    A. that workers in industry want to live close to their jobs
    B. an increase in the number of elderly people living in the region
    C. the inability of many families to afford the large lots necessary to build private homes
    D. the new zoning ordinance made it easier to build apartments

12. According to the above paragraph, the apartment construction boom

    A. increased the population density in the core
    B. spurred a population shift to the suburbs
    C. did not halt the outward flow of the population from the core
    D. was most significant in the outer areas of the region

Questions 13-14.

DIRECTIONS: Questions 13 and 14 are to be answered in accordance with the following paragraphs.

The city's economy has its own dynamics, and there is only so much the government can do to shape it. But that margin is critically important. If the city uses its points of leverage, it can generate a large number of jobs and good jobs, jobs that lead to advancement.

As a major employer itself, the city can upgrade the jobs it offers and greatly improve its services to the public if it does so. Since highly skilled professionals will always be in short supply, the city must train more paraprofessionals to take over routine tasks. Equally important, it must provide them with a realistic job ladder so they can move on up — nurse's aide to certified nurse, for example, teacher's aide to teacher. The training programs for such upgrading will require a substantial public investment but the cost-benefit return should be excellent.

As a major purchaser of goods and services, the city can stimulate business enterprise in the ghetto. The growth of Black and Puerto Rican firms will produce more local jobs; it will also create the kind of managerial talent the ghetto needs.

New kinds of enterprise can be set up. In housing, for example, there is a huge backlog of rehabilitation work to be done and a large pool of unskilled manpower to be trained for it. Corporations can be formed to take over tenements, remodel, maintain, and operate them, as in the Brownsville Home Maintenance Program. Grocery cooperatives to bring food prices down are another possibility.

13. According to the above paragraphs, the city is the major employer and, by using its capacity, it can

    A. assist unskilled people with talent to move up on the job ladder
    B. create private enterprises that will renew all areas of the city in need of renewal
    C. eliminate poverty in the ghetto areas by selective purchase of goods and services
    D. have no influence on the economy of the city

13._____

14. According to the above paragraphs, one may REASONABLY conclude that

    A. the city has no power to influence the job market
    B. a by-product of strategic purchasing and employment and training practices can be the rehabilitation of housing and the lowering of food prices
    C. highly skilled professions, which are now in short supply, will no longer be needed after paraprofessionals are trained to take over routine jobs
    D. the city's major objective is to bring down food prices

14._____

15. 500 persons attended a public hearing at which a proposed public housing project was being considered. Less than half favored the project, while the majority opposed the project.
According to the above statement, it is REASONABLE to conclude that

    A. the proposal stimulated considerable community interest
    B. the public housing project was disapproved by the city because a majority opposed it

15._____

C. those who opposed the project lacked sympathy for needy persons
D. the supporters of the project were led by militants

16. A document was published by a public agency and distributed for discussion. The document contained data showing trends in the level of reading among freshmen college students and suggested that the high schools were not investing enough effort in overcoming retardation. It compared the costs of intensifying reading instruction in the secondary schools as compared to costs in college for such instruction.
According to the above statement, it is REASONABLE to conclude that

   A. the document proposed new programs
   B. the college students read better than high school students
   C. some college students need remedial reading
   D. the study was done by a consultant

17. A vacant lot close to a polluted creek is for sale. Two buyers compete. One owns an adjacent factory which provides 300 high paying unskilled jobs. He needs to expand or move from the city. If he expands, he will provide 300 additional jobs. The other is a community group in a changing residential area close by. They hope to stabilize the neighborhood by bringing in new housing. They could build an apartment building with 100 dwelling units on the lot.
According to the above paragraph, it is REASONABLE to conclude that

   A. jobs are more important than housing
   B. there is conflict between the factory owners and the neighborhood group
   C. the neighborhood group will not succeed in stabilizing the area by constructing new housing
   D. the polluted creek should be cleaned up

Questions 18-21.

DIRECTIONS: Questions 18 through 21, inclusive, refer to the phrases shown below. For each of the questions, select that phrase which BEST completes the sentence for that question.

   A. to increase training and educational opportunities
   B. to remove social ills by a slum clearance program
   C. to select the goals and values to which these resources should be directed
   D. to diminish drastic redevelopment, to provide opportunities to move within the area, or to move to new areas which can be assimilated to old objectives

18. In addition to concern with the rational allocation of resources, the urban planning process needs _____.

19. The early housing reformers emphasized the inadequate physical environment of the slums, understressed the connection between the social environment of the slums and the disorders they wanted to cure, and attempted _____.

20. The objective for assisting the transition to middle class status will mean intensified 20.____
efforts _____.

21. To provide a sense of continuity for those people whose residential areas are being 21.____
renewed, mainly working class, it is desirable _____.

Questions 22-25.

DIRECTIONS: For Questions 22 through 25, select that item from Column B that is MOST closely related to the item in Column A.

COLUMN A		COLUMN B	
22. City Map	A.	Citizen Participation	22.____
23. Revenue Sharing	B.	Block Grants	23.____
24. Opportunity Structure	C.	Streets	24.____
25. Public Hearing	D.	Upward Mobility	25.____

KEY (CORRECT ANSWERS)

1. B   11. B
2. D   12. C
3. C   13. A
4. C   14. B
5. D   15. A

6. D   16. C
7. D   17. B
8. A   18. C
9. D   19. B
10. A   20. A

21. D
22. C
23. B
24. D
25. A

EXAMINATION SECTION
TEST 1

DIRECTIONS: Each question or incomplete statement is followed by several suggested answers or completions. Select the one that BEST answers the question or completes the statement. *PRINT THE LETTER OF THE CORRECT ANSWER IN THE SPACE AT THE RIGHT.*

Questions 1-5.

DIRECTIONS: Questions 1 through 5 are based on the table shown below.

POPULATION, URBAN AND RURAL, BY RACE: 2000 TO 2020

In thousands, except percent. An urbanized area comprises at least 1 city of 50,000 inhabitants (central city) plus contiguous, closely settled areas (urban fringe). Data for 2000 and 2010 according to urban definition used in the 2010 census; 2020 data according to the 2020 definition.

YEAR AND AREA	TOTAL	WHITE	ALL OTHER	PERCENT DISTRIBUTION TOTAL	WHITE	ALL OTHER
2000, total population	151,326	135,150	16,176	100.0	100.0	100.0
Urban	96,847	86,864	9,983	64.0	64.3	61.7
Inside urbanized areas	69,249	61,925	7,324	45.8	45.8	45.3
Central cities	48,377	42,042	6,335	32.0	31.1	39.2
Urban fringe	20,872	19,883	989	13.8	14.7	6.1
Outside urbanized areas	27,598	24,939	2,659	18.2	18.5	16.4
Rural	54,479	48,286	6,193	36.0	35.7	38.3
2010, total population	179,323	158,832	20,491	100.0	100.0	100.0
Urban	125,269	110,428	14,840	69.9	69.5	72.4
Inside urbanized areas	95,848	83,770	12,079	53.5	52.7	58.9
Central cities	57,975	47,627	10,348	32.3	30.0	50.5
Urban fringe	37,873	36,143	1,371	21.1	22.8	8.4
Outside urbanized areas	29,420	26,658	2,762	16.4	16.8	13.5
Rural	54,054	48,403	5,651	30.1	30.5	27.6
2020, total population	203,212	177,749	25,463	100.0	100.0	100.0
Urban	149,325	128,773	20,552	73.5	72.4	80.7
Inside urbanized areas	118,447	100,952	17,495	58.3	56.8	68.7
Central cities	63,922	49,547	14,375	31.5	27.9	56.5
Urban fringe	54,525	51,405	3,120	26.8	28.9	12.3
Outside urbanized areas	30,878	27,822	3,057	15.2	15.7	12.0
Rural	53,887	48,976	4,911	26.5	27.6	19.3

1. The ratio of urban to rural population in 2000 was MOST NEARLY

   A. 3:1 B. 4:1 C. 2:1 D. 14:1

   1._____

2. According to the table, the trend of population inside urban areas has been

   A. towards greater concentration B. towards less concentration
   C. towards stabilization D. erratic

   2._____

3. Since 2000, the urban fringe white population has substantially increased while the urban fringe other population has

   A. slightly decreased
   B. greatly decreased
   C. remained the same
   D. increased moderately

4. Over the years, the percentage of the urban white population as compared with the percentage of the total urban population has

   A. remained relatively constant
   B. substantially decreased
   C. substantially increased
   D. varied

5. Select the one of the following which BEST describes the central city white population rate of decrease since 2000 as compared with the central city black population rate of increase.

   A. The central city white population rate of decrease has been greater than the central city black population rate of increase.
   B. The central city white and black populations have not increased to a significant degree.
   C. The central city white population rate of decrease has been equal to the central city black population rate of increase.
   D. The central city white population rate of decrease has been less than the central city black population rate of increase.

Questions 6-10.

DIRECTIONS: Questions 6 through 10 are to be answered on the basis of the table shown below.

STANDARDS FOR RECREATION AREAS

TYPE OF AREA	ACRES PER 1,000 POPULATION	SIZE OF SITE (ACRES) IDEAL	SIZE OF SITE (ACRES) MINIMUM	RADIUS OF AREA SERVED (MILES)
Playgrounds	1.5	4	2	0.5
Neighborhood parks	2.0	10	5	0.5
Playfields	1.5	15	10	1.5
Community parks	3.5	100	40	2.0
District parks	2.0	200	100	3.0
Regional parks and reservations	15.0	500-1,000	varies	10.0

6. What is the MINIMUM number of playfields that a community of 15,000 people may contain if the size of each is kept within the limits shown in the table?

   A. 4   B. 10   C. 6   D. 2

7. If, as far as possible, ideal sized playgrounds are built, how many IDEAL SIZED playgrounds should a community of 12,000 people contain?

   A. 4   B. 8   C. 1   D. 10

8. Approximately how many people can a community park of 200 acres serve? 8._____

   A. 120,000 B. 80,000 C. 55,000 D. 20,000

9. If only minimum sized neighborhood parks are built, how many will be required for a population of 20,000? 9._____

   A. 5 B. 2 C. 8 D. 12

10. A community of 75,000 persons is evenly distributed over a 5 square mile area. Of the following, the number and size of playgrounds that would BEST satisfy the standards is _____ playgrounds @ _____ acres each. 10._____

    A. 5; 7.5 B. 35; 3.5 C. 10; 10 D. 50; 1.5

11. The illustration shown at the right is an example of a 11._____

    A. simple grade separation
    B. simple interchange of a freeway with a highway
    C. three-level interchange
    D. *T* interchange

12. The practical MINIMUM number of cars per hour that can be carried per lane on a limited access roadway with uninterrupted flow is considered to be APPROXIMATELY 12._____

    A. 750 B. 1,500 C. 5,000 D. 10,000

13. A street that is open at only one end, with provision for a turn-around at the other, is called a 13._____

    A. local street   B. cul-de-sac
    C. loop street   D. minor street

14. Which of the following shopping center types is the local source of staple goods and daily services? 14._____

    A. Central Business District
    B. Regional Shopping Center
    C. Highway Strip Development
    D. Neighborhood Shopping Center

15. *Air rights* refers to the concept that 15._____

    A. all people are entitled to clean air
    B. vistas from apartments cannot be obstructed
    C. buildings can be constructed over railroads or highways
    D. buildings should be oriented towards the prevailing breezes

16. The one of the following LEAST likely to be considered an integral part of urban design is 16._____

    A. spatial forms   B. surfaces
    C. vistas   D. underground utilities

Questions 17-21.

DIRECTIONS: Questions 17 through 21 are based upon the table shown below.

LIVE BIRTHS, DEATHS, MARRIAGES, AND DIVORCES: 1940-1991

	Number (1,000)					Rate per 1,000 Population				
		DEATHS		MAR-	DIVOR-		DEATHS		MAR-	DIVOR-
YEAR	BIRTHS	TOTAL	INFANT	RIAGES	CES	BIRTHS	TOTAL	INFANT	RIAGES	CES
1940	2,777	697	(NA)	948	83	30.1	14.7	(NA)	10.3	0.9
1945	2,965	816	78	1,008	104	29.5	13.2	99.9	10.0	1.0
1950	2,950	1,118	130	1,274	171	27.7	13.0	85.8	12.0	1.6
1955	2,909	1,192	135	1,188	175	25.1	11.7	71.7	10.3	1.5
1960	2,618	1,327	142	1,127	196	21.3	11.3	64.6	9.2	1.6
1965	2,377	1,393	120	1,327	218	18.7	10.9	55.7	10.4	1.7
1970	2,559	1,417	111	1,596	264	19.4	10.8	47.0	12.1	2.0
1975	2,858	1,402	105	1,613	485	20.4	10.6	38.3	12.2	3.5
1980	3,632	1,452	104	1,667	385	24.1	9.6	29.2	11.1	2.6
1985	4,104	1,529	107	1,531	377	25.0	9.3	26.4	9.3	2.3
1990	4,258	1,712	111	1,523	393	23.7	9.5	26.0	8.5	2.2
1991	4,268	1,702	108	1,548	414	23.3	9.3	25.3	8.5	2.3

NA   Not Available

17. From 1940 to 1991, the birth rate has

    A. approximately doubled
    B. remained stable
    C. been reduced by 25%
    D. had two breaks in its downward progression

18. A comparison of the total population death rate to the infant death rate shows that

    A. the two rates have remained constant
    B. the infant death rate is greater
    C. the total population death rate has decreased at a faster rate
    D. infants had a greater chance to survive in 1965 than in 1980

19. In 1945, about one marriage out of 10 ended in divorce.
In which of the following years would the rate be LESS?

    A. 1985   B. 1965   C. 1950   D. 1940

20. The significance of the decrease in the infant death rate is that

    A. family size will increase
    B. family size will decrease
    C. family size will not be affected
    D. children will become a smaller percentage of the total population

21. According to the chart, the total death rate declined from 14.7 in 1940 to 9.3 in 1991, yet each year more people have died. This fact is MOST likely accounted for by

    A. poor reporting techniques
    B. the decrease in the mortality rate
    C. the increase of total population
    D. the increase of older people in the total population

22. The type of interchange pictured in the illustration shown at the right is called a _____ interchange.

    A. simple
    B. cloverleaf
    C. universal
    D. Bel Geddes

22.____

23. This type of interchange (pictured in the preceding question) is used when

    A. topographic conditions are difficult
    B. traffic volumes are heavy
    C. a major and minor road intersect
    D. two major roads intersect

23.____

24. The one of the following basic requirements which would NOT be considered an integral part of a comprehensive plan is

    A. a capital improvement program
    B. physical design proposals
    C. long-range policy statements
    D. social and economic considerations

24.____

Questions 25-28.

DIRECTIONS: Questions 25 through 28 are based on the data shown below, which indicates total housing units.

HOUSING UNITS: 1960 to 1990
NUMBER IN THOUSANDS

▥ TOTAL   ≡ INSIDE SMSA'S   ▢ IN CENTRAL CITIES

(SMSA's = Standard Metropolitan Statistical Areas)

1990
- Total: 68,679
- Inside SMSA's: 46,295
- In Central Cities: 22,594

1980
- Total: 58,326
- Inside SMSA's: 36,386
- In Central Cities: 19,622

1970
- Total: 45,983
- Inside SMSA's: 25,626
- In Central Cities: 15,120

1960
- Total: 37,326

25. The period of GREATEST production of housing units was 25.___

   A. 1950-60   B. 1980-90   C. 1970-80   D. 1960-70

26. The location of the LARGEST gains in housing units since 1960 was in the 26.___

   A. suburban areas   B. central cities
   C. SMSA's   D. rural areas

27. Contrary to many misconceptions, the above data shows that the central cities are 27.___

   A. losing population to the suburbs
   B. keeping pace with the overall housing development
   C. showing strong development trends
   D. growing, but at a decreasing rate

28. Based on the above data, which of the following statements is MOST accurate? 28.____

   A. The housing stock is rapidly becoming outdated.
   B. More new homes are located in suburban areas than in central cities.
   C. The housing supply is rapidly catching up to the demand.
   D. The majority of the population is located in the SMSA's.

29. The name of the long-range schedule of major projects and their estimated costs over a period of 5-10 years is the 29.____

   A. budget
   B. comprehensive plan
   C. capital improvement program
   D. input-output program

30. *Cost Benefit Analysis* is a method used to 30.____

   A. determine budget compliance
   B. compare costs and benefits of a particular investment
   C. evaluate productivity in school construction
   D. establish social benefits for a neighborhood

31. A *workable program* is a SIGNIFICANT element of a(n) 31.____

   A. urban renewal program
   B. comprehensive plan
   C. capital improvement program
   D. urban design program

32. Which of the following would NOT be considered a major type of municipal planning agency in the United States? 32.____

   A. An independent planning commission
   B. The planning department
   C. A community development department
   D. A local renewal agency

33. Townhouses are MOST closely related to which of the following types of residential construction? 33.____

   A. Garden apartments   B. Row houses
   C. High-rise complexes   D. Semi-attached houses

34. The one of the following which could NOT be considered an accessory use in a residence district is a 34.____

   A. garage   B. greenhouse
   C. dwelling   D. storage shed

35. The ratio of parking space to retail floor area in a major regional shopping center would MOST often be 35.____

   A. 1:1   B. 3:1   C. 6:1   D. 10:1

KEY (CORRECT ANSWERS)

1.	C	16.	D
2.	A	17.	C
3.	D	18.	B
4.	A	19.	D
5.	D	20.	C
6.	D	21.	C
7.	A	22.	B
8.	C	23.	D
9.	C	24.	A
10.	B	25.	C
11.	A	26.	A
12.	B	27.	D
13.	B	28.	B
14.	D	29.	C
15.	C	30.	B

31. A
32. D
33. B
34. C
35. B

TEST 2

DIRECTIONS: Each question or incomplete statement is followed by several suggested answers or completions. Select the one that BEST answers the question or completes the statement. *PRINT THE LETTER OF THE CORRECT ANSWER IN THE SPACE AT THE RIGHT.*

1. When the term *density* is commonly employed as a measure of land use, it refers to the   1.____

    A. number of persons
    B. land coverage
    C. number of buildings
    D. number of dwelling units

2. The *City Beautiful* movement was an outgrowth of the   2.____

    A. Bauhaus School in 1920
    B. Chicago World's Fair in 1893
    C. N.Y.C. Zoning Ordinance of 1916
    D. planning concepts of Emilio Sitte

3. The American Greenbelt towns were built to   3.____

    A. create open space
    B. establish independent satellite communities
    C. establish residential *dormitory* communities
    D. disperse urban population

4. The FIRST United States Housing Act was passed by Congress in   4.____

    A. 1929   B. 1949   C. 1941   D. 1937

5. A specific ratio of permissible floor space to lot area is known as   5.____

    A. floor area ratio
    B. open space ratio
    C. sky exposure plane
    D. lot coverage

6. A *protective covenant* can BEST be described as a(n)   6.____

    A. zoning ordinance
    B. easement
    C. fire insurance policy
    D. deed restriction

7. Underground utility lines are PREFERRED by most planners rather than overhead lines because underground lines   7.____

    A. are more accessible for maintenance
    B. cost less
    C. are not visible
    D. are laid in proper easements

8. If a local street right-of-way is 50 feet, the paved width of the street is GENERALLY _____ feet.   8.____

    A. 18   B. 26   C. 44   D. 50

9. The term *zero population growth* refers to the concept that

   A. the population will eventually become extinct
   B. married couples will not bear children
   C. each family will produce only two children
   D. parents will be subject to a planned schedule of parenthood

10. The MOST common dimensions of a half-acre residential lot are

    A. 100 ft. x 100 ft.
    B. 100 ft. x 200 ft.
    C. 120 ft. x 150 ft.
    D. 200 ft. x 200 ft.

11. As a general rule, large street trees should be planted

    A. 25 feet apart
    B. 50-75 feet apart
    C. 150-200 feet apart
    D. spaced randomly

12. A key regulation of a zoning ordinance relates to the

    A. architectural style of a building
    B. slope of a site
    C. height and bulk of buildings
    D. subsoil conditions

13. Under which one of the following authorities are zoning ordinances adopted by local communities?

    A. Police power
    B. Community power
    C. Will of the people
    D. Common law

14. MOST state enabling laws require that zoning regulations be based upon a

    A. land use plan
    B. base map
    C. comprehensive plan
    D. topographical map

15. The OBJECTIVE of an *interim zoning ordinance* is to

    A. zone only a portion of the community for a special purpose
    B. maintain existing conditions until a more comprehensive ordinance is prepared
    C. create a special district
    D. allow greater freedom in interpretation and utilization of the zoning regulations

16. A *non-conforming* use is

    A. a use which requires special approval to remain
    B. a building that does not comply with yard or bulk regulations
    C. one that is not permitted in a specific district
    D. a building which is structurally unsafe

17. A variance is granted by a board of appeals to

    A. obtain financial relief
    B. provide a balance of power
    C. test community opinion
    D. relieve practical difficulty and hardship

18. Which of the following zoning regulations, taken by itself, would permit the MOST floor area of building on a specific lot?
A

    A. floor area ratio of 3:1
    B. maximum lot coverage of 60%
    C. maximum building height of 50 feet
    D. parking ratio of 2:1

19. Sewers used to carry rain or surface water to a body of water so as to prevent flooding are called _____ sewers.

    A. sanitary   B. storm   C. combined   D. overflow

20. The *Garden City* concept was made famous through a book written by

    A. Sir Patrick Abercombie
    B. Patrick Geddes
    C. Ebenezer Howard
    D. Sir Raymond Unwin

21. *Broadacre City* was advocated as a concept of urban development by

    A. F.L. Wright
    B. Corbusier
    C. Saarinen
    D. Geddes

22. The man who can BEST be associated with the planning principle of *high density-low coverage* is

    A. Wright
    B. VanderRohe
    C. Saarinen
    D. Corbusier

23. The AVERAGE number of persons per household in the United States in 1970 was MOST NEARLY

    A. 2.0   B. 2.5   C. 3.0   D. 3.5

24. Which of the following methods would be the MOST accurate in making population projections?

    A. Migration and natural increase
    B. Apportionment
    C. School enrollment
    D. Geometric extrapolation

25. According to the 1990 census, the total population of the United States was MOST NEARLY _____ million persons.

    A. 190   B. 200   C. 280   D. 350

26. After the amounts of different land uses in a medium-size city have been tabulated, which of the following percentages of the total developed land would USUALLY be utilized for streets?

    A. 12%   B. 20%   C. 30%   D. 8%

27. During the past twenty years, the MOST significant factor causing reorientation of traditional urban land use patterns has been

   A. express highway construction
   B. airport development
   C. new schools
   D. permissive zoning ordinances

28. The fundamental objective of MOST suburban communities in attracting new industries is to

   A. increase local employment opportunities
   B. attract minority groups to relocate
   C. establish a balanced land use pattern
   D. increase tax income

29. Which of the following terms is NOT considered to be part of the street classification system?

   A. Major street
   B. Right-of-way
   C. Local street
   D. Cul-de-sac

30. The USUAL purpose for providing a water tower in a municipal water supply system is to

   A. establish a constant pressure
   B. increase the supply of water
   C. increase water pressure
   D. provide a reserve supply

31. The neighborhood unit concept, which includes the elementary school as its major element, was FIRST advocated in 1929 by

   A. Clarence Stein
   B. Henry Wright
   C. Clarence Perry
   D. N. Engelhardt

32. In the past few years, the type of housing which has received the LEAST amount of consideration in resolving the housing problem is

   A. cluster housing
   B. urban renewal
   C. public housing
   D. middle-income housing

33. *Performance standards* have become an INTEGRAL part of zoning ordinances relating to

   A. road construction
   B. industrial districts
   C. parking garages
   D. commercial areas

34. The legal concept upon which the exercise of *condemnation* is based is called the

   A. *due process* clause of the Constitution
   B. police power
   C. power of eminent domain
   D. general community welfare

35. In which of the following situations would the granting of a zoning variance be considered as IMPROPER action? A(n)

   A. serious topographic condition
   B. undersized lot held prior to zoning
   C. subsurface water condition
   D. economic loss due to a zone change

KEY (CORRECT ANSWERS)

1. D
2. B
3. C
4. D
5. A

6. D
7. C
8. B
9. C
10. B

11. B
12. C
13. A
14. C
15. B

16. C
17. D
18. B
19. B
20. C

21. A
22. D
23. B
24. A
25. C

26. C
27. A
28. D
29. B
30. A

31. C
32. C
33. B
34. C
35. D

TEST 3

DIRECTIONS: Each question or incomplete statement is followed by several suggested answers or completions. Select the one that BEST answers the question or completes the statement. *PRINT THE LETTER OF THE CORRECT ANSWER IN THE SPACE AT THE RIGHT.*

1. The MAJOR objective of cluster zoning is to provide 1.___

    A. greater densities
    B. a variety of housing types
    C. open space
    D. racial balance

2. One tool in combating the problems of *spread city* is to provide 2.___

    A. improved mass transportation systems
    B. more major highways
    C. more single-family detached houses
    D. more community facilities

3. The Environmental Protection Agency has issued national air quality standards for six common pollutants. The one of the following pollutants NOT included is 3.___

    A. sulfur oxides   B. carbon monoxide
    C. sulfur dioxide   D. hydrocarbon oxides

4. The national air quality standards have been issued in two parts: primary and secondary standards. A PRIMARY standard is designed to 4.___

    A. protect public health
    B. protect public welfare
    C. establish ambient air quality
    D. prevent damage to the environment

5. The MAJOR source of air pollution in many urban areas, according to the Environmental Protection Agency, is 5.___

    A. emissions from new plants
    B. fossil-fueled steam-generating plants
    C. motor vehicles
    D. large incinerators

6. A technique designed for the analysis of national economies and which employs an industry interaction model appearing in the form of a multi-sector or industrial matrix is called 6.___

    A. economic base theory
    B. industrial complex analysis
    C. calculated forecasting
    D. input-output theory

7. The traditional master plan, with its strong emphasis on physical improvements, is being more frequently replaced by

   A. policies planning
   B. normative planning
   C. quantitative analysis
   D. flexible planning

8. *Advocate planning* involves the planner in

   A. participating on a federal level to influence local officials
   B. working within the planning unit to obtain his desired goals
   C. working as a citizen, often as a protagonist against the local government
   D. preparing mathematical models of urban development

9. Of the following, the type of commercial development which is LEAST likely to be planned is a

   A. regional shopping center
   B. local shopping complex
   C. highway strip development
   D. central business district

10. The *official map* of a community designates all of the following EXCEPT

    A. street right-of-ways
    B. parks and playgrounds
    C. residential areas
    D. school sites

11. Land use intensity standards are MOST appropriately utilized with the development of

    A. standard subdivisions
    B. planned unit developments
    C. mobile home parks
    D. high-rise residential complexes

12. A topographic map does NOT generally express

    A. climatic conditions
    B. easements
    C. boundary lines and distances
    D. existing buildings

13. Clarence Stein contributed GREATLY to the development of

    A. the concept of the balanced community
    B. the design of Reston
    C. high-rise residential complexes
    D. the Radburn Plan

14. In site development, a 10% grade is considered MAXIMUM for

    A. streets and roads
    B. play fields
    C. building sites
    D. parking lots

15. The Model Cities Program includes all of the following EXCEPT

   A. job training in construction work
   B. local control of programs
   C. physical and social rehabilitation of a community
   D. new city design and development

16. HUD's *Operation Breakthrough* program encouraged

   A. fireproof buildings
   B. innovative prefabricated systems of construction
   C. speed of building erection
   D. a socio-economic assault on the housing program

17. A condominium can BEST be described as a

   A. high-rise residential complex with a complete range of amenities
   B. variation of cooperative ownership
   C. planned unit development with open space
   D. building with full ownership of the dwelling unit and common ownership of public areas

18. A MAJOR advantage of a leaching cesspool is that it

   A. can be used where ground water is two feet below grade
   B. can be used close to potable water
   C. requires a minimum of land area
   D. is limited in capacity

19. Land which rises 2 feet vertically to 5 feet horizontally has a slope of

   A. 2.5%   B. 20%   C. 25%   D. 40%

20. The MAJOR advantage of a subsoil disposal bed for sewage disposal is that it

   A. may be used in any soil except that rated as impervious
   B. is more economical to build
   C. requires less land area than that of a treatment plant
   D. may have a ground water level less than 2 feet below grade

21. To achieve the GREATEST amount of open space in the siting of houses, the one of the following patterns that a planner would MOST probably choose is a _____ pattern.

   A. gridiron   B. court
   C. cluster   D. free-form

22. The maximum distance a child should be required to walk to an elementary school is GENERALLY considered to be _____ mile.

   A. 1/4   B. 1/2   C. 3/4   D. 1

23. Modern industrial parks most often will include all of the following amenities EXCEPT

   A. landscaping and screening
   B. employee parking areas
   C. utilities and services
   D. multi-story structures

24. The BEST source of aerial photographs that provide the greatest coverage of the United States by a single agency is the

   A. Soil Conservation Service
   B. U.S. National Ocean Survey
   C. National Park Service
   D. Agricultural Stabilization Conservation Service

25. Terrain analysis is MOST closely related to the study of

   A. landforms
   B. drainage
   C. soil
   D. land erosion

26. Riparian rights deal with property that is located

   A. over mineral resources
   B. along a body of water
   C. over railroad tracks
   D. over a right-of-way

27. The ADVANTAGE of a *stol* port is that it

   A. can be located near another airport
   B. is not government regulated
   C. accommodates business and pleasure aircraft
   D. requires a short runway

28. One square mile contains EXACTLY _____ acres.

   A. 316   B. 444   C. 640   D. 1,000

29. The one of the following methods of refuse disposal that causes the LEAST air pollution, if efficiently carried out, is

   A. open dumping
   B. land fill
   C. incineration
   D. compositing

30. Sewers which collect sewage only from the plumbing systems of buildings and carry it to a sewage treatment plant are called _____ sewers.

   A. sanitary
   B. storm
   C. combined
   D. constant-flow

KEY (CORRECT ANSWERS)

1.	C	16.	B
2.	A	17.	D
3.	C	18.	C
4.	A	19.	D
5.	C	20.	A
6.	D	21.	C
7.	A	22.	B
8.	C	23.	D
9.	C	24.	D
10.	C	25.	A
11.	B	26.	B
12.	A	27.	D
13.	D	28.	C
14.	A	29.	B
15.	D	30.	A

EXAMINATION SECTION
TEST 1

DIRECTIONS: Each of Questions 1 through 15 consists of a passage which contains one word that is incorrectly used because it is not in keeping with the meaning that the passage is evidently intended to convey. Determine which word is incorrectly used. Then select from the words lettered A, B, C, or D the word which, when substituted for the incorrectly used word, would BEST help to convey the meaning of the passage.

1. A manager must often operate systems that are quite complex, but these systems are an effective vehicle for management. Each system has an input, a process, and an output, and is a self-contained unit, but it is also related to a system of a wider and higher order as well as to its own sub-systems that represent the integration of several systems of the lower order. Thinking in terms of systems restricts his understanding of the multitudinous activities with which he must work, and it also enables him to see better the nature of the complex problems that he faces.

    A. isolation
    B. simplifies
    C. perpetuating
    D. constrains

1.____

2. Planning involves, first, the conceiving of goals and the development of alternative courses of future action to achieve the goals. Second, it involves the reduction of these alternatives from a very large number to a small number and finally to one approved course of action, the program. Budgeting probably plays a slight part in the first phase but an increasingly important and decisive part in the second. It facilitates the choice-making process by providing a basis for systematic comparisons among alternatives which take into account their total impacts on both the debit and the credit sides. It thus encourages, and provides some of the tools for, an increasing degree of precision in the planning process. Budgeting is the ingredient of planning which precedes the entire process.

    A. achievement
    B. improved
    C. immediate
    D. disciplines

2.____

3. In every instance the burden of proving each of the charges against the employee, which constitute the claimed misconduct or incompetence, must be upon the agency alleging the same. This simply means that it is incumbent upon the agency to establish each of the charges by a fair preponderance of the entire evidence. Unless the Hearing Officer is satisfied that the evidence has fairly and reasonably established the facts asserted by the agency, the agency has not sustained the burden of proof. The Hearing Officer must determine the admissibility of evidence where there is an objection to a question. Although at disciplinary hearings the presentation of the testimony is not limited by strict and. technical rules of evidence as in a court, nevertheless the Hearing Officer should at all times consider its relevance and materiality, and then make his determination on the basis of fairness.

    A. corroborate
    B. incredible
    C. disinterested
    D. obligatory

3.____

4. The examination of alternative means available for the accomplishment of a given program must proceed along lines somewhat different from the review of alternative programs. In the former, the budget officer should possess sufficient knowledge of operations, and of methods and procedures, to be able to challenge badly conceived projects and to ask the kinds of questions which call forth the orderly processes of administration. This is where budget review and organization and method analysis tend to conflict, and it is here that the reviewing officer who has had operating experience can be most effective in questioning and criticizing management techniques.

   A. personnel
   B. problems
   C. public
   D. merge

5. The employee is not required to submit a written answer to the charges of incompetency or misconduct. The fact that an employee does not choose to submit a written answer should not be taken to mean that he admits guilt. However, the answer provides a means for the accused employee, in writing and for the record, to plead guilty or not guilty to the various charges and specifications, to allege matters tending to disprove the charges, including his good character and reputation, to allege any incriminating circumstances and also to plead a favorable record of service and conduct which might tend to lessen the penalty. Upon receipt of the employee's written answer to the charges, the answer should be carefully analyzed and any allegations therein verified. It may also be necessary to gather new evidence for the hearing in relation to allegations contained in the answer.

   A. confidential
   B. mitigative
   C. particularize
   D. procedural

6. In an article in the Harvard Business Review ("Human Relations or Human Resources"), Raymond E. Miles expounded a human resources theory of management. He declared that a manager's job cannot be viewed as merely one of giving direction and obtaining cooperation; rather, it is one of creating an environment in which the total resources of his department can be utilized. In this environment, the manager shares information and modifies departmental decisions with his employees and encourages their self-direction, not to improve their role satisfactions but to improve the decision making and the total performance efficiency of the organization. Many decisions are made more efficiently by those directly involved in and affected by them. In fact, Miles added, the more important the decisions, the greater the manager's obligation to encourage subordinate self-direction.

   A. actuate
   B. appearance
   C. compulsion
   D. discusses

7. Each organization follows a particular philosophy of management selected from a spectrum ranging from authoritarian to participative. If it adopts an approach in which the manager makes all the decisions and passes them on to subordinates for consideration, it follows an authoritarian philosophy that determines its organization structure and climate. Its structure will follow closely the pattern of many levels of management, tight spans of control, and formal channels of communication. The direction of information flow will be downward, supervisors will have little trust in subordinates, and a high degree of emphasis will be placed on management controls.

   A. approve
   B. concentrated
   C. discretionary
   D. execution

8. Besides the ability to comprehend the magnitude of decisions the ability to deal with decision complexity also differs from person to person. Most human beings are discouraged only with a two-option decision, seeing reality in terms of black or white and hardly ever noticing the gray. Even when there is a choice of three or four pretty well-defined options, a human being will consciously or unconsciously reduce them to two. It takes a good deal of training and education plus a highly developed intellectual structure to handle multi-option decisions and to actively seek a third or fourth alternative.

   A. comfortable
   B. enlarging
   C. narrowly
   D. passive

9. Manpower planning, like finance; is a management function that cannot be delegated or decentralized. What has often been overlooked in studies of decentralization is that no successful firm has ever decentralized the financial function. Since there has rarely been more than one treasurer in a firm, the centralized, control of finances exercises an auxiliary power over all members in a decentralized organization. Just as the management of financial resources is regularly centralized, so the management of human and, in particular, managerial resources must be centralized and the primary responsibility accepted by the chief executive. In fact, he should consider the direction of the managerial manpower plan to be his top responsibility.

   A. concentration
   B. external
   C. subsidiary
   D. ultimate

10. One drawback of the participative-management approach is the lack of solid research to document its contentions. What has been collected is either inconclusive or negative. Laboratory experiments have repeatedly demonstrated that groups that are organized to counter interpersonal comfort, openness, familiarity, and cohesiveness perform poorly. At least one study, in a large insurance company, of different styles of management revealed that while greater acceptance of leadership and high morale were present in the division led by the manager who believes in democratic supervision, this division's performance results were no better than those achieved by the authoritarian leaders.

    A. disputed
    B. emphasise
    C. inconsistency
    D. resistance

11. An organization experiences continuous changes which, taken together, tend to follow a course that can be defined and projected as a trend. Thus, after a company has accumulated sufficient historical data, it is fairly simple to project certain manpower trends. For example, to estimate within a fairly close margin the number of managers who will retire, die, resign, or be discharged in the succeeding 12 months is not so difficult. What is much more difficult and should not even be tried is to predict the number of those individuals who will die, retire, or resign. Simply knowing that, according to present trends, the company must replace 23 managers in the next 12 months is a distinct advantage, and knowing within certain confidence limits how many must be replaced within the next five years affords an even greater advantage

    A. handicap
    B. names
    C. terminated
    D. withheld

12. To assess another person, one must first obtain an accurate description of him in relation to the task for which he is being considered, But, to describe a person accurately, we must obtain relevant information about him and this is the sensitive area. Precisely what information is relevant to the role he is asked to play? If it is relevant, have we the right to it? Are there not some personal areas that are open for public inspection? These quite difficult questions are made even more difficult by the unfortunate way they have been raised recently by government agencies. The mishandling of inquiries into the personal background of applicants for positions has been so widespread that it has been necessary to pass laws at all levels restricting the amount and the quality of information that an employer may seek to obtain from a job applicant.

    A. disclosure B. processing
    C. prohibition D. unavailable

13. An organization's goals must be based on an accurate appraisal of its manpower resources, otherwise they will be like the objectives announced by a last-place baseball-team manager in the spring no more than pious hopes set down for their inspirational value. Public officials are quite guilty in this respects establishing targets for full employment, tax reduction, and urban renewal that are totally attainable and hardly within the capacities of those on the payroll. Many businesses follow the same practice, establishing market-penetration or sales goals that are quite beyond the competence and the energy of their employees. Setting goals, therefore, must take into account the probable course of events that is likely to unfold inside and outside the organization. This prediction of future events is known as forecasting.

    A. estimates B. laxity
    C. tendency D. unrealistic

14. In some organizations, a silent conspiracy can prevail that masks the facts about the managerial situation. Older managers who feel threatened by their advancing age, their creeping obsolescence, or their rapidly changing environment may try to hide their heads in the sands of yesterday. To support themselves, they may try many maneuvers — hiding promising young men, promoting incompetence, or making a farce out of the performance evaluation program. Out of this mass anxiety an "establishment" is born, a highly structured "in" group that invalidates manpower rules designed to insure its own security. This is the system that old men cherish and young men rail a gainst, that blights an organization like a creeping cancer and slowly destroys it as, all the while, its presence remains unfelt until it is fatal.

    A. enforces B. erosion
    C. manipulate D. terminating

15. Z. Pietrowski found that the successful top executive strives more intensively for personal achievement, sets more difficult work goals for himself, can adapt emotionally to a variety of people, is more original, and has less insecurity and self-doubt. E. Ghiselli found in his study of 287 managers that the effective manager showed less need for job security than did less effective managers. The effective managers showed the strongest desire for self-actualization, for the opportunity to utilize their talents in customary ways. In summary, the studies indicate quite clearly that the successful manager has a total life pattern of successful endeavor.

    A. conspicuously B. creative
    C. effacement D. ineffectual

KEY (CORRECT ANSWERS)

1.	B	6.	D
2.	D	7.	D
3.	A	8.	A
4.	D	9.	D
5.	B	10.	B

11. B
12. D
13. D
14. A
15. B

TEST 2

DIRECTIONS: Each of the following questions consists of a paragraph which contains one word that is incorrectly used because it is not in keeping with the meaning that the paragraph is evidently intended to convey. Determine which word is incorrectly used. Select from the choices lettered A, B, C, and D the word which, when substituted for the incorrectly used work, would BEST help to convey the meaning of the paragraph.

1. Among the Housing Manager's over-all responsibilities in administering a project is the prevention of the development of conditions which might lead to termination of tenancy and eviction of a tenant. Where there appears to be doubt that a tenant is fully aware of his responsibilities and is thus jeopardizing his tenancy, the Housing Manager should acquaint him with these responsibilities. Where a situation involves behavior of a tenant or a member of his family, the Housing Manager should confirm, through discussions and referrals to social agencies, correction of the conditions before they reach a stage where there is no alternative but termination proceedings.

   A. coordinate B. identify
   C. assert   D. attempt

2. There is one almost universal administrative complaint. The budget is inadequate, Now, between adequacy and inadequacy lie all degrees of adequacy. Further, human wants are modest in relation to human resources. From these two facts we may conclude that the fundamental criterion of administrative decision must be a criterion Of efficiency (the degree to which the goals have been reached relative to the available resources) rather than a criterion of adequacy (the degree to which its goals have been reached). The task of the administrator is to maximize social values relative to limited resources.

   A. improve   B. simple
   C. limitless D. optimize

3. Leadership is a personality characteristic based to a large extent on the charisma the leader possesses for his followers. Thus his appeal must be to the emotional and the personal life of the group. A manager, on the other hand, has been entrusted with the responsibility of decision making, which has nothing whatsoever to do with leadership. It is not a personal trait, it is a role that is not administrative and based upon the process of choosing a course of action and committing the group's resources to it. The manager's function is to define goals and objectives, to select a course of action to achieve them, and to evaluate realistically the results of that action. There is little charisma in such a role. Leaders depend for their success on personality, a characteristic that has nothing to do with management. Consequently, leadership and management are most appropriately treated as separate phenomena that are effectively handled simultaneously but not necessarily by the same person.

   A. initiates B. limit
   C. purely   D. rational

4. Where it appears that any City employee may be guilty of corruption or wrongdoing, the Department of Investigation should be informed. The agency itself should then conduct the inquiry immediately only if the Department of Investigation so determines. If during an inquiry it appears that the corruption or wrongdoing may be more serious or widespread than originally suspected, the Department of Investigation should be recontacted immediately. In some instances, it may be necessary to hold the disciplinary hearing prior to the criminal proceedings and it is essential that the conduct of the criminal case not be unnecessarily warranted by the department trial. The transcript and all papers should be kept in a secure place and there should be no disclosure or publicity about what transpired without the approval of the Corpora- tion Counsel and the Commissioner of Investigation.

    A. superseded
    B. prejudiced
    C. premature
    D. concurrently

5. It is often easy to enumerate reasons why a housing enterprise succeeds or fails. With so many variables that appear to have a make-or-break impact upon the outcome, there is a natural tendency to over-emphasize the importance of the man, particularly the man in charge. Society subscribes to the idea that housing leadership is important, but society doesn't really believe it. Even top housing managers are dubious about the significance of their own roles in the success or failure of a public enterprise. When things go wrong, they tend to blame the system; when things go right, they modestly give credit to "the team." The only way to manage a housing organization effectively is to give managers authority to run it and then hold them strictly accountable for the results. This idea is hardly new to anyone, however rarely it is carried out in practice. But the idea breaks down because we know so little about picking men who have the capacity to manage large housing enterprises.

    A. coalesce
    B. disavows
    C. overlook
    D. wavering

6. The technological and social changes that have occurred in American economy during the rise of the Managerial Society have not only required much more highly trained managers, they have created intense competition for these same men from other sectors of the economy: from the government, from education, and from the nonprofit areas. In the decade between 1954 and 1964, the number of employees in the executive classes of the federal government jumped 58 percent. The result is an unprecedented demand for managers that is likely to continue unabated for the next three decades. If we assume that the shortage has been met in the same way as in technical fields, it is probable that a substantial number of managerial positions are filled by people not fully qualified or that the positions have been reinforced by the inclusion of duties incompatible with those of a manager. Since this latter strategy is most commonly employed, it is possible to assert that many managers are managers in name only.

    A. conflicting
    B. diluted
    C. eliminate
    D. incumbent

7. There is also a suspicion in some quarters that admin- istrators have a tendency to be imperialistic, that government officials have an inborn desire to spend more of the taxpayers' money, to hire more people, to build more buildings. Sometimes this charge is couched in more gentle terms, it is suggested that administrators tend to overestimate simply to be on the safe side, so that they will be able to retain some leeway in program administration. Again, there is no doubt that these charges and suspicions are justified in particular cases. The overzealous and overambitious are not unknown in our society, or in any society. But it would be difficult to demonstrate that these tendencies are more widespread in government than elsewhere. Very often, what looks like an overweening ambition may turn out to be regressive administration. The government official who seeks to expand his program may do so because he sees the need, because he would like to do a better job, because he is close to the beneficiaries of his program operations. 7.____

    A. responsive   B. fewer
    C. freedom   D. targets

KEY (CORRECT ANSWERS)

1. D
2. C
3. C
4. B
5. C
6. B
7. A

READING COMPREHENSION
UNDERSTANDING AND INTERPRETING WRITTEN MATERIAL

EXAMINATION SECTION

DIRECTIONS: Each question or incomplete statement is followed by several suggested answers or completions. Select the one that BEST answers the question or completes the statement. *PRINT THE LETTER OF THE CORRECT ANSWER IN THE SPACE AT THE RIGHT.*

TEST 1

Questions 1-2.

DIRECTIONS: Questions 1 and 2 are to be answered SOLELY on the basis of the following passage.

One of the biggest mistakes of government executives with substantial supervisory responsibility is failing to make careful appraisals of performance during employee probationary periods. Many a later headache could have been avoided by prompt and full appraisal during the early months of an employee's assignment. There is not much more to say about this except to emphasize the common prevalence of this oversight and to underscore that for its consequences, which are many and sad, the offending managers have no one to blame but themselves.

1. According to the above passage, probationary periods are
    A. a mistake and should not be used by supervisors with large responsibilities
    B. not used properly by government executives
    C. used only for those with supervisory responsibility
    D. the consequence of management mistakes

2. The one of the following conclusions that can MOST appropriately be drawn from the above passage is that
    A. management's failure to appraise employees during their probationary period is a common occurrence
    B. there is not much to say about probationary periods because they are unimportant
    C. managers should blame employees for failing to use their probationary periods properly
    D. probationary periods are a headache to most managers

Questions 3-7.

DIRECTIONS: Questions 3 through 7 are to be answered SOLELY on the basis of the passage preceding each question.

3. Things may not always be what they seem to be. Thus, the wise supervisor should analyze his problems and determine whether there is something there that does not meet the eye. For example, what may seem on the surface to be a personality clash between two subordinates may really be a problem of faulty organization, bad communication, or bad scheduling.
Which one of the following statements BEST supports this passage?
   A. The wise supervisor should avoid personality clashes.
   B. The smart supervisor should figure out what really is going on.
   C. Bad scheduling is the result of faulty organization.
   D. The best supervisor is the one who communicates effectively.

4. Some supervisors, under the pressure of meeting deadlines, become harsh and dictatorial to their subordinates. However, the supervisor most likely to be effective in meeting deadlines is one who absorbs or cushions pressures from above. According to the above passage, if a supervisor wishes to meet deadlines, it is MOST important that he
   A. be informative to his superiors
   B. encourage personal initiative among his subordinates
   C. become harsh and dictatorial to his subordinates
   D. protects his subordinates from pressures from above

5. When giving instructions, a supervisor must always make clear his meaning, leaving no room for misunderstanding. For example, a supervisor who tells a subordinate to do a task *as soon as possible* might legitimately be understood to mean either *it's top priority* or *do it when you can*. Which of the following statements is BEST supported by the above passage?
   A. Subordinates will attempt to avoid work by deliberately distorting instructions.
   B. Instructions should be short, since brief instructions are the clearest.
   C. Less educated subordinates are more likely to honestly misunderstand instructions.
   D. A supervisor should give precise instructions that cannot be misinterpreted.

6. Practical formulas are often suggested to simplify what a supervisor should know and how he should behave, such as the four F's (be firm, fair, friendly, and factual). But such simple formulas are really broad principles, not necessarily specific guides in a real situation. According to the above passage, simple formulas for supervisory behavior
   A. are superior to complicated theories and principles
   B. not always of practical use in actual situations
   C. useful only if they are fair and factual
   D. would be better understood if written in clear language

7. Many management decisions are made far removed from the actual place of operations. Therefore, there is a great need for reliable reports and records and, the larger the organization, the greater is the need for such reports and records. According to the above passage, management decisions made far from the place of operations are
   A. dependent to a great extent on reliable reports and records
   B. sometimes in error because of the great distances involved
   C. generally unreliable because of poor communications
   D. generally more accurate than on-the-scene decisions

Questions 8-9.

DIRECTIONS: Questions 8 and 9 are to be answered SOLELY on the basis of the following passage.

A supervisor who is seeking to influence the behavior of others, whether these others are subordinates, superiors, or colleagues, soon becomes aware of the importance of their attitudes. He may be surprised at some of the attitudes they have and wonder how they can hold some of the views they do - if these views differ from his own. He may be perplexed when others do not change their attitudes even after he has presented facts that obviously should cause them to change.

8. Of the following, the MAIN implication of the above passage is that
   A. behavior is influenced by factual data
   B. interaction with others is based on factual data
   C. rank and intelligence determine behavior
   D. interpretation of facts is controlled by attitude

9. The one of the following statements MOST directly supported by the above paragraph is:
   A. A competent supervisor is firm in his views yet retains an open mind
   B. Influencing the behavior of others is usually the most difficult problem in effective supervision
   C. A particular viewpoint may seem unusual to a supervisor holding a contrary opinion
   D. Organizational success depends upon supervisory motivation

Questions 10-13.

DIRECTIONS: Questions 10 through 13 are to be answered SOLELY on the basis of the following passage.

Top public officials, who feel they have tried to improve conditions for their employees, are often bewildered, hurt, or angered when these employees want to do something on their own through union membership. These officials gain little, however, by regarding unionization as an insult or as evidence of failure on their part. The real challenge and opportunity for top officials is to deal constructively with the labor organization which their employees have *duly* chosen to represent them.

10. The author of the above passage MOST likely considers top management to be
    A. corrupt   B. independent
    C. entrenched   D. paternalistic

11. The above passage points out that certain top public officials are LIKELY to be
    A. disturbed that employees wish to be unionized
    B. aware of the actual needs of their employees
    C. convinced that labor organizations are ineffectual in gaining benefits
    D. unable to deal constructively with individual employees

12. The tenor of the above passage suggests that
    A. top officials should deal positively with the labor organization
    B. intelligent management practices usually eliminate labor union activities
    C. the labor movement has often opposed enlightened management policies
    D. labor and management have had a long history of disagreement

13. As used in the above passage, the word *duly* means MOST NEARLY
    A. properly or legally
    B. forcefully or sincerely
    C. openly or publicly
    D. precisely or carefully

Questions 14-17.

DIRECTIONS: Questions 14 through 17 are to be answered SOLELY on the basis of the following passage.

The mental attitude of the employee toward safety is exceedingly important in preventing accidents. All efforts designed to keep safety on the employee's mind and to keep accident prevention a live subject in the office will help substantially in a safety program. Although it may seem strange, it is common for people to be careless. Therefore, safety education is a continuous process.

Safety rules should be explained, and the reasons for their rigid enforcement should be given to employees. Telling employees to be careful or giving similar general safety warnings and slogans is probably of little value. Employees should be informed of basic safety fundamentals. This can be done through staff meetings, informal suggestions to employees, movies, and safety instruction cards. Safety instruction cards provide the employees with specific suggestions about safety and serve as a series of timely reminders helping to keep safety on the minds of employees. Pictures, posters, and cartoon sketches on bulletin boards that are located in areas continually used by employees arouse the employees' interest in safety. It is usually good to supplement this type of safety promotion with intensive individual follow-up.

14. The above passage implies that the LEAST effective of the following safety measures is
    A. rigid enforcement of safety rules
    B. getting employees to think in terms of safety
    C. elimination of unsafe conditions in the office
    D. telling employees to stay alert at all times

15. The reason given by the above passage for maintaining ongoing safety education is that
    A. people are often careless
    B. office tasks are often dangerous
    C. the value of safety slogans increases with repetition
    D. safety rules change frequently

16. Which one of the following safety aids is MOST likely to be preferred by the above passage?
    A
    A. cartoon of a man tripping over a carton and yelling, *Keep aisles clear!*
    B. poster with a large number one and a caption saying, *Safety First*
    C. photograph of a very neatly arranged office
    D. large sign with the word *THINK* in capital letters

17. Of the following, the BEST title for the above passage is
    A. BASIC SAFETY FUNDAMENTALS
    B. ENFORCING SAFETY AMONG CARELESS EMPLOYEES
    C. ATTITUDES TOWARD SAFETY
    D. MAKING EMPLOYEES AWARE OF SAFETY

Questions 18-21.

DIRECTIONS: Questions 18 through 21 are to be answered SOLELY on the basis of the following passage.

An employee who has been a member of the retirement system continuously for at least two years may thereafter borrow an amount not exceeding forty percent of the amount of his accumulated contributions in the retirement system, provided that he can repay the amount borrowed, with interest, before he reaches age sixty-three by additional deductions of eight percent from his compensation at the time it is paid. The rate of interest payable on such loan shall be three percent higher than the rate of regular interest creditable to his retirement account. The amount borrowed, with interest, shall be repaid in equal installments by deduction from the member's compensation at the time it is paid, but such installments must be equal to at least four percent of the member's compensation.

Each loan shall be insured by the retirement system against the death of the member, as follows: from the twenty-fifth through the fiftieth day after making the loan, thirty percent of the present value of the loan is insured; from the fifty-first through the seventy-fifth day, sixty percent of the present value of the loan is insured; on and after the seventy-sixth day, all of the present value of the loan is insured. Upon the death of the member, the amount of insurance payable shall be credited to his accumulated contributions to the retirement system.

Instead of a loan, any member who cancels his rate of contribution may withdraw from his account, and may restore in any year he chooses, any sum in excess of the maximum in his annuity savings account and due to his account at the end of the calendar year in which he was entitled to cancel his rate of contribution.

18. Based on the information in the above passage, a member may obtain a loan
    A. in any amount not exceeding forty percent of his accumulated contributions in the system
    B. if he has contributions in excess of the maximum in his annuity savings account
    C. if he will remain a member of the retirement system until age 63
    D. once during his first two years of membership and then at any time thereafter

6 (#1)

19. According to the information in the above passage, the interest rate paid by a member who borrows from the retirement system is
    A. 4% of his earnable compensation
    B. 8% of his earnable compensation
    C. lower than the interest rate creditable to his retirement account
    D. higher than the interest rate creditable to his retirement account

19._____

20. Suppose that a member of the retirement system obtained a loan on July 15 of this year and died on October 2 when the present value of her loan was $800. Based on the information in the above passage, this member will have _____ her accumulated contributions to the retirement system.
    A. $480 credited to   B. $480 deducted from
    C. $800 credited to   D. $800 deducted from

20._____

21. Based on the information in the above passage, a member who has excess funds in his retirement account may with- draw funds from the retirement system
    A. if he has cancelled his rate of contribution
    B. if he restores the funds within one year of withdrawal
    C. when he retires
    D. if he leaves city service

21._____

Questions 22-25.

DIRECTIONS: Questions 22 through 25 are to be answered SOLELY on the basis of the following passage.

Upon the death of a member or former member of the retirement system, there shall be paid to his estate, or to the person he had nominated by written designation, his accumulated deductions. In addition, if he is a member who is in city service, there shall be paid a sum consisting of: an amount equal to the compensation he earned while a member during the three months immediately preceding his death, or, if the total amount of years of allowable service exceeds five, there shall be paid an amount equal to the compensation he earned while a member during the six months immediately preceding his death; and the reserve-for-increased-take-home-pay, if any. Payment for the expense of burial, not exceeding two hundred and fifty dollars, may be made to the relative or friend who, in the absence or failure of the designated beneficiary, assumes this responsibility.

Until the first retirement benefit payment has been made, where a member has not selected an option, the member will be considered to be in city service, and the death benefits provided above will be paid instead of the retirement allowance. The member, or upon his death his designated beneficiary, may provide that the actuarial equivalent of the benefit otherwise payable in a lump sum shall be paid in the form of an annuity payable in installments; the amount of such annuity is determined at the time of the member's death on the basis of the age of the beneficiary at that time.

22. Suppose that a member who has applied for retirement benefits without 22._____
selecting an option dies before receiving any payments.
According to the information in the above passage, this member's beneficiary would be entitled to receive
    A. an annuity based on the member's age at the time of his death
    B. a death benefit only
    C. the member's retirement allowance only
    D. the member's retirement allowance, plus a death benefit payment in a lump sum

23. According to the information in the above passage, the amount of the benefit 23._____
payable upon the death of a member is based, in part, on the
    A. length of city service during which the deceased person was a member
    B. number of beneficiaries the deceased member had nominated
    C. percent of the deceased member's deductions for social security
    D. type of retirement plan to which the deceased member belonged

24. According to the information in the above passage, which one of the following 24._____
statements concerning the payment of death benefits is CORRECT?
    A. In order for a death benefit to be paid, the deceased member must have previously nominated, in writing, someone to receive the benefit.
    B. Death benefits are paid upon the death of members who are in city service.
    C. A death benefit must be paid in one lump sum.
    D. When a retired person dies, his retirement allowance is replaced by a death benefit payment.

25. According to the information in the above passage, the amount of annuity 25._____
payments made to a beneficiary in monthly installments in lieu of a lump sum payment is determined by the
    A. length of member's service at the time of his death
    B. age of the beneficiary at the time of the member's death
    C. member's age at retirement
    D. member's age at the time of his death

KEY (CORRECT ANSWERS)

1.	B	11.	A	21.	A
2.	A	12.	A	22.	B
3.	B	13.	A	23.	A
4.	D	14.	D	24.	B
5.	D	15.	A	25.	B
6.	B	16.	A		
7.	A	17.	D		
8.	D	18.	A		
9.	C	19.	D		
10.	D	20.	C		

TEST 2

DIRECTIONS: Each question or incomplete statement is followed by several suggested answers or completions. Select the one that BEST answers the question or completes the statement. *PRINT THE LETTER OF THE CORRECT ANSWER IN THE SPACE AT THE RIGHT.*

Questions 1-4.

DIRECTIONS: Questions 1 through 4 are to be answered SOLELY on the basis of the following passage.

Depreciation -- Any reduction from the upper limit of value. An effect caused by deterioration and/or obsolescence. Deterioration is evidenced by wear and tear, decay, dry rot, cracks, encrustations, or structural defects. Obsolescence is divisible into two parts, functional or economic. Functional obsolescence may be due to poor planning, mechanical inadequacy or overadequacy, functional inadequacy or overadequacy due to size, style, or age. It is evidenced by conditions within the property. Economic obsolescence is caused by changes external to the property, such as neighborhood infiltrations of inharmonious groups or property uses, legislation, etc. It is also the actual decline in market value of the improvement to land from the time of purchase to the time of sale.

1. According to the above passage, a form of physical deterioration can be caused by
    A. termite infestation
    B. zoning regulations
    C. inadequate wiring
    D. extra high ceilings

2. According to the above passage, a form of economic obsolescence may be caused by
    A. structural defects
    B. poor architectural design
    C. changes in zoning regulations
    D. chemical reactions

3. According to the above passage, the statement which BEST explains the meaning of depreciation is that it is a loss in value
    A. caused only by economic obsolescence
    B. resulting from any cause
    C. caused only by wear and tear
    D. resulting from conditions or changes external to the property

4. According to the above passage, the lack of air conditioning in warm climates is
    A. a form of physical deterioration
    B. a form of functional obsolescence
    C. a form of economic obsolescence
    D. not a form of depreciation

Questions 5-8.

DIRECTIONS: Questions 5 through 8 are to be answered SOLELY on the basis of the following passage.

2 (#2)

In determining the valuation of income-producing property, the capitalization of income is accepted as a proper approach to value. Income-producing property is bought and sold for the purpose of making money. How much an investor would pay would, of course, depend on how much he could earn on his investment. The amount he would earn on his investment is called a return. The amount of return depends on the degree of risk involved.

If one has $100,000 to invest, it can be put in a bank account at perhaps a 5 percent return. In the bank, the money is relatively safe so the return is lower. If the money were invested by purchasing a block of stores in a depressed area, of course, one would not be satisfied with a 5 percent return. This is what the capitalization of income comes down to - the better the return, the higher the risk. This is the approach an experienced real estate investor uses in determining what he would pay for property.

5. According to the above passage, which one of the following investments would an experienced real estate investor with $100,000 MOST likely choose? A(n)
   A. apartment building in a slum area yielding a 6 percent return
   B. office building rented to professionals yielding a 6 percent return
   C. shopping center in a depressed area yielding a 10 percent return
   D. warehouse rented on a long-term lease to a major corporation yielding a 10 percent return

5._____

6. According to the above passage, in the capitalization of income, the relationship between the degree of risk and the rate of return GENERALLY is expected to be
   A. indeterminate
   B. variable
   C. inverse
   D. direct

6._____

7. According to the above passage, in purchasing income-producing property, the one of the following which would NOT be a factor influencing an experienced real estate investor is the
   A. socio-economic characteristics of the area in which the property is located
   B. rate of return on investment
   C. original cost of the property
   D. degree of risk involved

7._____

8. According to the above passage, the property listed below which would be LEAST likely to be valued by the capitalization of income is a(n)
   A. apartment house with no vacancies
   B. office building rented to 70 percent of capacity
   C. shopping center with several new tenants
   D. vacant lot located next to a factory

8._____

Questions 9-12.

DIRECTIONS: Questions 9 through 12 are to be answered SOLELY on the basis of the following passage.

The cost approach is used by assessors mainly in valuing one-family homes and properties of a special nature which are not commonly bought and sold and do not produce an income.

There are three aspects to the cost approach to valuation. The first is the actual cost of construction. Where the property has recently been built, the cost of constructing the property is relevant. It, however, may not be a true test as to its value. The building may have been constructed so as to serve the special needs of the owner. What it costs to construct may not truly reflect its value; it may be worth more or less. If it is income-producing property, the income may be more or less than expected. It may be sold for more or less than it cost to build.

The second aspect is replacement cost and applies to older structures. It involves the construction of a similar type of building with the same purpose. It does not require the use of the same materials or design.

Reproduction cost is the third aspect, and it also applies to older structures. It involves construction with the exact same materials and design. The cost in the two latter aspects is construction at today's prices with an allowance made for depreciation from the day the original building was constructed.

9. According to the above passage, which one of the following is a CORRECT statement concerning the cost approach to valuation?
   A. In determining value by the replacement and reproduction cost methods, an allowance must be made for depreciation from the day the building was originally constructed.
   B. The cost approach method is the best method to apply in valuing an office building.
   C. When a structure has been recently built, its actual cost is the best method of determining its value.
   D. The fact that a structure has been built to meet the special needs of the occupant is a relevant factor in valuation.

10. An assessor, in valuing a ten-year-old apartment house, finds that its original construction cost was $1,200,000. In capitalizing its net income, he realizes a valuation of $800,000. In using the replacement cost method and allowing for depreciation, the assessor arrives at a valuation of $900,000.
    According to the above passage, which one of the following valuations is LEAST acceptable for this apartment house?
    A. $1,200,000   B. $800,000
    C. $900,000   D. $850,000

11. The construction cost of a recently built structure is relevant to value, but may not be a true test of value. According to the above passage, which one of the following statements CORRECTLY explains why this is true?
    A. The builder may not know how to construct economically.
    B. A building can depreciate very quickly.
    C. The building may have been built to satisfy certain unique specifications.
    D. Cost-of-construction is not an accepted method of valuation.

12. According to the above passage, which one of the following statements CORRECTLY defines the essential difference between the replacement cost and reproduction cost aspects of the cost approach?   12.____
    A. Replacement cost is used only in assessing older buildings; reproduction cost is used only when the building has been recently constructed.
    B. Reproduction cost does not include any allowance for depreciation; replacement cost allows for depreciation from the date of construction of the original building.
    C. Replacement cost involves construction with the same exact materials; reproduction cost does not require the use of the same materials.
    D. Reproduction cost involves construction with the exact same materials and design; replacement cost does not require the use of the same materials and design.

Questions 13-18.

DIRECTIONS: Questions 13 through 18 are to be answered SOLELY on the basis of the following passage.

Realty, because of fixity in investment, immobility in location, and necessity for shelter purposes, lends itself readily to economic controls when such are deemed essential to serve social or political ends, or where the interest of health, safety, and morality of community population or the nation at large warrants it. Realty has consistently been recognized as a form of private property which is sufficiently invested with public interest to warrant its control either under the police power of a sovereign state and its branches of government or by direct and statutory legislation enacted within the framework of the governmental constitution.

Whenever war or catastrophe causes a sudden shifting of population or suspension of building operations, or both, an imbalance is brought about in the supply and demand for housing. This imbalance in housing demand and supply creates conditions of insecurity and instability among the tenants who fear indiscriminate eviction or unwarranted upward rental adjustments. It is this background of possible exploitation during times of economic stress and strain that underlies the enactment of emergency rent control legislation.

Although rent control has been in effect in many communities, particularly the larger metropolitan communities, since the end of World War II, the attitude of all levels of government is to view this form of legislation as temporary and to hasten, as far as their power permits, a return to normal relations between landlords and tenants.

13. According to the above passage, the reason that realty can conveniently be subjected to controls is due to   13.____
    A. public interest   B. site immobility
    C. population shifts   D. moral considerations

14. The above passage includes as a justification for the imposition of economic controls all of the following EXCEPT   14.____
    A. threats to physical safety
    B. socio-political considerations
    C. dangers to health in the community
    D. requirements of police powers

15. According to the above passage, a LIKELY cause for a cessation of construction might be a
    A. natural disaster
    B. change in the demand for housing
    C. change in the supply of housing
    D. demographic fluctuations

16. According to the above passage, of the following, a tenant's insecurity would MOST likely result in his fear of
    A. reduction in necessary services
    B. loss in equity
    C. rent increases
    D. condemnation proceedings

17. According to the above passage, indiscriminate evictions by landlords during periods of economic difficulties constitute
    A. unlawful acts   B. justifiable measures
    C. desirable actions   D. exploitation of tenants

18. According to the above passage, economic controls of realty have been in effect on a widespread basis since
    A. 1918   B. 1945
    C. 1953   D. 1964

Questions 19-22.

DIRECTIONS: Questions 19 through 22 are to be answered SOLELY on the basis of the following passage.

In capitalizing the net income of property to produce a value, certain expenses are permitted to be deducted from gross income. Even though the premises may be fully rented, it is proper to deduct from the gross income an allowance for vacancy. All expenses attributable to the maintenance and upkeep of the premises are deductible. These include heat, light and power, water and sewers, wages or employees and expenses attributable to wages, insurance, repairs and maintenance, supplies and materials, legal and accounting fees, telephone, rental commission, advertising, and so forth. If the premises are furnished, a reserve for the depreciation of personal property is deductible. A capital improvement to the building is not a deductible expense. Real estate taxes should not be deducted as an expense. Instead, taxes should be factored as part of the overall capitalization rate.

It is proper to allow an expense for management of the building even in cases where the owner himself is manager. But payments of interest and principal of the mortgage are not a properly deductible expense. Real property is appraised free and clear of all encumbrances. Otherwise, two identical buildings located next to each other might be valued differently because one has a greater mortgage than the other.

19. According to the above passage, the one of the following which is NOT a proper deductible expense during the year in which the expense is incurred is the cost for
    A. advertising to rent the premises
    B. accounting fees
    C. utilities
    D. putting in central air conditioning

19._____

20. According to the above passage, the one of the following statements concerning deductible expenses which is CORRECT is that
    A. a vacancy allowance is a proper deductible expense even though the premises may be fully rented
    B. real estate taxes are a proper deductible expense
    C. if the owner manages his own property, he cannot charge a management fee as a deductible expense
    D. payments for interest and principal of the mortgage are proper deductible expenses

20._____

21. According to the above passage, two identical adjacent buildings CANNOT receive different valuations because of differences in their
    A. mortgages   B. net income
    C. leases   D. management fees

21._____

22. According to the above passage, an owner of furnished premises may set aside a reserve as a deductible expense for all of the following EXCEPT
    A. refrigerators   B. carpeting
    C. bookcases   D. walls

22._____

Questions 23-25.

DIRECTIONS: Questions 23 through 25 are to be answered SOLELY on the basis of the following passage.

The standard for assessment in the state is contained in Section 306 of the Real Property Tax Law. It states that all real property in each assessing unit shall be assessed at the full value thereof. However, the courts of the state have not required assessors to assess at 100% of full value. Assessments of property for real estate tax purposes at less than full value are not invalid if they are made at a uniform percentage of full value throughout the assessing district. In assessing real property, full value is equivalent to market value.

In determining market value of real property for tax purposes, every element which can reasonably affect value of property ought to be considered, and the main considerations should be given to actual sales of the subject or similar property, cost to produce or reproduce the property, capitalization of income therefrom, and the combination of these factors.

23. According to the above passage, the one of the following statements which is INCORRECT is that all real property in each assessing unit
    A. must be assessed at full value
    B. shall be assessed at full value or at a uniform percentage of full value
    C. may be assessed at 50% of full value
    D. may be assessed at 100% of full value

23._____

24. According to the above passage, the one of the following elements of value which should be given the LEAST consideration in determining market value is
    A. actual or comparable sales
    B. reproduction cost
    C. amount of mortgage
    D. capitalization of income

25. According to the above passage, the basis for the legality of assessing units, making assessments at a uniform percentage of full value rather than at full value is
    A. Section 306 of the Real Property Tax Law
    B. decisions of the state courts
    C. judgments of individual assessors
    D. decisions of municipal executives

KEY (CORRECT ANSWERS)

1.	A	11.	C
2.	C	12.	D
3.	B	13.	B
4.	B	14.	D
5.	D	15.	A
6.	D	16.	C
7.	C	17.	D
8.	D	18.	B
9.	A	19.	D
10.	A	20.	A

21.	A
22.	D
23.	A
24.	C
25.	B

TEST 3

DIRECTIONS: Each question or incomplete statement is followed by several suggested answers or completions. Select the one that BEST answers the question or completes the statement. *PRINT THE LETTER OF THE CORRECT ANSWER IN THE SPACE AT THE RIGHT.*

Questions 1-4.

DIRECTIONS: Questions 1 through 4 are to be answered SOLELY on the basis of the following passage.

Although zoning is a phase of city planning and is concerned with land use control of private property, zoning powers are better known and more generally applied than most city planning powers. Zoning powers predict the formulation of a master plan and even the formation of the planning commission itself. The widespread application of zoning powers is evident from a survey conducted by the International City Managers' Association. As reported in the 2015 MUNICIPAL YEARBOOK, 98 percent of all cities in excess of ten thousand population had enacted comprehensive zoning ordinances governing the utilization of privately owned land. Since 60 percent of all urban land is generally held under private ownership, the impact of zoning laws upon income and value of real property is most significant.

1. According to the above passage, in relation to the powers of city planning, zoning powers are
   A. not as familiar to the general public
   B. formulated subsequent to the establishment of the powers of the planning commission
   C. more general in their application
   D. likely to develop as a result of the community's master plan

1.____

2. According to the above passage, if there are 200 cities in the United States with a population exceeding 10,000 persons, the number of such cities LIKELY to have enacted comprehensive zoning laws is
   A. 190   B. 192
   C. 194   D. 196

2.____

3. According to the above passage, for each 400 acres of urban land, it is LIKELY that the amount of land which would be privately owned would be ____ acres.
   A. 220   B. 240
   C. 260   D. 280

3.____

4. Of the following, the one whose land use is MOST likely to be affected by zoning controls, according to the above passage, is
   A. Sears Department Store
   B. the Port Authority terminal
   C. the New York Public Library at 42nd Street
   D. the Federal Building

4.____

Questions 5-7.

DIRECTIONS: Questions 5 through 7 are to be answered SOLELY on the basis of the following passage.

Apartments located in rehabilitated old law tenement houses are designated as *off-site apartments*. The purpose of such apartments is to provide temporary housing accommodations for the relocation of persons and families living on sites which are to

95

be used for future housing projects who can not otherwise be relocated. A family shall be permitted to continue to occupy an off-site apartment for a period of two years from the date of its admission and shall be required to move out at the termination of such two-year period. However, no proceedings shall be undertaken to remove any tenant now in occupancy of an off-site apartment until after May 9, 2015.

A family shall, however, be required to remove from an off-site apartment prior to the expiration of the periods and date enumerated above if it refuses to accept an available apartment in a public housing project for which it is eligible; or, as a tenant in occupancy, it fails to execute any lease required by management or it fails to comply with other requirements, standard procedures, or rules promulgated by management.

5. A tenant occupying an off-site apartment refuses to renew his lease for one year because he expects to move into a new apartment house within six months. This tenant may
   A. be required to move before his new apartment is ready
   B. be required to move before his new apartment is ready only if his occupancy in the off-site apartment exceeds two years
   C. not be required to move before his new apartment is ready
   D. not be required to move prior to May 9, 2015

5._____

6. According to the above passage, if a family living on a site can be relocated to an apartment in a public housing project, it is
   A. eligible for an off-site apartment near its present dwelling
   B. not eligible for any off-site apartment
   C. eligible for an off-site apartment if it has been living in its present home for at least two years
   D. permitted to continue in occupancy for at least two more years

6._____

7. According to the above passage, a tenant admitted to an off-site apartment on October 1, 2013 is FIRST subject to removal after
   A. October 1, 2015
   B. May 9, 2015
   C. he has been investigated and found to be ineligible for an apartment in the public housing project
   D. he refuses to sign a lease on the apartment or after September 30, 2015, whichever comes first

7._____

Questions 8-14.

DIRECTIONS: Questions 8 through 14 are to be answered SOLELY on the basis of the following passage.

From a nationwide point of view, the need for new housing units during the years immediately ahead will be determined by four major factors. The most important factor is the net change in household formations -- that is, the difference between the number of new households that are formed and the number of existing households that are dissolved, whether by death or other circumstances. During the 2010's, as the children born during the '80's and 90's come of age and marry, the total number of households is expected to increase at a rate of more than 1,000,000 annually. The second factor affecting the need for new housing units is *removals* -- that is, existing units that are demolished, damaged beyond repair, or otherwise removed from the housing supply. A third factor is the number of existing vacancies. To some extent, vacancies can satisfy the housing demand caused by increases in total number of households or by removals, although population shifts that are already underway mean that some areas will have a surfeit of vacancies and other areas will be faced with serious shortages of housing. A final factor, and one that has only recently assumed major importance, is the increasing demand for second homes. These may take any form from a shack in the woods for a city dweller to a pied-a-terre in the city for a suburbanite. Whatever the form, however, it is certain that increasing leisure time, rising amounts of discretionary income, and improvements in transportation are leading more and more Americans to look on a second home not as a rich man's luxury but as the common man's right.

8. The above passage uses the term *housing units* to refer to
    A. residences of all kinds
    B. apartment buildings only
    C. one-family houses only
    D. the total number of families in the United States

9. The above passage uses the word *removals* to mean
    A. the shift of population from one area to another
    B. vacancies that occur when families move
    C. financial losses suffered when a building is damaged or destroyed
    D. former dwellings that are demolished or can no longer be used for housing

10. The expression *pied-a-terre* appears in the next-to-last sentence in the above passage.
    A person who is not familiar with the expression should be able to tell from the way it is used here that it PROBABLY means
    A. a suburban home owned by a commuter
    B. a shack in the woods
    C. a second home that is used from time to time
    D. overnight lodging for a traveler in a strange city

11. Of the factors described in the above passage as having an important influence on the demand for housing, which factor, taken alone, is LEAST likely to encourage the construction of new housing?
    The
    A. net change in household formations
    B. destruction of existing housing
    C. existence of vacancies
    D. use of second homes

12. Based on the above passage, the TOTAL increase in the number of households during the 2010's is expected to be MOST NEARLY
    A. 1,000,000   B. 10,000,000
    C. 100,000,000   D. 1,000,000,000

13. Which one of the following conclusions could MOST logically be drawn from the information given in the above passage?
    A. The population of the United States is increasing at the rate of about 1,000,000 people annually.
    B. There is already a severe housing shortage in all parts of the country.
    C. The need for additional housing units is greater in some parts of the country than in others.
    D. It is still true that only wealthy people can afford to keep up more than one home.

14. Which one of the following conclusions could NOT logically be drawn from the information given in the above passage?
    A. The need for new housing will be even greater in the 2020's than in the 2010's.
    B. Demolition of existing housing must be taken into account in calculating the need for new housing construction.
    C. Having a second home is more common today than it was in the 1970's.
    D. Part of the housing needs of the 2010's can be met by vacancies.

Questions 15-18.

DIRECTIONS: Questions 15 through 18 are to be answered SOLELY on the basis of the following passage.

A city may expand by growing vertically through the replacement of lower buildings with higher ones; or by filling in open spaces between settled areas; or by extending the existing settled area. When the settled area is expanded, growth may take several forms, the most important forms being concentric circle or ring growth around the central nucleus; axial growth, with prongs or fingerlike extensions moving out along main transportation routes; and suburban growth, with the establishment of islands of settlements before the expansion of the main city area. These types of expansion are characteristic of most large cities. Baltimore was for a long time a good example of ring growth, whereas New York, Chicago, and Detroit illustrate axial and suburban growth.

15. The title that BEST expresses the theme of the above passage is
    A. FORMS OF CITY EXPANSION
    B. MAJOR METROPOLITAN PROBLEMS
    C. METHODS OF URBAN PLANNING
    D. SUBURBAN GROWTH IN AMERICA

16. The one of the following which is an example of vertical growth is the
    A. settlement of year-round residents along the upper Hudson River
    B. restoration of former rooming houses to their original brownstone condition
    C. subdivision of large estates into small lot semidetached houses
    D. erection of the Empire State Building in New York City

17. A city that grew as a concentric circle is
    A. Baltimore   B. New York
    C. Chicago   D. Detroit

18. When the author speaks of axial growth, he refers to a situation where 18._____
    A. expansion is primarily into rural areas until suburbs are thereby created
    B. small towns and villages are consolidated by gradually growing until one large city is created
    C. the direction in which a city expands is determined by the location of major highways
    D. the number of new buildings is greater than the number of old buildings demolished

Questions 19-21.

DIRECTIONS: Questions 19 through 21 are to be answered SOLELY on the basis of the following passage.

Incentive zoning is an affirmative tool that has widespread applications. The Zoning Resolution which became effective in 1998 substantially reduced the amount of floor space that a developer could put up on a given size lot and increased the light and air. In the Trump Building, which was built under the old legislation, the floor space is 27 times the size of the lot. The maximum ratio allowed for buildings now without a special permit is 18.

The 1998 zoning ordinance provided incentives to developers to devote part of the plot to public plazas or arcades. This space is needed to supplement the sidewalks, which in many cases are as narrow as they were when the midtown area was lined with brownstone or brickfront houses.

While the newer zoning has produced plazas, it has not of itself proved to be a sufficient development control. Stretches of Third Avenue and the Avenue of the Americas, for example, have been almost completely redeveloped in the last few years. This massive private investment has produced several fine individual buildings. The total environment produced, however, has been disappointing in a number of respects, and there is nowhere near the amenity that there could have been.

19. According to the above passage, the use of incentive zoning has NOT been entirely successful because it 19._____
    A. has discouraged redevelopment
    B. has encouraged massive private development along Third Avenue
    C. has been ineffective in controlling overall redevelopment
    D. has not significantly increased the number of parks and plazas being built

20. According to the above passage, one might conclude that before the 1998 Zoning Resolution was passed, 20._____
    A. buildings on a given site were required to have greater setbacks
    B. the amount of private investment in development was significantly smaller than it is today
    C. no controls on development existed
    D. the provision of parks and plazas was less frequent

21. In the context of the above passage, the word *amenity* means 21.____
    A. compliance with regulations
    B. correction of undesirable environmental aspects
    C. responsiveness to guidelines and incentives
    D. pleasant or desirable features

Questions 22-24.

DIRECTIONS: Questions 22 through 24 are to be answered SOLELY on the basis of the following passage.

Physical design plays a very significant role in crime rate. Crime rate has been found to increase almost proportionately with building height. The average number of crimes is much greater in higher buildings than in lower ones (equal to or less than six stories). What is most interesting is that in buildings of six stories or less, the project size or total number of units does not make a difference. It seems that although larger projects encourage crime by fostering feelings of anonymity, isolation, irresponsibility, and lack of identity with surroundings, evidence indicates that larger projects encompassed in low buildings seem to offset what we may assume to be factors conducive to high crime rates. High-rise projects not only experience a higher rate of crime within the buildings, but a greater proportion of the crime occurs in the interior public spaces of these buildings as compared with those of the lower buildings. Lower buildings have more limited public space than higher ones. A criminal probably perceives that the interior public areas of buildings are where his victims are most vulnerable and where the possibility of his being seen or apprehended is minimal. Placement of elevators, entrance lobbies, fire stairs, and secondary exits all are factors related to the likelihood of crimes taking place in buildings. The study of all of these elements should bear some weight in the planning of new projects.

22. According to the above passage, which of the following BEST describes the relationship between building size and crime? 22.____
    A. Larger projects lead to a greater crime rate.
    B. Higher buildings tend to increase the crime rate.
    C. The smaller the number of project apartments in low buildings, the higher the crime rate.
    D. Anonymity and isolation serve to lower the crime rate in small buildings.

23. According to the above passage, the likelihood of a criminal attempting a mugging in the interior public portions of a high-rise building is GOOD because 23.____
    A. tenants will be constantly flowing in and out of the area
    B. there is easy access to fire stairs and secondary exits
    C. there is a good chance that no one will see him
    D. tenants may not recognize the victims of crime as their neighbors

24. Which of the following is IMPLIED by the above passage as an explanation for the fact that the crime rate is lower in large low-rise housing projects than in large high-rise projects?
    A. Tenants know each other better and take a greater interest in what happens in the project.
    B. There is more public space where tenants are likely to gather together.
    C. The total number of units in a low-rise project is fewer than the total number of units in a high-rise project.
    D. Elevators in low-rise buildings travel quickly, thus limiting the amount of time in which a criminal can act.

25. The financing of housing represents two distinct forms of costs. One is the actual capital invested, and the other is the interest rate which is charged for the use of capital. In fixing rents, the interest rate which capital is expected to yield plays a very important part. On the basis of this statement, it would be MOST correct to state that
    A. the financing of housing represents two distinct forms of capital investment
    B. reducing the interest rate charged for the use of capital is not as important as economies in construction in achieving lower rentals
    C. in fixing rents, the interest rate is expected to yield capital gains, justifying the investment
    D. the actual capital invested and the interest rate charged for use of this capital are factors in determining housing costs

KEY (CORRECT ANSWERS)

1.	C	11.	C
2.	D	12.	B
3.	B	13.	C
4.	A	14.	A
5.	A	15.	A
6.	B	16.	D
7.	D	17.	A
8.	A	18.	C
9.	D	19.	C
10.	C	20.	D

21.	D
22.	B
23.	C
24.	A
25.	D

READING COMPREHENSION
UNDERSTANDING AND INTERPRETING WRITTEN MATERIAL
EXAMINATION SECTION
TEST 1

DIRECTIONS: Each question or incomplete statement is followed by several suggested answers or completions. Select the one that BEST answers the question or completes the statement. *PRINT THE LETTER OF THE CORRECT ANSWER IN THE SPACE AT THE RIGHT.*

Questions 1-3.

DIRECTIONS: Questions 1 through 3 are to be answered SOLELY on the basis of the following paragraph.

The aging housing inventory presents a broad spectrum of conditions, from good upkeep to unbelievable deterioration. Buildings, even relatively good buildings, are likely to have numerous minor violations rather than the gross and evident sanitary violations of an earlier age. Except for the serious violations in a relatively small number of slum buildings, the task is to deal with masses of minor violations that, though insignificant in themselves, amount in the aggregate to major deprivations of health and comfort to tenants. Caused by wear and tear, by the abrasions of time, and aggravated by neglect, these conditions do not readily yield to the dramatic *vacate and restore* measures of earlier times. Moreover, the lines between *good* and *bad* housing have become blurred in many parts of our cities; we find a range of *shades of gray* blending into each other. Different kinds of code enforcement efforts may be required to deal with different degrees of deterioration.

1. The above passage suggests that code enforcement efforts may have to be

   A. developed to cope with varying levels of housing dilapidation
   B. aimed primarily at the serious violations in slum buildings
   C. modeled on the *vacate and restore* measures of earlier times
   D. modified to reduce unrealistic penalties for petty violations

1.____

2. According to the above passage, during former times some buildings had sanitary violations which were

   A. irreparable and minor
   B. blurred and gray
   C. flagrant and obvious
   D. insignificant and numerous

2.____

3. According to the above passage, the aging housing stock presents a

   A. great number of rent-controlled buildings
   B. serious problem of tenant-caused deterioration
   C. significant increase in buildings without intentional violations
   D. wide range of physical conditions

3.____

Questions 4-5.

DIRECTIONS: Questions 4 and 5 are to be answered SOLELY on the basis of the following passage.

In general, housing code provisions relating to the safe and sanitary maintenance of dwelling units prescribe the maintenance required for foundations, walls, ceilings, floors, windows, doors, stairways, and also the facilities and equipment required in other sections. The more recent codes have, in addition, extensive provisions designed to ensure that the unit be maintained in a rat-free and rat-proof condition. Also, as an example of new approaches in code provisions, one proposed Federal model housing code prohibits the landlord from terminating vital services and utilities except during temporary emergencies or when actual repairs or maintenance are in process. This provision may be used to prevent a landlord from turning off utility services as a technique of self-help eviction or as a weapon against rent strikes.

4. According to the above passage, the more recent housing codes have extensive provisions designed to

    A. maintain a reasonably fire-proof living unit
    B. prohibit tenants from participating in rent strikes
    C. maintain the unit free from rats
    D. prohibit tenants from using lead-based paints

4.____

5. According to the above passage, one housing code would permit landlords to terminate vital services during

    A. a rent strike
    B. an actual eviction
    C. a temporary emergency
    D. the planning of repairs and maintenance

5.____

Questions 6-8.

DIRECTIONS: Questions 6 through 8 are to be answered SOLELY on the basis of the following passage.

City governments have long had building codes which set minimum standards for building and for human occupancy. The code (or series of codes) makes provisions for standards of lighting and ventilation, sanitation, fire prevention, and protection. As a result of demands from manufacturers, builders, real estate people, tenement owners, and building-trades unions, these codes often have established minimum standards well below those that the contemporary society would accept as a rock-bottom minimum. Codes often become outdated so that meager standards in one era become seriously inadequate a few decades later as society"s concept of a minimum standard of living changes. Out-of-date codes, when still in use, have sometimes prevented the introduction of new devices and modern building techniques. Thus, it is extremely important that building codes keep pace with changes in the accepted concept of a minimum standard of living.

6. According to the above passage, all of the following considerations in building planning would probably be covered in a building code EXCEPT

   A. closet space as a percentage of total floor area
   B. size and number of windows required for rooms of differing sizes
   C. placement of fire escapes in each line of apartments
   D. type of garbage disposal units to be installed

7. According to the above passage, if an ideal building code were to be created, how would the established minimum standards in it compare to the ones that are presently set by city governments?
   They would

   A. be lower than they are at present
   B. be higher than they are at present
   C. be comparable to the present minimum standards
   D. vary according to the economic group that sets them

8. On the basis of the above passage, what is the reason for difficulties in introducing new building techniques?

   A. Builders prefer techniques which represent the rock-bottom minimum desired by society.
   B. Certain manufacturers have obtained patents on various building methods to the exclusion of new techniques.
   C. The government does not want to invest money in techniques that will soon be outdated.
   D. New techniques are not provided for in building codes which are not up-to-date.

Questions 9-11.

DIRECTIONS: Questions 9 through 11 are to be answered SOLELY on the basis of the following paragraph.

When constructed within a multiple dwelling, such storage space shall be equipped with a sprinkler system and also with a system of mechanical ventilation in no way connected with any other ventilating system. Such storage space shall have no opening into any other part of the dwelling except through a fireproof vestibule. Any such vestibule shall have a minimum superficial floor area of fifty square feet, and its maximum area shall not exceed seventy-five square feet. It shall be enclosed with incombustible partitions having a fire-resistive rating of three hours. The floor and ceiling of such vestibule shall also be of incombustible material having a fire-resistive rating of at least three hours. There shall be two doors to provide access from the dwelling, to the car storage space. Each such door shall have a fire-resistive rating of one and one-half hours and shall be provided with a device to prevent the opening of one door until the other door is entirely closed.

9. According to the above paragraph, the one of the following that is REQUIRED in order for cars to be permitted to be stored in a multiple dwelling is a(n)

   A. fireproof vestibule   B. elevator from the garage
   C. approved heating system   D. sprinkler system

10. According to the above paragraph, the one of the following materials that would NOT be acceptable for the walls of a vestibule connecting a garage to the dwelling portion of a building is

    A. 3" solid gypsum blocks
    B. 4" brick
    C. 4" hollow gypsum blocks, plastered both sides
    D. 6" solid cinder concrete blocks

10.____

11. According to the above paragraph, the one of the following that would be ACCEPTABLE for the width and length of a vestibule connecting a garage that is within a multiple dwelling to the dwelling portion of the building is

    A. 3'8" x 13'0"
    B. 4'6" x 18'6"
    C. 4'9" x 14'6"
    D. 4'3" x 19'3"

11.____

Questions 12-13.

DIRECTIONS: Questions 12 and 13 are to be answered SOLELY on the basis of the following paragraph.

It shall be unlawful to place, use, or maintain in a condition intended, arranged, or designed for use, any gas-fired cooking appliance, laundry stove, heating stove, range or water heater or combination of such appliances in any room or space used for living or sleeping in any new or existing multiple dwelling unless such room or space has a window opening to the outer air or such gas appliance is vented to the outer air. All automatically operated gas appliances shall be equipped with a device which shall shut off automatically the gas supply to the main burners when the pilot light in such appliance is extinguished. A gas range or the cooking portion of a gas appliance incorporating a room heater shall not be deemed an automatically operated gas appliance. However, burners in gas ovens and broilers which can be turned on and off or ignited by non-manual means shall be equipped with a device which shall shut off automatically the gas supply to those burners when the operation of such non-manual means fails.

12. According to the above paragraph, an automatic shut-off device is NOT required on a gas

    A. hot water heater
    B. laundry dryer
    C. space heater
    D. range

12.____

13. According to the above paragraph, a gas-fired water heater is permitted

    A. only in kitchens
    B. only in bathrooms
    C. only in living rooms
    D. in any type of room

13.____

Questions 14-18.

DIRECTIONS: Questions 14 through 18 are to be answered SOLELY on the basis of the information contained in the statement below.

No multiple dwelling shall be erected to a height in excess of one and one-half times the width of the widest street on which it faces, except that above the level of such height, for each one foot that the front wall of such dwelling sets back from the street line, three feet shall be added to the height limit of such dwelling, but such dwelling shall not exceed in maximum height three feet plus one and three-quarter times the width of the widest street on which it faces.

Any such dwelling facing a street more than one hundred feet in width shall be subject to the same height limitations as though such dwelling faced a street one hundred feet in width.

14. The MAXIMUM height of a multiple dwelling set back five feet from the street line and facing a 60 foot wide street is ___ feet.

    A. 60   B. 90   C. 105   D. 165

15. The MAXIMUM height of a multiple dwelling set back six feet from the street line and facing a 120 foot wide street is _____ feet.

    A. 198   B. 168   C. 120   D. 105

16. The MAXIMUM height of a multiple dwelling is

    A. 100 ft.   B. 150 ft.   C. 178 ft.   D. unlimited

17. The MAXIMUM height of a multiple dwelling set back 10 feet from the street line and facing a 110 foot wide street is ___ feet.

    A. 178   B. 180   C. 195   D. 205

18. The MAXIMUM height of a multiple dwelling set back eight feet from the street line and facing a 90 foot wide street is ___ feet.

    A. 135   B. 147   C. 178   D. 159

Questions 19-23.

DIRECTIONS: Questions 19 through 23 are to be answered SOLELY on the basis of the following statement.

The number of persons accommodated on any story in a lodging house shall not be greater than the sum of the following components,

   a. 22 persons for each full multiple of 22 inches in the smallest clear width for each means of egress approved by the department, other than fire escapes
   b. 20 persons for each lawful fire escape accessible from such story.

19. The MAXIMUM number of persons that may be accommodated on a story in a lodging house depends on the

    A. number of lawful fire escapes *only*
    B. number of approved means of egress *only*
    C. smallest clear width in each approved means of egress *only*
    D. number of lawful fire escapes and sum total of smallest clear widths in each approved means of egress

20. The MAXIMUM number of persons that may be accommodated on a story of a lodging house having one lawful fire escape and a sum total of 44 inches in the smallest clear widths of the two approved means of egress is

    A. 20   B. 22   C. 42   D. 64

21. The MAXIMUM number of persons that may be accommodated on a story of a lodging house having two lawful fire escapes and a sum total of 60 inches in the smallest clear width of the approved means of egress is

    A. 64 B. 84 C. 100 D. 106

22. The MAXIMUM number of persons that may be accommodated on a story of a lodging house having one lawful fire escape and a sum total of 33 inches in the smallest clear width of the approved means of egress is

    A. 42 B. 53 C. 64 D. 73

23. The MAXIMUM number of persons that may be accommodated on a story of a lodging house having two lawful fire escapes and two approved means of egress, with 40 inches and 44 inches in the smallest clear widths, respectively, is

    A. 84 B. 104 C. 106 D. 108

Questions 24-25.

DIRECTIONS: Questions 24 and 25 are to be answered SOLELY on the basis of the following paragraph.

Though the recent trend toward apartment construction may appear to be the Region's response to large-lot zoning and centralized industry, it really is not. It is mainly a function of the age of the population. Most of the apartments are occupied by one- and two-person families young people out of school but without a family of their own and older people whose children have grown. Both groups have been increasing in number; and, in this Region, they characteristically live in apartments. It is this increased demand for apartments and the simultaneous decrease in demand for one-family houses that dramatically raised the percentage of building permits issued for multi-family housing units from 36 percent in 1977 to 67 percent in 1981. The fact that three-fourths of the apartments were built in the Core between 1977 and 1981 at the same time as the Core was losing population underscores the failure of the apartment boom to slow the outward spread of the population.

24. According to the above paragraph, one of the reasons for the increase in the number of building permits issued for multi-family construction in the City Metropolitan Region is

    A. that workers in industry want to live close to their jobs
    B. an increase in the number of elderly people living in the Region
    C. the inability of many families to afford the large lots necessary to build private homes
    D. the new zoning ordinance made it easier to build apartments

25. According to the above paragraph, the apartment construction boom

    A. increased the population density in the Core
    B. spurred a population shift to the suburbs
    C. did not halt the outward flow of the population from the Core
    D. was most significant in the outer areas of the Region

KEY (CORRECT ANSWERS)

1. A
2. C
3. D
4. C
5. C

6. A
7. B
8. D
9. D
10. B

11. C
12. D
13. D
14. C
15. B

16. C
17. A
18. D
19. D
20. D

21. B
22. A
23. C
24. B
25. C

TEST 2

DIRECTIONS: Each question or incomplete statement is followed by several suggested answers or completions. Select the one that BEST answers the question or completes the statement. *PRINT THE LETTER OF THE CORRECT ANSWER IN THE SPACE AT THE RIGHT.*

Questions 1-4.

DIRECTIONS: Questions 1 through 4 are to be answered SOLELY on the basis of the following paragraph.

Although the suburbs have provided housing and employment for millions of additional families since 1950, many suburban communities have maintained controls over the kinds of families who can live in them. Suburban attitudes have been formed by reaction against a perception of crowded, harassed city life and threatening alien city people. As population, taxable income, and jobs have left the cities for the suburbs, the *urban crisis* of substandard housing, declining levels of education and public services, and decreasing employment opportunities has been created. The crisis, however, is not urban at all, but national, and in part a result of the suburban policy that discourages outward movement by the urban poor.

1. According to the above paragraph, the quality of urban life

   A. is determined by public opinion in the cities
   B. has worsened in recent years
   C. is similar to rural life
   D. can be changed by political means

1.____

2. According to the above paragraph, suburban communities have

   A. tried to show that the urban crisis is really a national crisis
   B. avoided taking a position on the urban crisis
   C. been involved in causing the urban crisis
   D. been the innocent victims of the urban crisis

2.____

3. According to the above paragraph, the poor have

   A. become increasingly sophisticated in their attempts to move to the suburbs
   B. generally been excluded from the suburbs
   C. lost incentive for betterment of their living conditions
   D. sought improvement of the central cities

3.____

4. As used in the above paragraph, the word perception means MOST NEARLY

   A. development   B. impression
   C. opposition   D. uncertainty

4.____

Questions 5-8.

DIRECTIONS: Questions 5 through 8 are to be answered SOLELY on the basis of the following paragraph.

The concentration of publicly assisted housing in central cities -- because the suburbs do not want them and effectively bar them -- is usually rationalized by a solicitous regard for keeping intact the city neighborhoods cherished by low-income groups. If one accepted this as valid, the devotion of minorities to blighted city neighborhoods in preference to suburban employment and housing would be an historic first. Certainly no such devotion was visible among the millions who have deserted their city neighborhoods in the last 25 years even if it meant an arduous daily trip from the suburbs to their jobs in the cities.

5. The writer implies that MOST poor people 5.____

   A. prefer isolation   B. fear change
   C. are angry   D. seek betterment

6. The general tone of the paragraph is BEST characterized as 6.____

   A. uncertain   B. skeptical   C. evasive   D. indifferent

7. As used in the above paragraph, the word <u>rationalize</u> means MOST NEARLY 7.____

   A. dispute   B. justify   C. deny   D. locate

8. According to the above paragraph, publicly assisted housing is concentrated in the central cities PRIMARILY because 8.____

   A. city dwellers are unable to find satisfactory housing
   B. deterioration of older housing has increased in recent years
   C. suburbanites have opposed the movement of the poor to the suburbs
   D. employment opportunities have decreased in the suburbs

Questions 9-11.

DIRECTIONS: Questions 9 through 11 are to be answered SOLELY on the basis of the following paragraph.

In recent years, new and important emphasis has been placed upon the maximum use of conservation and rehabilitation techniques in carrying out programs of urban renewal and revitalization. In urban renewal projects where existing structures are hopelessly deteriorated or land uses are incompatible with the community's overall plans, the entire area may be acquired, cleared, and sold for redevelopment. However, where existing structures are basically sound but have deteriorated to the point where they are a <u>blighting</u> influence on the neighborhood, they may be salvaged through a program of rehabilitation and reconditioning.

9. According to the above paragraph, the one of the following which is MOST likely to cause area-wide razing of the buildings in urban renewal programs is 9.____

   A. a program of rehabilitation and reconditioning
   B. concerted insistence by landlords and tenants that certain buildings be bulldozed
   C. an inability of community groups to agree on priorities for staged clearance
   D. land use contrary to the community's general plan

10. According to the above paragraph, rehabilitation of structures may take place if 10.____

    A. new conservation and rehabilitation techniques are used
    B. salvaging all the buildings in the entire area is hopeless
    C. the community wishes to preserve historic structures
    D. the existing buildings are structurally sound

11. As used in the above paragraph, the word <u>blighting</u> means MOST NEARLY   11._____

    A. ruining   B. infrequent   C. recurrent   D. traditional

Questions 12-13.

DIRECTIONS: Questions 12 and 13 are to be answered SOLELY on the basis of the following paragraphs.

We must also find better ways to handle the relocation of people uprooted by projects. In the past, many renewal plans have foundered on this problem, and it is still the most difficult part of the community development. Large-scale replacement of low-income residents -- many ineligible for public housing -- has contributed to deterioration of surrounding communities. However, thanks to changes in housing authority procedures, relocation has been accomplished in a far more satisfactory fashion. The step-by-step community development projects we advocate in this plan should bring further improvement.

But additional measures will be necessary. There are going to be more people to be moved; and, with the current shortage of apartments, large ones especially, it is going to be tougher to find places to move them to. The city should have more freedom to buy or lease housing that comes on the market because of normal turnover and make it available to relocatees.

12. According to the above paragraphs, one of the reasons a neighborhood may deteriorate is that   12._____

    A. there is a scarcity of large apartments
    B. step-by-step community development projects have failed
    C. people in the given neighborhood are uprooted from their homes
    D. a nearby renewal project has an inadequate relocation plan

13. From the above paragraphs, one might conclude that the relocation phase of community renewal has been improved.   13._____

    A. by changes in housing authority procedures
    B. by development of step-by-step community development projects
    C. through expanded city powers to buy housing for relocation
    D. by the addition of huge sums of money

Questions 14-15.

DIRECTIONS: Questions 14 and 15 are to be answered SOLELY on the basis of the following paragraphs.

Provision of decent housing for the lower half of the population (by income) was thus taken on as a public responsibility. Public housing was to assist the poorest quarter of urban families while the 221(d)(3) Housing Program would assist the next quarter. But limited funds meant that the supply of subsidized housing could not stretch nearly far enough to help this half of the population. Who were to be left out in the rationing process which was accomplished by the sifting of applicants for housing on the part of public and private authorities?

Discrimination on the grounds of race or color is not allowed under Federal law. In all sections of the country, encouragingly, housing programs are found which follow this law to the letter. Yet, housing programs in some cities still suffer from the residue of racial segregation policies and attitudes that for years were condoned or even encouraged.

Some sifting in the 221(d)(3) Housing Program follows the practice of many public housing authorities, the imposition of requirements with respect to character. This is a delicate matter. To fill a project overwhelmingly with broken families, alcoholics, criminals, delinquents, and other problem tenants would hardly make it a wholesome environment. Yet the total exclusion of such families is hardly an acceptable alternative. To the extent this exclusion is practiced, the very people whose lives are described in order to persuade lawmakers and the public to instigate new programs find the door shut in their faces when such programs come into being. The proper balance is difficult to achieve, but society's neediest families surely should not be totally denied the opportunities for rejuvenation in subsidized housing.

14. From the above paragraphs, it can be assumed that the 221(d)(3) Housing Program

    A. served a population earning more than the median income
    B. served a less affluent population than is served by public housing
    C. excludes all problem families from its projects
    D. is a subsidized housing program

15. According to this text, the provision of housing for the poor

    A. has not been completely accomplished with public monies
    B. is never influenced by segregationist policies
    C. is limited to providing housing for only the neediest families
    D. is primarily the responsibility of the Federal government

16. Five hundred persons attended a public hearing at which a proposed public housing project was being considered. Less than half favored the project while the majority opposed the project.
    According to the above statement, it is REASONABLE to conclude that

    A. the proposal stimulated considerable community interest
    B. the public housing project was disapproved by the city because a majority opposed it
    C. those who opposed the project lacked sympathy for needy persons
    D. the supporters of the project were led by militants

17. A vacant lot close to a polluted creek is for sale. Two buyers compete. One owns an adjacent factory which provides 300 high paying unskilled jobs. He needs to expand or move from the city. If he expands, he will provide 300 additional jobs. The other is a community group in a changing residential area close by. They hope to stabilize the neighborhood by bringing in new housing. They would build an apartment building with 100 dwelling units on the lot.
    According to the above paragraph, it is REASONABLE to conclude that

    A. jobs are more important than housing
    B. there is conflict between the factory owners and the neighborhood group
    C. the neighborhood group will not succeed in stabilizing the area by constructing new housing
    D. the polluted creek should be cleaned up

18. The housing authority faces every problem of the private developer, and it must also assume responsibilities of which private building is free. The authority must account to the community; it must conform to federal regulations; it must provide durable buildings of good standard at low cost; it must overcome the prejudices against public operations, of contractors, bankers, and prospective tenants. These authorities are being watched by anti-housing enthusiasts for the first error of judgment or the first evidence of high costs, to be torn to bits before a Congressional committee.
On the basis of this statement, it would be MOST correct to state that

   A. private builders do not have the opposition of contractors, bankers, and prospective tenants
   B. Congressional committees impede the progress of public housing by petty investigations
   C. a housing authority must deal with all the difficulties encountered by the private builder
   D. housing authorities are no more immune from errors in judgment than private developers

19. Another factor that has considerably added to the city's housing crisis has been the great influx of low-income workers and their families seeking better employment opportunities during wartime and defense boom periods. The circumstances of these families have forced them to crowd into the worst kind of housing and have produced on a renewed scale the conditions from which slums flourish and grow.
On the basis of this statement, one would be justified in stating that

   A. the influx of low-income workers has aggravated the slum problem
   B. the city has better employment opportunities than other sections of the country
   C. the high wages paid by our defense industries have made many families ineligible for tenancy in public housing projects
   D. the families who settled in the city during wartime and the defense build-up brought with them language and social customs conducive to the growth of slums

20. Much of the city felt the effects of the general postwar increase of vandalism and street crime, and the greatly expanded public housing program was no exception. Projects built in congested slum areas with a high incidence of delinquency and crime were particularly subjected to the depredations of neighborhood gangs. The civil service watchmen who patrolled the projects, unarmed and neither trained nor expected to perform police duties, were unable to cope with the situation.
On the basis of this statement, the MOST accurate of the following statements is:

   A. Neighborhood gangs were particularly responsible for the high incidence of delinquency and crime in congested slum areas having public housing programs
   B. Civil service watchmen who patrolled housing projects failed to carry out their assigned police duties
   C. Housing projects were not spared the effects of the general postwar increase of vandalism and street crime
   D. Delinquency and crime affected housing projects in slum areas to a greater extent than other dwellings in the same area

21. Another peculiar characteristic of real estate is the absence of liquidity. Each parcel is a discrete unit as to size, location, rental, physical condition, and financing arrangements. Each property requires investigation, comparison of rents with other properties, and individualized haggling on price and terms.
On the basis of this statement, the LEAST accurate of the following statements is:

21.____

   A. Although the size, location, and rent of parcels vary, comparison with rents of other properties affords an indication of the value of a particular parcel
   B. Bargaining skill is the essential factor in determining the value of a parcel of real estate
   C. Each parcel of real estate has individual peculiarities distinguishing it from any other parcel
   D. Real estate is not easily converted to other types of assets

22. In part, at least, the charges of sameness, monotony, and institutionalism directed at public housing projects result from the degree in which they differ from the city's normal housing pattern. They seem alike because their very difference from the usual makes them stand apart.
In many respects, there is considerably more variety between public housing projects than there is between different streets of apartment houses or tenements throughout the city.
On the basis of this statement, it would be LEAST accurate to state that:

22.____

   A. There is considerably more variety between public housing projects than there is between different streets of tenements throughout the city
   B. Public housing projects differ from the city's normal housing pattern to the degree that sameness, monotony, and institutionalism are characteristic of public buildings
   C. Public housing projects seem alike because their deviation from the usual dwellings draws attention to them
   D. The variety in structure between public housing projects and other public buildings is related to the period in which they were built

23. The amount of debt that can be charged against the city for public housing is limited by law. Part of the city's restricted housing means goes for cash subsidies it may be required to contribute to state-aided projects. Under the provisions of the state law, the city must match the state's contributions in subsidies; and while the value of the partial tax exemption granted by the city is counted for this purpose, it is not always sufficient.
On the basis of this statement, it would be MOST accurate to state that:

23.____

   A. The amount of money the city may spend for public housing is limited by annual tax revenues
   B. The value of tax exemptions granted by the city to educational, religious, and charitable institutions may be added to its subsidy contributions to public housing projects
   C. The subsidy contributions for state-aided public housing projects are shared equally by the state and the city under the provisions of the state law
   D. The tax revenues of the city, unless supplemented by state aid, are insufficient to finance public housing projects

24. Maintenance costs can be minimized and the useful life of houses can be extended by building with the best and most permanent materials available. The best and most permanent materials in many cases are, however, much more expensive than materials which require more maintenance. The most economical procedure in home building has been to compromise between the capital costs of high quality and enduring materials and the maintenance costs of less desirable materials.
    On the basis of this statement, one would be justified in stating that:

    A. Savings in maintenance costs make the use of less durable and less expensive building materials preferable to high quality materials that would prolong the useful life of houses constructed from them
    B. Financial advantage can be secured by the home builder if he judiciously combines costly but enduring building materials with less desirable materials which, however, require more maintenance
    C. A compromise between the capital costs of high quality materials and the maintenance costs of less desirable materials makes it easier for a home builder to estimate construction expenditures
    D. The most economical procedure in home building is to balance the capital costs of the most permanent materials against the costs of less expensive materials that are cheaper to maintain

24.____

25. Personnel selection has been a critical problem for local housing authorities. The pool of qualified workers trained in housing procedures is small, and the colleges and universities have failed to grasp the opportunity for enlarging it. While real estate experience makes a good background for management of a housing project, many real estate men are deplorably lacking in understanding of social and governmental problems. Social workers, on the other hand, are likely to be deficient in business judgment.
    On the basis of this statement, it would be MOST accurate to state that:

    A. Colleges and universities have failed to train qualified workers for proficiency in housing procedures
    B. Social workers are deficient in business judgment as related to the management of a housing project
    C. Real estate experience makes a person a good manager of a housing project
    D. Local housing authorities have been critical of present methods of personnel selection

25.____

KEY (CORRECT ANSWERS)

1.	B	11.	A
2.	C	12.	D
3.	B	13.	A
4.	B	14.	D
5.	D	15.	A
6.	B	16.	A
7.	B	17.	B
8.	D	18.	C
9.	D	19.	A
10.	D	20.	C

21.	B
22.	B
23.	C
24.	B
25.	A

EXAMINATION SECTION
TEST 1

DIRECTIONS: Each question or incomplete statement is followed by several suggested answers or completions. Select the one that BEST answers the question or completes the statement. *PRINT THE LETTER OF THE CORRECT ANSWER IN THE SPACE AT THE RIGHT.*

1. When assigning work, it would be BEST for a supervisor to

    A. allow each employee to select the tasks he or she does best
    B. assign all unimportant work to the slower employees
    C. assign the more tiring tasks to the newer employees
    D. assign tasks based on the abilities of employees

2. You have been supervising ten people for 16 months. During that time, your employees have never reported any problems to you.
    It is likely that

    A. you are doing such a good job there is no room for improvement
    B. since your staff is small, the chances of problems arising are smaller than in a larger unit
    C. for some reason your staff is reluctant to discuss problems with you
    D. your employees are very competent, and are handling all of the problems well by themselves

3. Your supervisor informs you that three of your fifteen employees have complained to her about your inconsistent methods of supervision.
    You should

    A. offer to attend a supervisory training program
    B. first ask her if it is proper for her to allow these employees to go over your head
    C. ask her what specific acts have been considered inconsistent
    D. explain that you have purposely been inconsistent because of the needs of these three employees

4. On short notice, a supervisor must ask her staff to work overtime.
    Of the following, it would be BEST to

    A. explain they would be doing her a personal favor which she would appreciate a great deal
    B. explain why it is necessary
    C. reassure them that they can take the time off in the near future
    D. remind them that working overtime occasionally is part of the job requirement

5. One of your employees has begun reporting to work late on the average of twice a week.
    You should

    A. send a memo to everyone in your unit, stressing that lateness cannot be tolerated
    B. privately discuss the matter with the employee to determine if there are any unusual circumstances causing the behavior
    C. bring the issue up at the next staff meeting, without singling out any employee
    D. ask one of your employees to discuss the matter with the individual

6. One of your employees submitted an application for acceptance into a career development workshop two months ago and has heard nothing. The individual tells you that when one of her co-workers submitted an application, he received a reply a week later. Which is the BEST response for you to make?

    A. "This is obviously a case of discrimination. I'll bring it to the affirmative action officer immediately."
    B. "Next time you submit a request for something of this nature, let me know and I will write a cover letter that will carry more weight."
    C. "Perhaps it was an oversight. Why don't you call the organization and ask why you've heard nothing?"
    D. "It looks like you won't be accepted this year. Be sure to try again next year."

7. In order to meet deadlines, a supervisor should

    A. schedule the work and keep informed of its progress
    B. delegate work
    C. hire temporary personnel
    D. know the capabilities of his or her most reliable employees

8. Your supervisor has given instructions to your employees, in your absence, that differ from those you had given them. You should

    A. have your employees follow your instructions
    B. have your employees follow your supervisor's instructions
    C. discuss the matter with your supervisor
    D. discuss the matter with your employees and find out which method they think is best

9. You have found it necessary to return an assignment completed by one of your employees so that several changes can be made. The employee objects to making these changes. The MOST appropriate action for you to take FIRST is to

    A. inform the employee that he or she is free to object to your supervisor
    B. ask if the employee has carefully read your proposed changes
    C. calmly state that your decision is final and further discussion will most likely be useless
    D. allow the employee to present his or her objections against making the changes

10. You are preparing a vacation schedule for your employees. The factor which is LEAST important for you to consider in setting up the schedule is

    A. the competence of each employee
    B. the vacation preference of each employee
    C. the anticipated workload in the unit
    D. how essential each employee's services will be during the vacation period

11. Among the problems that confront a new supervisor in relation to her or his employees, the one which requires the MOST unusual degree of skill and diplomacy is

    A. changing established ideas
    B. calling attention to mistakes
    C. gaining the respect of employees
    D. training new employees

12. Of the following, the BEST indication of high morale in a supervisor's unit would be that the   12.____

    A. unit never has to work overtime
    B. supervisor often enjoys staying late to plan work for the following day
    C. unit gives expensive birthday presents to each other
    D. employees are willing to give first priority to attaining group objectives, subordinating personal desires they may have

13. In the satisfactory handling of an employee's complaint which is fancied rather than real, the complaint should be considered   13.____

    A. not very important since it has no basis in fact
    B. as important as a grievance grounded in fact
    C. an attempt by the employee to create trouble
    D. an indication of a psychological problem on the part of the employee

14. You are attempting to teach a new employee in your unit how to change a typewriter ribbon. The employee is having a great deal of difficulty changing the ribbon, even though you have always found it simple to do.   14.____
    Before you spend more time instructing the individual, you should

    A. ask if the employee working nearest would take responsibility for changing the ribbon in the future
    B. tell the employee that you never found this difficult, and ask what he or she finds difficult about it
    C. review each of the steps you have already explained and determine whether the individual understands them
    D. tell the employee that you will continue after lunch because you are getting irritable

15. An employee you supervise frequently protests when receiving any assignment that requires the typing of tabular material, although she then performs the task competently. Her protests are causing resentments among the other employees and interfering with their work. You should   15.____

    A. arrange to give such assignments to her when no other employees are present
    B. threaten to formally discipline her if she continues to protest
    C. explain the effect her actions are having on the other employees' performance and ask for her cooperation
    D. ask one of the employees who is upset by her behavior to speak with her

16. Lax supervision has been blamed largely on the unwillingness of supervisors to supervise their employees.   16.____
    The CHIEF reason for this unwillingness to supervise is based MAINLY on the supervisors'

    A. failure to accept modern concepts of proper supervision
    B. doubt of their ability to keep pace with modern techniques and developments in supervision
    C. fear of complaints from employees, and the supervisors' wish to avoid unpleasantness
    D. inability to adhere to the same high standards of performance which are required of employees

17. The appraisal of employees and their performance is an integral part of the supervisor's job. There is wide agreement that several basic principles must be taken into account by supervisors involved in the appraisal process in order to perform this function correctly. The one of the statements below that LEAST represents a basic principle of the appraisal process is appraisal(s)

    A. should be based more on performance of definite tasks than on personality considerations
    B. of long-range potential should rely heavily on subjective judgment of that potential
    C. involves the use of value judgments by the supervisor and does, therefore, require reference to pre-established standards
    D. should aim at emphasizing employees' strengths rather than weaknesses

18. Of the following, it is LEAST essential for a supervisor to issue written instructions in assigning work to an employee when the

    A. instructions will be passed on to others
    B. supervisor will be present to check the quality of the work
    C. assignment involves much detail
    D. employee has often misinterpreted instructions

19. Although accuracy and speed are both important in the performance of work, accuracy should be considered more important MAINLY because

    A. most supervisors insist on accurate work
    B. much time is lost in correcting errors
    C. a rapid rate of work cannot be maintained for any length of time
    D. speedy workers are often inaccurate

20. If an employee has done a complicated task well, his or her supervisor should

    A. tell the employee that he or she has done a good job
    B. call a staff meeting to see if anyone has suggestions for improving future performance of the task
    C. avoid commending the employee, as performing competently is what they are paid to do
    D. confide in the employee that he or she is the best worker in your unit

21. You are a newly appointed supervisor in a large office. It had been the practice in that office for the employees to take an unauthorized coffee break at 10:00 A.M. You have been successful in stopping this practice, and for one week no one had gone out for coffee at 10:00 A.M. One day a stenographer comes over to you at 10:15 A.M., appearing to be ill. She states that she does not feel well and that she would like to go out for a cup of tea. She asks your permission to leave the office for a few minutes.
    You should

    A. telephone and have a cup of tea delivered to her
    B. permit her to go out
    C. refuse her permission, explaining that you do not wish to set a bad example
    D. tell her she can leave for an early lunch

22. A clerk in your unit performs work quickly but carelessly. The head of another unit this employee wishes to transfer to asks you for your opinion of the employee's work.
It would be BEST for you to

   A. emphasize the employee's good points and downplay the bad
   B. allow the employee to begin with a clean record by avoiding any criticism
   C. state that the employee works quickly but carelessly
   D. warn the unit head that he or she would be making a big mistake by hiring the employee

23. You wish to reprimand a worker for neglect of duty. It would NOT be good practice to

   A. allow yourself a cooling off period of several days before you administer the reprimand
   B. give the employee a chance to reply to your criticism
   C. be very specific about the particular act for which you are reprimanding the employee
   D. reprimand the employee when you are alone with him or her

24. One of the employees you supervise has just put up a small poster in her work area that two of your eight employees find obscene and distasteful. While you do not like the poster either, it does not upset you. The two employees already have complained to you about the poster.
Of the following, you should

   A. have the two employees talk to the individual and explain why they are offended
   B. privately explain to the individual that her poster is causing some problems and seek her cooperation in removing it
   C. do nothing, as the employee has the right to express her feelings
   D. compromise and allow her to display the poster half of the time

25. One of the most effective ways to build a sense of employee pride, teamwork, and motivation is for the supervisor to seek advice, suggestions, and information from employees concerning ways in which work should be solved. Many experiments in group decision making have indicated that work groups can help the supervisor in improving decision making. Where employees feel that they are really part of a team and that they have a significant influence on the decisions that are made, they are more likely to accept the decisions and to seek new solutions to future difficult problems. According to the above passage, a supervisor should

   A. almost always follow the advice of his or her employees in handling difficult problems
   B. always seek advice from employees when handling difficult problems
   C. keeps his thoughts to himself
   D. look to employees for assistance in decision making

KEY (CORRECT ANSWERS)

1. D
2. C
3. C
4. B
5. B

6. C
7. A
8. C
9. D
10. A

11. A
12. D
13. B
14. C
15. C

16. C
17. B
18. B
19. B
20. A

21. B
22. C
23. A
24. B
25. D

TEST 2

DIRECTIONS: Each question or incomplete statement is followed by several suggested answers or completions. Select the one that BEST answers the question or completes the statement. *PRINT THE LETTER OF THE CORRECT ANSWER IN THE SPACE AT THE RIGHT.*

1. You have just had a private discussion with an employee with an offending poster. You have explained that her poster is causing some problems and have asked for her cooperation in removing it. She has politely refused to do so, saying looking at it cheers her up, and she's been depressed lately.
   You should

   A. wait a day or two to see if the incident *blows over* before deciding whether to take any further action
   B. call in the two disgruntled employees within the hour and let them know they will have to live with the poster, as you are not going to *act as a censor in the office*
   C. check agency policies to see if it is legal to have posters in work areas
   D. firmly but politely instruct the employee to take the poster down, as it is interfering with the work of the unit

   1.____

2. Of the following, if a supervisor has an employee who is lacking in self-confidence but is otherwise capable, the supervisor should

   A. give the employee a forceful pep talk
   B. overly praise the employee to increase his or her confidence
   C. find out if the condition is caused by home problems
   D. compliment the employee's work whenever possible

   2.____

3. An employee reprimanded for poor performance tells her supervisor that her recent behavior has been due to a serious family problem. The supervisor suggests several programs which may be able to help her.
   The action of the supervisor was

   A. *inappropriate;* the supervisor should not involve herself in the personal affairs of her subordinates
   B. *appropriate;* personal problems frequently affect job performance
   C. *inappropriate;* the employee may consider the supervisor responsible for the subsequent action of the social agencies
   D. *appropriate;* the discussion with the supervisor will in itself tend to solve the problem

   3.____

4. Your supervisor informs you that the employee turnover rate in your office is well above the norm and must be reduced.
   Which one of the following initial steps would be LEAST appropriate in attempting to overcome this problem?

   A. Decide to be more lenient about performance standards and about employee requests for time off, so that your office will gain a reputation as a good place to work
   B. Discuss the problem with a few of your employees whose judgment you trust to see if they can provide insight into the underlying causes of the problem

   4.____

C. Review the records of employees who have left during the past year to see if they can shed some light on the underlying causes of the problem
D. Carefully review your training procedures to see if they can be improved

5. The management principle that each employee should be under the direct control of one immediate supervisor at any one time is known as the principle of

   A. chain of command
   B. span of control
   C. unity of command
   D. homogeneous assignment

6. The employees of a unit have been wasteful in the use of office supplies.
Of the following, the MOST desirable action for the supervisor to take to reduce this waste is to

   A. determine the average quantity of supplies used daily by each employee
   B. find out which employees have been most wasteful and reprimand those employees
   C. discuss this matter at a conference with the staff, pointing out the necessity for, and methods of, eliminating waste
   D. issue supplies for an assignment at the time the assignment is made, and limit the quantity to the amount needed for that assignment only

7. You supervise nineteen employees in a unit which is located directly across from the commissioner's office. One of your new employees has a habit of *showing off* whenever the commissioner is nearby. You have just heard other employees laughing about this behavior among themselves. You like the new employee and would like the employee to be accepted by the others.
Of the following, you should

   A. discuss the situation with two of the older employees, and seek their cooperation in being a little more tolerant
   B. talk with the new employee and gently explain the situation
   C. discuss the situation with your most trusted employees and ask them to talk to the others
   D. do nothing

8. One of your employees comes to you and complains of sexual harassment by your supervisor. The employee has frequently complained about minor issues in the six months she has been there. You have known your supervisor for thirteen years and respect him a great deal. Of the following, you should

   A. firmly let the employee know what a serious allegation she is bringing against your supervisor
   B. let the employee know you will take her concerns seriously
   C. call your supervisor and give him a chance to prepare a defense
   D. inform the employee that she had better have concrete proof for a charge of this nature

9. The one of the following which is usually the POOREST reason for transferring an employee is to

   A. grant a doctor's request that the employee work nearer to his or her home
   B. take care of changes in workload

C. relieve the monotony of work assignments
D. discipline the employee

10. A good way for a supervisor to retain the confidence of his or her employees is to

    A. say as little as possible
    B. check work frequently
    C. make no promises unless they will be fulfilled
    D. never hesitate in giving an answer to any question

11. Your supervisor has discovered a serious error in work done by your unit under your supervision.
    Of the following, it would be BEST to

    A. assure your supervisor it will not happen again
    B. state that mistakes are unavoidable because your unit is understaffed
    C. assure your supervisor you will find out how the mistake occurred so that you can prevent it from happening again
    D. assure your supervisor that you will investigate and then reprimand the employee responsible

12. Good supervision is essentially a matter of

    A. patience in supervising workers
    B. care in selecting workers
    C. skill in human relations
    D. fairness in disciplining workers

13. It is MOST important for an employee who has been assigned a monotonous task to

    A. perform this task before doing other work
    B. ask another employee to help
    C. perform this task only after all other work has been completed
    D. take measures to prevent mistakes in performing the task

14. One of your employees has violated a minor agency regulation.
    The FIRST thing you should do is to

    A. warn the employee that you will have to take disciplinary action if it should happen again
    B. ask the employee to explain his or her actions
    C. inform your supervisor and wait for advice
    D. write a memo describing the incident and place it in the employee's personnel file

15. Your unit head has issued orders changing working procedures that your staff disagrees with.
    It would be BEST for you to tell your employees that

    A. you do not like the changes either, but the unit head wouldn't listen to you
    B. they should write a memo detailing their complaints to the unit head
    C. nothing can be done, even though you feel they are correct
    D. you will discuss your objections with the unit head

16. One of your employees tells you that he feels you give him much more work than the other employees, and he is having trouble meeting your deadlines.
You should

     A. ask if he has been under a lot of non-work related stress lately
     B. review his recent assignments to determine if he is correct
     C. explain that this is a busy time, but you are dividing the work equally
     D. tell him that he is the most competent employee and that is why he receives more work

17. It is generally considered proper that the number of employees immediately supervised by a higher, upper echelon supervisor should be

     A. equal to the number of employees supervised by a lower level supervisor
     B. larger than the number supervised by a lower level supervisor
     C. smaller than the number supervised by a lower level supervisor
     D. none of the above

18. Some managers propose that work assignments be made by assigning a varied set of tasks to a group of employees and then allowing the group to decide for itself how to organize the work to be done.
The one of the following which is considered to be the CHIEF advantage of this system is that it

     A. encourages employees to specialize in the work they are assigned to do
     B. reduces the amount of control employees have over their work
     C. increases the employees' job satisfaction
     D. reduces the number of skills the employee is required to learn

19. You find that have unjustly reprimanded one of your subordinates.
You should

     A. ignore the matter, but be more careful in the future
     B. readily admit your mistake to the employee
     C. admit your mistake at your next staff meeting, so that your employees will know how fair you are
     D. admit your mistake, but blame the misunderstanding on your supervisor

20. An experienced, self-confident employee carelessly omitted an essential operation on a job assigned to her. As a result, the completion of an important urgent report was delayed for several hours. A few days later, a relatively inexperienced, sensitive co-worker made a similar careless mistake with similar negative results. The supervisor of the two employees was more gentle in reprimanding the latter than the former employee. The supervisor's action in administering reprimands of unequal severity to these two subordinates was

     A. *inappropriate,* because fairness requires that subordinates responsible for like mistakes receive reprimands of like severity
     B. *appropriate,* because supervisors should consider the temperament of subordinates when reprimanding them
     C. *appropriate,* because subordinates who accept greater responsibilities must likewise accept the consequent greater penalties for their mistakes
     D. *inappropriate,* because more experienced employees benefit less, in general, from reprimands than less experienced employees

21. You have just overheard a tense discussion in the cafeteria between two of your best employees. One of them has owed the other $40 for several months and has not paid it back or even mentioned the debt. The employees do not realize that you have overheard them.
    During that week, you should

    A. not discuss the matter with either of them
    B. discuss the matter with both of them, as the conflict may adversely affect their job performance
    C. discuss the matter with the one who has not paid back the money
    D. put a clever but meaningful cartoon up on your wall about the importance of paying back debts to friends

22. You have been supervising twenty employees for three months. You suspect that one of your employees, who has worked in the unit longer than anyone else, has perfected the *art of looking busy.* You wish to find out how much work she is really accomplishing.
    Of the following, it would be LEAST appropriate to

    A. have a frank discussion with the employee about her performance
    B. set specific time limits on when you would like to get work back from her
    C. try to observe her more carefully while she is working
    D. be more careful when monitoring her work output

23. The supervisor of a central files bureau which has fifty employees customarily spends a considerable portion of time in spot-checking the files, reviewing material being transferred from active to inactive files, and similar activities.
    From the viewpoint of the department management, the MOST pertinent evaluation which can be made on the basis of this information is that the

    A. supervisor is conscientious and hardworking
    B. bureau may need additional staff
    C. supervisor has not made a sufficient delegation of authority and responsibility
    D. bureau needs an in-service training course as the work of its employees requires an abnormal amount of review

24. You have just been appointed as supervisor of ten employees. The supervisor you are replacing demanded that her subordinates accept their assignments without question. She refused to allow them to exercise initiative in carrying out assignments, and maintained a constant check on their work performance.
    The MOST appropriate policy for you to adopt would be to

    A. gradually remove the controls you consider too strict and provide opportunities for your staff to participate in formulating work plans and procedures
    B. continue her rigid policies, as the employees are used to this
    C. discontinue all strict controls immediately and give the employees complete freedom in carrying out their assignments
    D. ask your employees what method of supervision they would prefer

25. In any public agency, the top administrative officials are concerned largely with the work of overall creative planning with respect to the anticipated progress of the agency. The first-line supervisors, on the other hand, are concerned largely with the control of current action for the execution of current jobs.
On the basis of this passage, a first-line supervisor would be CHIEFLY responsible for

    A. increasing or decreasing the responsibilities of his or her unit to reflect changes in the policies of the agency
    B. modifying the work assignments of his or her present staff to handle a seasonal variation in the activities of the unit
    C. revising the procedure that is used for transmitting instructions from the head of the agency to the unit heads
    D. raising and lowering the production goals of his or her unit as often as necessary to adjust them to the abilities of employees

KEY (CORRECT ANSWERS)

1.	A	11.	C
2.	D	12.	C
3.	B	13.	D
4.	A	14.	B
5.	C	15.	D
6.	C	16.	B
7.	D	17.	C
8.	B	18.	C
9.	D	19.	B
10.	C	20.	B

21. A
22. A
23. C
24. A
25. B

EXAMINATION SECTION
TEST 1

DIRECTIONS: Each question or incomplete statement is followed by several suggested answers or completions. Select the one that BEST answers the question or completes the statement. *PRINT THE LETTER OF THE CORRECT ANSWER IN THE SPACE AT THE RIGHT.*

1. When a supervisor requests a subordinate to prepare a report, he should not only indicate the areas to be covered in the report but should also indicate to the subordinate

    A. for whom it is intended and its purpose
    B. the conclusions he expects to reach
    C. the decision that he will make based on the facts presented
    D. why that subordinate was chosen to prepare it

   1.____

2. The MOST accurate of the following principles of education and learning for a supervisor to keep in mind when planning a training program for the assistant supervisors under her supervision is that

    A. assistant supervisors, like all other individuals, vary in the rate at which they learn new material and in the degree to which they can retain what they do learn
    B. experienced assistant supervisors who have the same basic college education and agency experience will be able to learn new material at approximately the same rate of speed
    C. the speed with which assistant supervisors can learn new material after the age of forty is half as rapid as at ages twenty to thirty
    D. with regard to any specific task, it is easier and takes less time to break an experienced assistant supervisor of old, unsatisfactory work habits than it is to teach him new, acceptable ones

   2.____

3. Assume that you are a supervisor and that you are planning to train a group of experienced investigators in certain specific skills which they need in their daily work.
The one of the following methods which may *generally* be expected to be MOST valuable in ascertaining the effectiveness of the training program is to

    A. administer an objective examination to these investigators prior to conducting the training program and an equivalent form of the examination after the program and compare the results
    B. evaluate and compare the work records of these investigators with regard to these skills prior to and after completion of the training program
    C. hold a staff meeting with the investigators after the training program is completed and allow them to discuss frankly their opinions of the values they derived from the various parts of the training
    D. prepare an objective and detailed questionnaire covering the program, have the investigators answer without identifying themselves, and analyze the answers given

   3.____

4. A supervisor has received orders for a work assignment to be carried out by his unit. He has firmly decided on methods for carrying out this assignment which he believes will lead to its completion both properly and expeditiously. He has no intention whatsoever of changing his mind. After he has reached his decision, he calls a staff conference to discuss various alternative methods of carrying out the assignments without making clear that he has already decided upon the method to be used.
To hold a conference of this type would GENERALLY be a

   A. *good* idea, ecause his subordinates are likely to carry the assignment through better if they believe that they devised the methods used
   B. *good* idea, because the staff will have the opportunity and be properly motivated to gain knowledge and experience in methodology without endangering staff performance
   C. *poor* idea, because it would be a failure on the part of the supervisor to show the firm leadership which his unit has a right to expect
   D. *poor* idea, because the discovery by the staff that they had not actually participated in deciding upon methods to be used would have an adverse effect upon their morale

5. Supervisors are frequently faced with the necessity of training old employees in new tasks. An employee inexperienced in a task is much more likely to make a mistake than one who is experienced in it.
In delegating authority to an old employee to perform a new task, a supervisor should GENERALLY

   A. delegate the authority as soon as the subordinate gains minimum competence, allowing him to make mistakes which will not do major damage to the client or to the agency program
   B. delegate the authority as soon as the subordinate gains minimum competence but supervise him closely, enough so that he will not have the opportunity to make even minor mistakes
   C. make the delegation of authority dependent upon the importance which the client places upon the problems involved
   D. withhold the authority until the employee has become experienced in performing the task

6. A supervisor has been transferred from supervision of one group of units to another group of units. She spends the first three weeks in her new assignment in getting acquainted with her new subordinates, their problems, and their work. In this process, she notices that some of the records and forms which are submitted to her by two of the assistant supervisors are carelessly or improperly prepared.
The BEST of the following actions for the supervisor to take in this situation is to

   A. carefully check the work submitted by these assistant supervisors during an additional three weeks before taking any more positive action
   B. confer with these offending workers and show each one where her work needs improvement and how to go about achieving it
   C. institute an in-service training program specifically designed to solve such a problem and instruct the entire subordinate staff in proper work methods
   D. make a note of these errors for documentary use in preparing the annual service rating reports and advise the workers involved to prepare their work more carefully

7. A supervisor, who was promoted to this position a year ago, has supervised a certain assistant supervisor for this one year. The work of the assistant supervisor has been very poor because he has done a minimum of work, refused to take sufficient responsibility, been difficult to handle, and required very close supervision. Apparently due to the increasing insistence by his supervisor that he improve the caliber of his work, the assistant supervisor tenders his resignation, stating that the demands of the job are too much for him. The opinion of the previous supervisor, who had supervised this assistant supervisor for two years, agrees substantially with that of the new supervisor. Under such circumstances, the BEST of the following actions the supervisor can take in general is to

   A. recommend that the resignation be accepted and that he be rehired should he later apply when he feels able to do the job
   B. recommend that the resignation be accepted and that he not be rehired should he later so apply
   C. refuse to accept the resignation but try to persuade the assistant supervisor to accept psychiatric help
   D. refuse to accept the resignation, promising the assistant supervisor that he will be less closely supervised in the future since he is now so experienced

8. After completing a conference with a supervisor concerning the ramifications of a complex problem, an employee informs the supervisor that she feels that her assistant supervisor is too strict in her handling of all the workers under her supervision, especially in comparison with the other assistant supervisors.
The one of the following actions which is *generally* BEST for the supervisor to take is to

   A. advise the worker in a friendly fashion to apply for a transfer to a unit which has a more lenient supervisor
   B. caution the employee that complaining about a fellow employee behind her back is frowned upon by higher authority as it is a sign of disloyalty
   C. inform the employee that she, the supervisor, will investigate the complaint to determine whether or not it has any validity
   D. tell the worker that the closer and stricter a supervisor is, the better and more completely trained will be her subordinate staff

9. Rumors have arisen to the effect that one of the investigators under your supervision has been attending classes at a local university during afternoon hours when he is supposed to be making field visits.
The BEST of the following ways for you to approach this problem is to

   A. disregard the rumors since, like most rumors, they probably have no actual foundation in fact
   B. have a discreet investigation made in order to determine the actual facts prior to taking any other action
   C. inform the investigator that you know what he has been doing and that such behavior is overt derelection of duty and is punishable by dismissal
   D. review the investigator's work record, spot check his performance, and take no further action unless the quality of his work is below average for the unit

10. A supervisor must consider many factors in evaluating a worker whom he has supervised for a considerable time. In evaluating the capacity of such a worker to use independent judgment, the one of the following to which the supervisor should *generally* give MOST consideration is the worker's

A. capacity to establish good relationships with people (clients, colleagues)
B. educational background
C. emotional stability
D. the quality and judgment shown by the worker in previous work situations known to the supervisor

11. A supervisor is conducting a special meeting with the assistant supervisors under her supervision to read and discuss some major complex changes in the rules and procedures. She notices that one of the assistant supervisors who is normally attentive at meetings seems to be paying no attention to what is being said. The supervisor stops reading the rules and asks the assistant supervisor a couple of questions about the changed procedure, to which she gets satisfactory answers.
The BEST action of the following for the supervisor to take at the meeting is to

   A. advise the assistant supervisor gently but firmly that these changes are complex and that her undivided attention is required in order to fully comprehend them
   B. avoid further embarrassment to the assistant supervisor by asking the group as a whole to pay more attention to what is being read
   C. discontinue the questioning and resume reading the procedure
   D. politely request the assistant supervisor to stop giving those present the impression that she is uninterested in what goes on about her

12. A supervisor becomes aware that one of her very competent experienced workers never takes notes during an interview with a client except to note an occasional name, address, or date. When asked about this practice by the supervisor, the worker states that she has a good memory for important details and has always been able to satisfactorily record an interview after the client has left.
It would *generally* be BEST for the supervisor to handle this situation by

   A. discussing with her that more extensive note-taking may sometimes be desirable with a client who believes note-taking to be evidence that his problem will receive serious consideration
   B. agreeing with this practice since note-taking interferes with the establishment of a proper worker-client relationship
   C. explaining that, since interviewing is an art form rather than an exact science, a good worker must devise her own personal rules for interviewing and not be bound by general principles
   D. warning the worker that memory is too uncertain a thing to be relied upon and, therefore, notes should be taken during an interview of all matters

13. When an experienced subordinate who has the authority and information necessary to make a decision on a certain difficult matter brings the matter to his supervisor without having made the decision, it would *generally* be BEST for the supervisor to

   A. agree to make the decision for the subordinate after the subordinate has explained why he finds it difficult to make the decision and after he has made a recommendation
   B. make the decision for the subordinate, explaining to him the reasons for arriving at the decision
   C. refuse to make the decision, but discuss the various alternatives with the subordinate in order to clarify the issues involved
   D. refuse to make the decision, explaining to the subordinate that he is deemed to be fully qualified and competent to make the decision

14. The one of the following instances when it is MOST important for an upper-level supervisor to follow the chain of command is when he is

   A. communicating decisions
   B. communicating information
   C. receiving suggestions
   D. seeking information

15. Experts in the field of personnel relations feel that it is generally a bad practice for subordinate employees to become aware of pending or contemplated changes in policy or organizational set-up via the *grapevine* CHIEFLY because

   A. evidence that one or more responsible officials have proved untrustworthy will undermine confidence in the agency
   B. the information disseminated by this method is seldom entirely accurate and generally spreads needless unrest among the subordinate staff
   C. the subordinate staff may conclude that the administration feels the staff cannot be trusted with the true information
   D. the subordinate staff may conclude that the administration lacks the courage to make an unpopular announcement through official channels

16. In order to maintain a proper relationship with a worker who is assigned to staff rather than line functions, a line supervisor should

   A. accept all recommendations of the staff worker
   B. include the staff worker in the conferences called by the supervisor for his subordinates
   C. keep the staff worker informed of developments in the area of his staff assignment
   D. require that the staff worker's recommendations be communicated to the supervisor through the supervisor's own superior

17. Of the following, the GREATEST disadvantage of placing a worker in a staff position under the direct supervision of the supervisor whom he advises is the possibility that the

   A. staff worker will tend to be insubordinate because of a feeling of superiority over the supervisor
   B. staff worker will tend to give advice of the type which the supervisor wants to hear or finds acceptable
   C. supervisor will tend to be mistrustful of the advice of a worker of subordinate rank
   D. supervisor will tend to derive little benefit from the advice because to supervise properly he should know at least as much as his subordinate

18. One factor which might be given consideration in deciding upon the optimum span of control of a supervisor over his immediate subordinates is the position of the supervisor in the hierarchy of the organization.
   It is GENERALLY considered proper that the number of subordinates immediately supervised by a higher, upper echelon supervisor

   A. is unrelated to and tends to form no pattern with the number supervised by lower-level supervisors
   B. should be about the same as the number supervised by a lower-level supervisor
   C. should be larger than the number supervised by a lower-level supervisor
   D. should be smaller than the number supervised by a lower-level supervisor

19. An important administrative problem is how precisely to define the limits on authority that is delegated to subordinate supervisors.
    Such definition of limits of authority should be

    A. as precise as possible and practicable in all areas
    B. as precise as possible and practicable in areas of function, but should allow considerable flexibility in the area of personnel management
    C. as precise as possible and practicable in the area of personnel management, but should allow considerable flexibility in the areas of function
    D. in general terms so as to allow considerable flexibility both in the areas of function and in the areas of personnel management

20. The LEAST important of the following reasons why a particular activity should be assigned to a unit which performs activities dissimilar to it is that

    A. close coordination is needed between the particular activity and other activities performed by the unit
    B. it will enhance the reputation and prestige of the unit supervisor
    C. the unit makes frequent use of the results of this particular activity
    D. the unit supervisor has a sound knowledge and understanding of the particular activity

21. In a conference on difficult cases between a recently appointed supervisor and an experienced, above-average employee, the MOST valuable of the following services that the supervisor can offer the employee is a

    A. detached point of view
    B. knowledge of human needs
    C. knowledge of the agency's basic rules and regulations
    D. willingness to make decisions

22. A supervisor is put in charge of a special unit. She is exceptionally well qualified for this assignment by her training and experience. One of her very close personal friends has been working for some time in this unit. Both the supervisor and worker are certain that the rest of the employees in the unit, many of whom have been in the bureau for a long time, know of this close relationship.
    Under these circumstances, the MOST advisable action for the supervisor to take is to

    A. ask that either she be allowed to return to her old assignment or, if that cannot be arranged, that her friend be transferred to another unit in the center
    B. avoid any overt sign of favoritism by acting impartiall and with greater reserve when dealing with this employee than with the rest of the staff
    C. discontinue any socializing with this employee either inside or outside the office so as to eliminate any gossip or dissatisfaction
    D. talk the situation over with the employee and arrive at a mutually acceptable plan of proper office decorum

23. A supervisor who wishes to attain established objectives should concentrate on

    A. determining whether management is operating at maximum effectiveness
    B. making suggestions for improving the organization
    C. planning work assignments
    D. securing salary increases for needy employees

24. A usually competent employee complains that he does not understand the procedures to be followed in performing a certain task although the supervisor has explained them twice and has demonstrated them.
Of the following, the BEST course of action for the supervisor to take is to

   A. ask the employee whether he has any problems which are bothering him
   B. assign someone else to the job
   C. explain the procedures again and demonstrate at the same time
   D. have the employee perform the job while he watches and gives additional instructions

25. GENERALLY, in order to be completely qualified as a supervisor, a person

   A. should be able to perform exceptionally well at least one of the jobs he supervises and have some knowledge of the others
   B. must have an intimate working knowledge of all facets of the jobs which he supervises
   C. should know the basic principles and procedures of the jobs he supervises
   D. need know little or nothing of the jobs which he supervises as long as he knows the principles of supervision

---

KEY (CORRECT ANSWERS)

1.	A	11.	C
2.	A	12.	A
3.	B	13.	C
4.	D	14.	A
5.	A	15.	B
6.	B	16.	C
7.	B	17.	B
8.	C	18.	D
9.	B	19.	A
10.	D	20.	B

21. A
22. A
23. C
24. D
25. C

TEST 2

DIRECTIONS: Each question or incomplete statement is followed by several suggested answers or completions. Select the one that BEST answers the question or completes the statement. *PRINT THE LETTER OF THE CORRECT ANSWER IN THE SPACE AT THE RIGHT.*

1. Your superior has asked you to notify employees of an important change in one of the operating procedures described in the manual. Every employee presently has a copy of this manual.
   Which of the following is *normally* the MOST practical way to get the employees to understand such a change?

   A. Notify each employee individually of the change and answer any questions he might have
   B. Send a written notice to key personnel, directing them to inform the people under them
   C. Call a general meeting, distribute a corrected page for the manual, and discuss the change
   D. Send a memo to employees describing the change in general terms and asking them to make the necessary corrections in their copies of the manual

   1.____

2. A supervisor was directed by the head of his division to report figures for overtime wages. The supervisor asked a clerk under his supervision to give him the figures, and he passed the clerk's figures along to his superior without questioning them. It was then discovered that the clerk had carelessly supplied the wrong information. Who can PROPERLY be held responsible for the mistake, the supervisor or the payroll clerk?

   A. Only the supervisor because he should have known that the clerk would be careless
   B. Only the clerk because it should be unnecessary for supervisors to check the work of their subordinates except for work which is unusually complex or important
   C. Neither of them because it is perfectly understandable that such mistakes will occur from time to time
   D. Both of them because the person to whom a task is delegated is responsible to the supervisor who delegated the task, and the supervisor is responsible to his superior

   2.____

3. As a supervisor, it is necessary for you to show a new employee how to enter information on standard forms that he will have to prepare. These forms have a number of blanks to be filled in, but the job is fairly simple once a person becomes familiar with it.
   The BEST way to show the new employee how to do the job is to

   A. explain how to do it and have him fill out a few forms, helping him with any difficulties
   B. give him a completed form to use as a model and tell him to do all the others exactly the same way
   C. put him on his own immediately and assume that he will learn for himself through trial and error
   D. give him several dozen completed forms to read and ask him to check back with you in a few hours when he feels ready to start work

   3.____

4. Suppose that a usually competent employee whom you supervise has suddenly begun having difficulty completing his assignments. You ask the employee to speak to you privately about this situation, and he agrees that he would appreciate this opportunity because of a problem he is having.
Of the following, which one would be the BEST technique for you to use in speaking with him?

    A. Criticize the employee's performance as soon as he mentions his difficulty in completing his assignments
    B. Listen patiently to what the employee has to say before making any comments on your own
    C. Refuse to discuss any personal factors which the employee mentions when he tries to explain his recent work difficulty
    D. Allow the employee to argue with you but plan your attack and defense carefully

4.____

5. A certain supervisor does not compliment members of his staff when they come up with good ideas. He feels that coming up with good ideas is part of the job and does not merit special attention.
This supervisor's practice is

    A. *poor,* because recognition for good ideas is a good motivator
    B. *poor,* because the staff will suspect that the supervisor has no good ideas of his own
    C. *good,* because it is reasonable to assume that employees will tell their supervisor of ways to improve office practice
    D. *good,* because the other members of the staff are not made to seem inferior by comparison

5.____

6. An employee under your supervision complains about a decision you have made in assigning work in the office. You consider the matter to be unimportant, but it seems to be very important to him. He is excited and very angry. Of the following, the MOST appropriate action for you to take FIRST is to

    A. listen to the details of his complaint
    B. refer him to your superior
    C. tell him to *cool off* before discussing the matter
    D. tell him to settle it with the other employees

6.____

7. An experienced employee complains to his unit supervisor that the latter's continual, very close supervision of his work is unnecessary and annoying. The unit supervisor has been recently appointed.
Of the following, it would *generally* be BEST for the unit supervisor to

    A. agree to discontinue all supervision if the employee will agree, if he has any problems, to consult the supervisor
    B. assure the employee that close supervision is necessary but should not be taken personally
    C. consider with the employee what aspects of the supervision could be reduced
    D. explain that he is supervising closely only until he learns what the job is all about

7.____

8. A supervisor had a clerk assigned to help him review records. One day the supervisor asked the clerk to continue checking the records, and the clerk said, *No, I'm not doing any more of that today.*
   In this instance, the supervisor should IMMEDIATELY

   A. ask the clerk why he will not check the records
   B. ask another clerk to do the job
   C. tell the clerk he must do it or be transferred
   D. contact his own supervisor

9. Assume that you have been assigned to supervise other employees. You find that one of your subordinates makes many mistakes whenever he prepares a particular report. Of the following, the MOST desirable course of action for you to follow FIRST in such a situation is to

   A. retrain the subordinate in the preparation of the report
   B. transfer the subordinate to another unit
   C. tell the subordinate to improve or resign
   D. give the employee different duties

10. Some employees of a department have sent an anonymous letter containing many complaints to the department head. Of the following, what is this MOST likely to show about the department?

    A. It is probably a good place to work.
    B. Communications are probably poor.
    C. The complaints are probably unjustified.
    D. These employees are probably untrustworthy.

11. Of the following, the BEST reason for rotating employee work assignments is that such rotation

    A. challenges the ingenuity of supervisors in making assignments
    B. gives each employee a chance at both desirable and undesirable assignments
    C. creates specialists among all employees
    D. increases the competitive spirit among employees

12. Although an employee under your supervision frequently protests when receiving a monotonous assignment, he nevertheless performs the assigned task efficiently. His protests, however, disturb the other employees and interfere with their work.
    Of the following actions you may take in handling this employee, the MOST desirable one is for you to

    A. point out to him the effect of his conduct on the staff's work and request his cooperation in accepting such assignments
    B. arrange to issue such assignments to him when the other members of the staff are not present
    C. inform him that you will request his transfer to another unit unless he puts a halt to his unjustifiable protests
    D. ask other members of the staff to tell him that he is disturbing them by his protests

13. A supervisor has had several problems with a clerk who assists him. He calls the clerk in for a discussion of the matters.
    Which of the following should comprise the MAJOR part of the discussion?

    A. All the things the clerk has done wrong
    B. The most recent things the clerk has done wrong
    C. The things the clerk has done well in addition to the things he has done wrong
    D. The clerk's previous experience and personal problems

14. Assume that certain work processed in your office is then sent to another office for further processing. One of the employees in your office tells you that the supervisor in the other office has been complaining about your office's method of handling the work.
    Of the following, the MOST appropriate action for you to take is to

    A. get all the details from the employee and then speak to the other supervisor
    B. ignore the situation and continue to do the best you can
    C. remind the supervisor that it is not his function to evaluate your work
    D. refrain from reporting the matter to your superior

15. It is the practice in your department to make objective evaluations of the performance of different units. This requires looking at the results achieved by a particular unit during a specified period of time; for instance, the number of applications processed, the number of inquiries answered, the number of inspections made, and so forth.
    Of the following, the BEST method of evaluating the performance of each unit is to compare its results with the

    A. results achieved by all units of the same size that are performing other kinds of work
    B. goals that the unit was reasonably expected to meet during the specified period
    C. performance of the same unit during a similar period of time four or five years earlier
    D. amount of money spent to achieve these results

16. It is possible that you may be asked to submit a brief written evaluation of the work of several employees under your supervision.
    Such an evaluation should *normally* give LEAST emphasis to an employee's

    A. attendance record, including tardiness and absence
    B. ability to grasp new assignments and carry them out effectively
    C. educational background and previous employment experience
    D. ability to get along with co-workers

17. Of the following leadership characteristics, the one that is *generally* considered PRIMARY for a supervisor is the ability to

    A. achieve good working relations with fellow supervisors
    B. get subordinates to air their personal problems
    C. take action to get the job done
    D. plan his work efficiently

18. A recently appointed supervisor is placed in charge of a district which includes several senior employees. He finds that while these subordinates are able to learn new tasks and methods, some of them tend to take longer to learn procedural changes than newer, younger workers.
Of the following, the MAIN reason for this is that senior workers

    A. are embarrassed by younger workers' intelligence
    B. have to *unlearn* what was taught them in the past
    C. form learning blocks when they are supervised by a younger person
    D. are more interested in doing the work than in academic discussions

19. Which of the following is *generally* considered to be the MOST desirable way for a supervisor to begin a discussion of an employee's performance with the employee?

    A. Accentuate the positive by giving credit where credit is due
    B. Encourage the employee to suggest ways in which he can improve
    C. Point out specific instances of poor performance
    D. Suggest training programs that the employee may be interested in

20. For a supervisor to use consultative supervision with his subordinates effectively, it is ESSENTIAL that he

    A. accept the fact that his formal authority will be weakened by the procedure
    B. admit that he does not know more than all his men together and that his ideas are not always best
    C. utilize a committee system so that the procedure is orderly
    D. make sure that all subordinates are consulted so that no one feels left out

21. During a conversation with his supervisor, a subordinate begins to discuss what appears to the supervisor to be a deep-seated personality problem that has been bothering the subordinate.
For the supervisor to suggest to the subordinate the possibility of professional help would NORMALLY be

    A. *undesirable;* the necessity of requiring professional help would automatically disqualify the subordinate from being promoted in the future
    B. *desirable;* generally a supervisor can be of limited assistance in personally solving deep-seated personality problems
    C. *undesirable;* since the supervisor was approached by the employee, it is his responsibility as a supervisor to help the employee solve his problem
    D. *desirable;* in accordance with the Civil Service Commission regulations, a supervisor is not allowed to get involved in subordinates' personal problems

22. When a new method of performing a job operation is to be instituted, the one of the following approaches which will MOST generally gain acceptance of the change by subordinates is to

    A. hold a friendly, informal meeting after the change has been implemented to explain the advantages of the new method
    B. consult the subordinates involved in the change as early as possible in the planning stage
    C. work closely with just one of the subordinates who will be affected by the change so that others need not be taken off the job

D. implement the change, instruct employees fully in the new method, and then follow up on results

23. Of the following, the supervisory practice which is LEAST likely to produce a favorable work environment is that the supervisor

    A. takes an active interest in subordinates
    B. does not tolerate mistakes, regardless of who has made the mistake
    C. gives praise when justified
    D. disciplines individuals in accordance with their violation of the rules

23.____

24. When a supervisor finds it necessary to let a subordinate know that he is dissatisfied with the subordinate's level of performance, which of the following tactics would *usually* prove MOST effective in improving the subordinate's performance?

    A. The supervisor should be angry when criticizing in order to prevent the mistakes from recurring.
    B. Once criticism has been made, the supervisor should be sure to continuously impress the seriousness of the mistakes upon the subordinate.
    C. When making his criticism, the supervisor should guard against referring to any work that was well done since this would reduce the effect of his criticism.
    D. The supervisor should focus his criticism on the mistakes being made and should avoid downgrading the subordinate personally.

24.____

25. Of the following, the BEST descriptive statement of an effective supervisor is *generally* that he

    A. works alongside his subordinates on the same type of work
    B. catches all errors when they are made
    C. gives many specific work orders and few general work orders
    D. devotes much of his time to long-range activities, such as planning and improving human relations

25.____

KEY (CORRECT ANSWERS)

1.	C	11.	B
2.	D	12.	A
3.	A	13.	C
4.	B	14.	A
5.	A	15.	B
6.	A	16.	C
7.	C	17.	C
8.	A	18.	B
9.	A	19.	A
10.	B	20.	D

21. B
22. B
23. B
24. D
25. D

EXAMINATION SECTION
TEST 1

DIRECTIONS: Each question or incomplete statement is followed by several suggested answers or completions. Select the one that BEST answers the question or completes the statement. *PRINT THE LETTER OF THE CORRECT ANSWER IN THE SPACE AT THE RIGHT.*

1. Which one of the following is LEAST likely to be an area or cause of trouble in the use of staff personnel?

    A. Misunderstanding of the role the staff personnel are supposed to play as a result of vagueness of definition of their duties and authority
    B. Tendency of staff personnel almost always to be older than line personnel at comparable salary levels with whom they must deal
    C. Selection of staff personnel who fail to have simultaneously both competence in their specialities and skill in staff work
    D. The staff person fails to understand mixed staff and operating duties

2. Which of the following is generally NOT a valid statement with respect to the supervisory process?

    A. General supervision is more effective than close supervision.
    B. Employee-centered supervisors lead more effectively than do production-centered supervisors.
    C. Employee satisfaction is directly related to productivity.
    D. Low-producing supervisors use techniques that are different from high-producing supervisors.

3. Which of the following is the MOST essential element for proper evaluation of the performance of subordinate supervisors?

    A. Careful definition of each supervisor's specific job responsibilities and of his progress in meeting mutually agreed upon work goals
    B. System of rewards and penalties based on each supervisor's progress in meeting clearly defined performance standards
    C. Definition of personality traits, such as industry, initiative, dependability, and cooperativeness, required for effective job performance
    D. Breakdown of each supervisor's job into separate components and a rating of his performance on each individual task

4. The PRINCIPAL advantage of specialization for the operating efficiency of a public service agency is that specialization

    A. reduces the amount of red tape in coordinating the activities of mutually dependent departments
    B. simplifies the problem of developing adequate job controls
    C. provides employees with a clear understanding of the relationship of their activities to the overall objectives of the agency
    D. reduces destructive competition for power between departments

5. A list of conditions which encourages good morale inside a work group would NOT include a

   A. high rate of agreement among group members on values and objectives
   B. tight control system to minimize the risk of individual error
   C. good possibility that joint action will accomplish goals
   D. past history of successful group accomplishment

6. Of the following, the MOST important factor to be considered in selecting a training strategy or program is the

   A. requirements of the job to be performed by the trainees
   B. educational level or prior training of the trainees
   C. size of the training group
   D. quality and competence of available training specialists

7. Of the following, the one which is considered to be LEAST characteristic of the higher ranks of management is

   A. that higher levels of management benefit from modern technology
   B. that success is measured by the extent to which objectives are achieved
   C. the number of subordinates that directly report to a manager
   D. the de-emphasis of individual and specialized performance

8. Assume that a manager is preparing a training syllabus to be used in training members of her staff.
   Which of the following would NOT be a valid principle of the learning process to consider when preparing this training syllabus?

   A. When a person has thoroughly learned a task, it takes a lot of effort to create a little more improvement.
   B. In complicated learning situations, there is a period in which an additional period of practice produces an equal amount of improvement in learning.
   C. The less a person knows about the task, the slower the initial progress.
   D. The more a person knows about the task, the slower the initial progress.

9. Which statement BEST illustrates when collective bargaining agreements are working well?

   A. Executives strongly support subordinate managers.
   B. The management rights clause in the contract is clear and enforced.
   C. Contract provisions are competently interpreted.
   D. The provisions of the agreement are properly interpreted, communicated, and observed.

10. An executive who wishes to encourage subordinates to communicate freely with him about a job-related problem should FIRST

    A. state his own position on the problem before listening to the subordinates' ideas
    B. invite subordinates to give their own opinions on the problem
    C. ask subordinates for their reactions to his own ideas about the problem
    D. guard the confidentiality of management information about the problem

11. The ability to deal constructively with intra-organizational conflict is an essential attribute of the successful manager.
    The one of the following types of conflict which would be LEAST difficult to handle constructively is a situation in which there is

    A. agreement on objectives, but disagreement as to the probable results of adopting the various alternatives
    B. agreement on objectives, disagreement on alternative courses of action, and relative certainty as to the outcome of one of the alternatives
    C. disagreement on objectives and on alternative courses of action, and relative certainty as to the outcome of one of the alternatives
    D. disagreement on objectives and on alternative courses of action, but uncertainty as to the outcome of the alternatives

12. Which of the following actions does NOT belong in a properly conducted grievance handling process?

    A. Gathering relevant information on why the grievance arose
    B. Formulating a personal judgment about the fairness or unfairness of the grievance at the time the grievance is presented
    C. Establishing tentative answers to the grievance
    D. Following up to see whether the solution has eliminated the difficulty

13. Grievances are generally defined as complaints expressed over work-related matters.
    Which one of the following is MOST important for managers to be aware of in connection with this definition?
    The

    A. fact that the definition fails to separate the subject of the grievance from the attitude of the grievant
    B. fact that anything in the organization may be the source of the grievance
    C. need to assume that dissatisfied people have adverse effects on productivity
    D. implication that management should be concerned about expressed grievances and unconcerned about unexpressed grievances

4 (#1)

14. In carrying out disciplinary action, the MOST important procedure for all managers to follow is to

   A. convince all levels of management on the need for discipline from the organization's viewpoint
   B. follow up on a disciplinary action and not assume that the action has been effective
   C. convince all executives that proper discipline is a legitimate tool for their use
   D. convince all executives that they need to display confidence in the organization's rules

14._____

15. Assume that an employee under your supervision is acquitted in court of criminal charges arising out of his employment.
Of the following statements concerning disciplinary action, which is MOST NEARLY correct?

   A. Disciplinary proceedings against the employee may not be held for the same offenses on which he was tried and acquitted.
   B. In a disciplinary action, the acquittal dispenses with the requirement that the employee be advised as to his constitutional rights.
   C. Civil Rights Law Section 79 prohibits the taking of any further punitive action by an employer if the offense did not involve official corruption.
   D. It is possible for the employee to be found guilty of the same offense when tried in a departmental hearing.

15._____

16. Work rules can be an effective tool in the process of personnel management.
The BEST practical definition for work rules is that they are

   A. minimum standards of conduct or performance that apply to individuals or groups at work in an organization
   B. prescriptions that serve to specialize employee behavior
   C. predetermined decisions about disciplinary action
   D. the major determinant of an organization's climate and the morale of its workforce

16._____

Questions 17-18

DIRECTIONS: Questions 17 and 18 pertain to identification of words that are incorrectly used because they are not in keeping with the meaning of the quotation. In answering each question, the first step is to read the passage and identify the incorrectly used word, and then select the word which, when substituted, BEST serves to convey the meaning of the quotation.

17. Among the Housing Manager's overall responsibilities in administering a project is the prevention of the development of conditions which might lead to termination of tenancy and eviction of a tenant. Where there appears to be doubt that a tenant is fully aware of his responsibilities and is thus jeopardizing his tenancy, the Housing Manager should acquaint him with these responsibilities. Where a situation involves behavior of a tenant or a member of his family, the Housing Manager should confirm, through discussions and referrals to social agencies, correction of the conditions before they reach a state where there is no alternative but termination proceedings.

    A. Coordinate
    B. Identify
    C. Assert
    D. Attempt

17._____

18. The one universal administrative complaint is that the budget is inadequate. Between adequacy and inadequacy lie all degrees of adequacy. Further, human wants are modest in relation to human resources. From these two facts we may conclude that the fundamental criterion of administrative decision must be a criterion of efficiency (the degree to which the goals have been reached relative to the available resources) rather than a criterion of adequacy (the degree to which its goals have been reached). The task of the manager is to maximize social values relative to limited resources.

    A. Improve
    B. Simple
    C. Limitless
    D. Optimize

18._____

Questions 19-21.
DIRECTIONS: Questions 19 through 21 are to be answered SOLELY on the basis of the following situation.

John Foley, a top administrator, is responsible for output in his organization. Because productivity had been lagging for two periods in a row, Foley decided to establish a committee of his subordinate managers to investigate the reasons for the poor performance and to make recommendations for improvements. After two meetings, the committee came to the conclusions and made the recommendations that follow.

Output forecasts had been handed down from the top without prior consultation with middle management and first level supervision. Lines of authority and responsibility had been unclear. The planning and control process should be decentralized.

After receiving the committee's recommendations, Foley proceeded to take the following actions. Foley decided he would retain final authority to establish quotas but would delegate to the middle managers the responsibility for meeting quotas.

After receiving Foley's decision, the middle managers proceeded to delegate to the first-line supervisors the authority to establish their own quotas. The middle managers eventually received and combined the first-line supervisors' quotas so that these conformed to Foley's.

19. Foley's decision to delegate responsibility for meeting quotas to the middle managers is inconsistent with sound management principles because

    A. Foley should not have involved himself in the first place
    B. middle managers do not have the necessary skills
    C. quotas should be established by the chief executive
    D. responsibility should not be delegated

19._____

20. The principle of co-extensiveness of responsibility and authority bears on Foley's decision.
    In this case, it implies that

    A. authority should exceed responsibility
    B. authority should be delegated to match the degree of responsibility
    C. both authority and responsibility should be retained and not delegated
    D. responsibility should be delegated, but authority should be retained

20._____

21. The middle managers' decision to delegate to the first-line supervisors the authority to establish quotas was INCORRECTLY reasoned because

    A. delegation and control must go together
    B. first-line supervisors are in no position to establish quotas
    C. one cannot delegate authority that one does not possess
    D. the meeting of quotas should not be delegated

21._____

22. If one attempts to list the advantages of the management-by-exception principle as it is used in connection with the budgeting process, several distinct advantages could be cited.
    Which of the following is NOT an advantage of this principle as it applies to the budgeting process?
    Management-by-exception

    A. saves time
    B. identifies critical problem areas
    C. focuses attention and concentrates effort
    D. escalates the frequency and importance of budget-related decisions

22._____

23. The MOST accurate description of a budget is that

    A. a budget is made up by an organization to plan its future activities
    B. a budget specifies in dollars and cents how much is spent in a particular time period
    C. a budget specifies how much the organization to which it relates estimates it will spend over a certain period of time
    D. all plans dealing with money are budgets

23._____

24. Of the following, the one which is NOT a contribution that a budget makes to organizational programming is that a budget

    A. enables a comparison of what actually happened with what was expected
    B. stresses the need to forecast specific goals and eliminates the need to focus on tasks needed to accomplish goals
    C. may illustrate duplication of effort between interdependent activities
    D. shows the relationship between various organizational segments

25. A line-item budget is a good control budget because

    A. it clearly specifies how the items being purchased will be used
    B. expenditures can be shown primarily for contractual services
    C. it clearly specifies what the money is buying
    D. it clearly specifies the services to be provided

KEY (CORRECT ANSWERS)

1.	B	11.	B
2.	C	12.	B
3.	A	13.	C
4.	B	14.	B
5.	B	15.	D
6.	A	16.	A
7.	A	17.	D
8.	D	18.	C
9.	D	19.	D
10.	B	20.	B

21. C
22. D
23. C
24. B
25. C

TEST 2

DIRECTIONS: Each question or incomplete statement is followed by several suggested answers or completions. Select the one that BEST answers the question or completes the statement. *PRINT THE LETTER OF THE CORRECT ANSWER IN THE SPACE AT THE RIGHT.*

1. The insights of Chester I. Barnard have influenced the development of management thought in significant ways. He is MOST closely identified with a position that has become known as the

    A. acceptance theory of authority
    B. principle of the manager's or executive's span of control
    C. *Theory X* and *Theory Y* dichotomy
    D. unit of command principle

    1._____

2. Certain conditions should exist to insure that a subordinate will decide to accept a communication as being authoritative.
Which of the following is LEAST valid as a condition which should exist?

    A. The subordinate understands the communication.
    B. At the time of the subordinate's decision, he views the communication as consistent with the organization's purpose and his personal interest.
    C. At the time of the subordinate's decision, he views the communication as more consistent with his personal purposes than with the organization's interest.
    D. The subordinate is mentally and physically able to comply with the communication.

    2._____

3. In exploring the effects that employee participation has on implementing changes in work methods, certain relationships have been established between participation and productivity.
It has MOST generally been found that highest productivity occurs in groups provided with

    A. participation in the process of change only through representatives of their group
    B. no participation in the change process
    C. full participation in the change process
    D. intermittent participation in the process of change

    3._____

4. The trend LEAST likely to occur in the area of employee-management relations is that

    A. employees will exert more influence on decisions affecting their interests
    B. technological change will have a stronger impact on organizations' human resources
    C. labor will judge management according to company profits
    D. government will play a larger role in balancing the interests of the parties in labor-management affairs

    4._____

5. Members of an organization must satisfy several fundamental psychological needs in order to be happy and productive.
The BROADEST and MOST basic needs are

   A. achievement, recognition, and acceptance
   B. competition, recognition, and accomplishment
   C. salary increments and recognition
   D. acceptance of competition and economic award

6. Morale has been defined as the capacity of a group of people to pull together steadily for a common purpose.
Morale thus defined is MOST generally dependent on

   A. job security
   B. group and individual self-confidence
   C. organizational efficiency
   D. physical health of the individuals

7. Which is the CORRECT order of steps to follow when revising office procedure?
To

   I. develop the improved method as determined by time and motion studies and effective workplace layout
   II. find out how the task is now performed
   III. apply the new method
   IV. analyze the current method

   The CORRECT answer is:
   A. IV, II, I, III
   B. II, I, III, IV
   C. I, II, IV, III
   D. II, IV, I, III

8. In contrast to broad spans of control, narrow spans of control are MOST likely to

   A. provide opportunity for more personal contact between superior and subordinate
   B. encourage decentralization
   C. stress individual initiative
   D. foster group of team effort

9. A manager is coaching a subordinate on the nature of decision-making. She could BEST define decision-making as

   A. choosing between alternatives
   B. making diagnoses of feasible ends
   C. making diagnoses of feasible means
   D. comparing alternatives

10. Of the following, the LEAST valid purpose of an organizational policy statement is to

    A. keep personnel from performing improper actions and functions on routine matters
    B. prevent the mishandling of non-routine matters
    C. provide management personnel with a tool that precludes the need for their use of judgment
    D. provide standard decisions and approaches in handling problems of a recurrent nature

11. Current thinking on bureaucratic organizations is that

    A. bureaucracy is on the way out
    B. bureaucracy, though not perfect, is unlikely to be replaced
    C. bureaucratic organizations are most effective in dealing with constant change
    D. bureaucratic organizations are most effective when dealing with sophisticated customers or clients

12. The development of alternate plans as a major step in planning will normally result in the planner's having several possible course of action available. GENERALLY, this is

    A. *desirable* since such development helps to determine the most suitable alternative and to provide for the unexpected
    B. *desirable* since such development makes the use of planning premises and constraints unnecessary
    C. *undesirable* since the planners should formulate only one way of achieving given goals at a given time
    D. *undesirable* since such action restricts efforts to modify the planning to take advantage of opportunities

13. Assume a manager carries out his responsibilities to his staff according to what is now known about managerial leadership.
    Which of the following statements would MOST accurately reflect his assumptions about proper management?

    A. Efficiency in operations results from allowing the human element to participate in a minimal way.
    B. Efficient operation results from balancing work considerations with personnel considerations.
    C. Efficient operation results from a work force committed to its self-interest.
    D. Efficient operation results from staff relationships that produce a friendly work climate.

14. Assume that a manager is called upon to conduct a management audit. To do this properly, he would have to take certain steps in a specific sequence. Which step should this manager take FIRST?

    A. Managerial performance must be surveyed.
    B. A method of reporting must be established.
    C. Management auditing procedures and documentation must be developed.
    D. Criteria for the audit must be established.

14._____

15. If a manager is required to conduct a scientific investigation of an organizational problem, the FIRST step he should take is to

    A. state his assumptions about the problem
    B. carry out a search for background information
    C. choose the right approach to investigate the validity of his assumptions
    D. define and state the problem

15._____

16. A manager would be correct to assert that the principle of delegation states that decisions should be made PRIMARILY

    A. by persons in an executive capacity qualified to make them
    B. by persons in a non-executive capacity
    C. at as low an organizational level of authority as practicable
    D. by the next lower level of authority

16._____

17. Of the following, which one is NOT regarded by management authorities as a fundamental characteristic of an ideal bureaucracy?

    A. Division of labor and specialization
    B. An established hierarchy
    C. Decentralization of authority
    D. A set of operating rules and regulations

17._____

18. As the number of subordinates in a manager's span of control increases, the actual number of possible relationships

    A. increases disproportionately to the number of subordinates
    B. increases in equal number to the number of subordinates
    C. reaches a stable level
    D. will first increase, then slowly decrease

18._____

19. Management experts generally believe that computer-based management information systems (MIS) have greater potential for improving the process of management than any other development in recent decades.
    The one of the following which MOST accurately describes the objectives of MIS is to

    A. provide information for decision-making on planning, initiating, and controlling the operations of the various units of the organization
    B. establish mechanization of routine functions such as clerical records, payroll, inventory, and accounts receivable in order to promote economy and efficiency
    C. computerize decision-making on planning, initiating, organizing, and controlling the operations of an organization
    D. provide accurate facts and figures on the various programs of the organization to be used for purposes of planning and research

20. The one of the following which is the BEST application of the *management-by-exception* principle is that this principle

    A. stimulates communication and aids in management of crisis situations, thus reducing the frequency of decision-making
    B. saves time and reserves top management decisions only for crisis situations, thus reducing the frequency of decision-making
    C. stimulates communication, saves time, and reduces the frequency of decision-making
    D. is limited to crisis-management situations

21. Generally, each organization is dependent upon the availability of qualified personnel.
    Of the following, the MOST important factor affecting the availability of qualified people to each organization is

    A. availability of public transportation
    B. the general rise in the educational levels of our population
    C. the rise of sentiment against racial discrimination
    D. pressure by organized community groups

22. A fundamental responsibility of all managers is to decide what physical facilities and equipment are needed to help attain basic goals.
    Good planning for the purchase and use of equipment is seldom easy to do and is complicated most by the fact that

    A. organizations rarely have stable sources of supply
    B. nearly all managers tend to be better at personnel planning than at equipment planning
    C. decisions concerning physical resources are made too often on an emergency basis rather than under carefully prepared policies
    D. legal rulings relative to depreciation fluctuate very frequently

23. In attempting to reconcile managerial objectives and an individual employee's goals, it is generally LEAST desirable for management to

    A. recognize the capacity of the individual to contribute toward realization of managerial goals
    B. encourage self-development of the employee to exceed minimum job performance
    C. consider an individual employee's work separately from other employees
    D. demonstrate that an employee advances only to the extent that he contributes directly to the accomplishment of stated goals

24. As a management tool for discovering individual training needs, a job analysis would generally be of LEAST assistance in determining

    A. the performance requirements of individual jobs
    B. actual employee performance on the job
    C. acceptable standards of performance
    D. training needs for individual jobs

25. One of the major concerns of organizational managers today is how the spread of automation will affect them and the status of their positions. Realistically speaking, one can say that the MOST likely effect of our newer forms of highly automated technology on managers will be to

    A. make most top-level positions superfluous or obsolete
    B. reduce the importance of managerial work in general
    C. replace the work of managers with the work of technicians
    D. increase the importance of and demand for top managerial personnel

KEY (CORRECT ANSWERS)

1.	A	11.	B
2.	C	12.	A
3.	C	13.	B
4.	C	14.	D
5.	A	15.	D
6.	B	16.	C
7.	D	17.	C
8.	A	18.	A
9.	A	19.	A
10.	C	20.	C

21. B
22. C
23. C
24. B
25. D

PHILOSOPHY, PRINCIPLES, PRACTICES, AND TECHNICS
OF
SUPERVISION, ADMINISTRATION, MANAGEMENT, AND ORGANIZATION

TABLE OF CONTENTS

	Page
MEANING OF SUPERVISION	1
THE OLD AND THE NEW SUPERVISION	1
THE EIGHT (8) BASIC PRINCIPLES OF THE NEW SUPERVISION	1
I. Principle of Responsibility	1
II. Principle of Authority	2
III. Principle of Self-Growth	2
IV. Principle of Individual Worth	2
V. Principle of Creative Leadership	2
VI. Principle of Success and Failure	2
VII. Principle of Science	3
VIII. Principle of Cooperation	3
WHAT IS ADMINISTRATION?	3
I. Practices Commonly Classed as "Supervisory"	3
II. Practices Commonly Classed as "Administrative"	3
III. Practices Commonly Classed as Both "Supervisory" and "Administrative"	4
RESPONSIBILITIES OF THE SUPERVISOR	4
COMPETENCIES OF THE SUPERVISOR	4
THE PROFESSIONAL SUPERVISOR-EMPLOYEE RELATIONSHIP	4
MINI-TEXT IN SUPERVISION, ADMINISTRATION, MANAGEMENT, AND ORGANIZATION	5
I. Brief Highlights	5
A. Levels of Management	6
B. What the Supervisor Must Learn	6
C. A Definition of Supervision	6
D. Elements of the Team Concept	6
E. Principles of Organization	6
F. The Four Important Parts of Every Job	7
G. Principles of Delegation	7
H. Principles of Effective Communications	7
I. Principles of Work Improvement	7
J. Areas of Job Improvement	7
K. Seven Key Points in Making Improvements	8

	L.	Corrective Techniques for Job Improvement	8
	M.	A Planning Checklist	8
	N.	Five Characteristics of Good Directions	9
	O.	Types of Directions	9
	P.	Controls	9
	Q.	Orienting the New Employee	9
	R.	Checklist for Orienting New Employees	9
	S.	Principles of Learning	10
	T.	Causes of Poor Performance	10
	U.	Four Major Steps in On-the-Job Instructions	10
	V.	Employees Want Five Things	10
	W.	Some Don'ts in Regard to Praise	11
	X.	How to Gain Your Workers' Confidence	11
	Y.	Sources of Employee Problems	11
	Z.	The Supervisor's Key to Discipline	11
	AA.	Five Important Processes of Management	12
	BB.	When the Supervisor Fails to Plan	12
	CC.	Fourteen General Principles of Management	12
	DD.	Change	12
II.	Brief Topical Summaries		13
	A.	Who/What is the Supervisor?	13
	B.	The Sociology of Work	13
	C.	Principles and Practices of Supervision	14
	D.	Dynamic Leadership	14
	E.	Processes for Solving Problems	15
	F.	Training for Results	15
	G.	Health, Safety, and Accident Prevention	16
	H.	Equal Employment Opportunity	16
	I.	Improving Communications	16
	J.	Self-Development	17
	K.	Teaching and Training	17
		1. The Teaching Process	17
		a. Preparation	17
		b. Presentation	18
		c. Summary	18
		d. Application	18
		e. Evaluation	18
		2. Teaching Methods	18
		a. Lecture	18
		b. Discussion	18
		c. Demonstration	19
		d. Performance	19
		e. Which Method to Use	19

PHILOSOPHY, PRINCIPLES, PRACTICES, AND TECHNICS OF SUPERVISION, ADMINISTRATION, MANAGEMENT, AND ORGANIZATION

MEANING OF SUPERVISION

The extension of the democratic philosophy has been accompanied by an extension in the scope of supervision. Modern leaders and supervisors no longer think of supervision in the narrow sense of being confined chiefly to visiting employees, supplying materials, or rating the staff. They regard supervision as being intimately related to all the concerned agencies of society, they speak of the supervisor's function in terms of "growth," rather than the "improvement" of employees.

This modern concept of supervision may be defined as follows: Supervision is leadership and the development of leadership within groups which are cooperatively engaged in inspection, research, training, guidance, and evaluation.

THE OLD AND THE NEW SUPERVISION

TRADITIONAL
1. Inspection
2. Focused on the employee
3. Visitation
4. Random and haphazard
5. Imposed and authoritarian
6. One person usually

MODERN
1. Study and analysis
2. Focused on aims, materials, methods, supervisors, employees, environment
3. Demonstrations, intervisitation, workshops, directed reading, bulletins, etc.
4. Definitely organized and planned (scientific)
5. Cooperative and democratic
6. Many persons involved (creative)

THE EIGHT (8) BASIC PRINCIPLES OF THE NEW SUPERVISION

I. Principle of Responsibility
   Authority to act and responsibility for acting must be joined.
   A. If you give responsibility, give authority.
   B. Define employee duties clearly.
   C. Protect employees from criticism by others.
   D. Recognize the rights as well as obligations of employees.
   E. Achieve the aims of a democratic society insofar as it is possible within the area of your work.
   F. Establish a situation favorable to training and learning.
   G. Accept ultimate responsibility for everything done in your section, unit, office, division, department.
   H. Good administration and good supervision are inseparable.

II. Principle of Authority
The success of the supervisor is measured by the extent to which the power of authority is not used.
  A. Exercise simplicity and informality in supervision
  B. Use the simplest machinery of supervision
  C. If it is good for the organization as a whole, it is probably justified.
  D. Seldom be arbitrary or authoritative.
  E. Do not base your work on the power of position or of personality.
  F. Permit and encourage the free expression of opinions.

III. Principle of Self-Growth
The success of the supervisor is measured by the extent to which, and the speed with which, he is no longer needed.
  A. Base criticism on principles, not on specifics.
  B. Point out higher activities to employees.
  C. Train for self-thinking by employees to meet new situations.
  D. Stimulate initiative, self-reliance, and individual responsibility
  E. Concentrate on stimulating the growth of employees rather than on removing defects.

IV. Principle of Individual Worth
Respect for the individual is a paramount consideration in supervision.
  A. Be human and sympathetic in dealing with employees.
  B. Don't nag about things to be done.
  C. Recognize the individual differences among employees and seek opportunities to permit best expression of each personality.

V. Principle of Creative Leadership
The best supervision is that which is not apparent to the employee.
  A. Stimulate, don't drive employees to creative action.
  B. Emphasize doing good things.
  C. Encourage employees to do what they do best.
  D. Do not be too greatly concerned with details of subject or method.
  E. Do not be concerned exclusively with immediate problems and activities.
  F. Reveal higher activities and make them both desired and maximally possible.
  G. Determine procedures in the light of each situation but see that these are derived from a sound basic philosophy.
  H. Aid, inspire, and lead so as to liberate the creative spirit latent in all good employees.

VI. Principle of Success and Failure
There are no unsuccessful employees, only unsuccessful supervisors who have failed to give proper leadership.
  A. Adapt suggestions to the capacities, attitudes, and prejudices of employees.
  B. Be gradual, be progressive, be persistent.
  C. Help the employee find the general principle; have the employee apply his own problem to the general principle.
  D. Give adequate appreciation for good work and honest effort.
  E. Anticipate employee difficulties and help to prevent them.
  F. Encourage employees to do the desirable things they will do anyway.
  G. Judge your supervision by the results it secures.

VII. Principle of Science
Successful supervision is scientific, objective, and experimental. It is based on facts, not on prejudices.
   A. Be cumulative in results.
   B. Never divorce your suggestions from the goals of training.
   C. Don't be impatient of results.
   D. Keep all matters on a professional, not a personal, level.
   E. Do not be concerned exclusively with immediate problems and activities.
   F. Use objective means of determining achievement and rating where possible.

VIII. Principle of Cooperation
Supervision is a cooperative enterprise between supervisor and employee.
   A. Begin with conditions as they are.
   B. Ask opinions of all involved when formulating policies.
   C. Organization is as good as its weakest link.
   D. Let employees help to determine policies and department programs.
   E. Be approachable and accessible—physically and mentally.
   F. Develop pleasant social relationships.

WHAT IS ADMINISTRATION

Administration is concerned with providing the environment, the material facilities, and the operational procedures that will promote the maximum growth and development of supervisors and employees. (Organization is an aspect and a concomitant of administration.)

There is no sharp line of demarcation between supervision and administration; these functions are intimately interrelated and, often, overlapping. They are complementary activities.

I. Practices Commonly Classed as "Supervisory"
   A. Conducting employees' conferences
   B. Visiting sections, units, offices, divisions, departments
   C. Arranging for demonstrations
   D. Examining plans
   E. Suggesting professional reading
   F. Interpreting bulletins
   G. Recommending in-service training courses
   H. Encouraging experimentation
   I. Appraising employee morale
   J. Providing for intervisitation

II. Practices Commonly Classified as "Administrative"
   A. Management of the office
   B. Arrangement of schedules for extra duties
   C. Assignment of rooms or areas
   D. Distribution of supplies
   E. Keeping records and reports
   F. Care of audio-visual materials
   G. Keeping inventory records
   H. Checking record cards and books

      I. Programming special activities
      J. Checking on the attendance and punctuality of employees

III. Practices Commonly Classified as Both "Supervisory" and "Administrative"
    A. Program construction
    B. Testing or evaluating outcomes
    C. Personnel accounting
    D. Ordering instructional materials

RESPONSIBILITIES OF THE SUPERVISOR

A person employed in a supervisory capacity must constantly be able to improve his own efficiency and ability. He represent the employer to the employees and only continuous self-examination can make him a capable supervisor.

Leadership and training are the supervisor's responsibility. An efficient working unit is one in which the employees work with the supervisor. It is his job to bring out the best in his employees. He must always be relaxed, courteous, and calm in his association with his employees. Their feelings are important, and a harsh attitude does not develop the most efficient employees.

COMPETENCES OF THE SUPERVISOR

    I. Complete knowledge of the duties and responsibilities of his position.
    II. To be able to organize a job, plan ahead, and carry through.
    III. To have self-confidence and initiative.
    IV. To be able to handle the unexpected situation and make quick decisions.
    V. To be able to properly train subordinates in the positions they are best suited for.
    VI. To be able to keep good human relations among his subordinates.
    VII. To be able to keep good human relations between his subordinates and himself and to earn their respect and trust.

THE PROFESSIONAL SUPERVISOR-EMPLOYEE RELATIONSHIP

There are two kinds of efficiency: one kind is only apparent and is produced in organizations through the exercise of mere discipline; this is but a simulation of the second, or true, efficiency which springs from spontaneous cooperation. If you are a manager, no matter how great or small your responsibility, it is your job, in the final analysis, to create and develop this involuntary cooperation among the people whom you supervise. For, no matter how powerful a combination of money, machines, and materials a company may have, this is a dead and sterile thing without a team of willing, thinking, and articulate people to guide it.

The following 21 points are presented as indicative of the exemplary basic relationship that should exist between supervisor and employee:

1. Each person wants to be liked and respected by his fellow employee and wants to be treated with consideration and respect by his superior.
2. The most competent employee will make an error. However, in a unit where good relations exist between the supervisor and his employees, tenseness and fear do not exist. Thus, errors are not hidden or covered up, and the efficiency of a unit is not impaired.

3. Subordinates resent rules, regulations, or orders that are unreasonable or unexplained.
4. Subordinates are quick to resent unfairness, harshness, injustices, and favoritism.
5. An employee will accept responsibility if he knows that he will be complimented for a job well done, and not too harshly chastised for failure; that his supervisor will check the cause of the failure, and, if it was the supervisor's fault, he will assume the blame therefore. If it was the employee's fault, his supervisor will explain the correct method or means of handling the responsibility.
6. An employee wants to receive credit for a suggestion he has made, that is used. If a suggestion cannot be used, the employee is entitled to an explanation. The supervisor should not say "no" and close the subject.
7. Fear and worry slow up a worker's ability. Poor working environment can impair his physical and mental health. A good supervisor avoids forceful methods, threats, and arguments to get a job done.
8. A forceful supervisor is able to train his employees individually and as a team, and is able to motivate them in the proper channels.
9. A mature supervisor is able to properly evaluate his subordinates and to keep them happy and satisfied.
10. A sensitive supervisor will never patronize his subordinates.
11. A worthy supervisor will respect his employees' confidences.
12. Definite and clear-cut responsibilities should be assigned to each executive.
13. Responsibility should always be coupled with corresponding authority.
14. No change should be made in the scope or responsibilities of a position without a definite understanding to that effect on the part of all persons concerned.
15. No executive or employee, occupying a single position in the organization, should be subject to definite orders from more than one source.
16. Orders should never be given to subordinates over the head of a responsible executive. Rather than do this, the officer in question should be supplanted.
17. Criticisms of subordinates should, whoever possible, be made privately, and in no case should a subordinate be criticized in the presence of executives or employees of equal or lower rank.
18. No dispute or difference between executives or employees as to authority or responsibilities should be considered too trivial for prompt and careful adjudication.
19. Promotions, wage changes, and disciplinary action should always be approved by the executive immediately superior to the one directly responsible.
20. No executive or employee should ever be required, or expected, to be at the same time an assistant to, and critic of, another.
21. Any executive whose work is subject to regular inspection should, wherever practicable, be given the assistance and facilities necessary to enable him to maintain an independent check of the quality of his work.

MINI-TEXT IN SUPERVISION, ADMINISTRATION, MANAGEMENT, AND ORGANIZATION

I. Brief Highlights

Listed concisely and sequentially are major headings and important data in the field for quick recall and review.

A. Levels of Management
Any organization of some size has several levels of management. In terms of a ladder, the levels are:

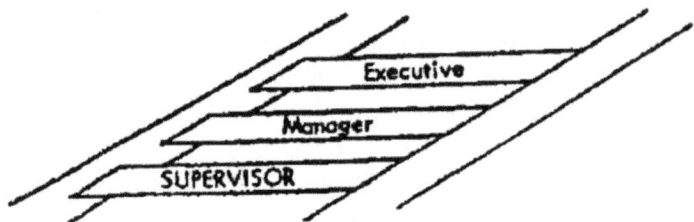

The first level is very important because it is the beginning point of management leadership.

B. What the Supervisor Must Learn
A supervisor must learn to:
1. Deal with people and their differences
2. Get the job done through people
3. Recognize the problems when they exist
4. Overcome obstacles to good performance
5. Evaluate the performance of people
6. Check his own performance in terms of accomplishment

C. A Definition of Supervisor
The term supervisor means any individual having authority, in the interests of the employer, to hire, transfer, suspend, lay-off, recall, promote, discharge, assign, reward, or discipline other employees or responsibility to direct them, or to adjust their grievances, or effectively to recommend such action, if, in connection with the foregoing, exercise of such authority is not of a merely routine or clerical nature but requires the use of independent judgment.

D. Elements of the Team Concept
What is involved in teamwork? The component parts are:
1. Members
2. A leader
3. Goals
4. Plans
5. Cooperation
6. Spirit

E. Principles of Organization
1. A team member must know what his job is.
2. Be sure that the nature and scope of a job are understood.
3. Authority and responsibility should be carefully spelled out.
4. A supervisor should be permitted to make the maximum number of decisions affecting his employees.
5. Employees should report to only one supervisor.
6. A supervisor should direct only as many employees as he can handle effectively.
7. An organization plan should be flexible.

8. Inspection and performance of work should be separate.
9. Organizational problems should receive immediate attention.
10. Assign work in line with ability and experience.

F. The Four Important Parts of Every Job
1. Inherent in every job is the *accountability* for results.
2. A second set of factors in every job is *responsibilities*.
3. Along with duties and responsibilities one must have the *authority* to act within certain limits without obtaining permission to proceed.
4. No job exists in a vacuum. The supervisor is surrounded by key *relationships*.

G. Principles of Delegation
Where work is delegated for the first time, the supervisor should think in terms of these questions:
1. Who is best qualified to do this?
2. Can an employee improve his abilities by doing this?
3. How long should an employee spend on this?
4. Are there any special problems for which he will need guidance?
5. How broad a delegation can I make?

H. Principles of Effective Communications
1. Determine the media.
2. To whom directed?
3. Identification and source authority.
4. Is communication understood?

I. Principles of Work Improvement
1. Most people usually do only the work which is assigned to them.
2. Workers are likely to fit assigned work into the time available to perform it.
3. A good workload usually stimulates output.
4. People usually do their best work when they know that results will be reviewed or inspected.
5. Employees usually feel that someone else is responsible for conditions of work, workplace layout, job methods, type of tools/equipment, and other such factors.
6. Employees are usually defensive about their job security.
7. Employees have natural resistance to change.
8. Employees can support or destroy a supervisor.
9. A supervisor usually earns the respect of his people through his personal example of diligence and efficiency.

J. Areas of Job Improvement
The areas of job improvement are quite numerous, but the most common ones which a supervisor can identify and utilize are:
1. Departmental layout
2. Flow of work
3. Workplace layout
4. Utilization of manpower
5. Work methods
6. Materials handling

7. Utilization
8. Motion economy

K. Seven Key Points in Making Improvements
1. Select the job to be improved
2. Study how it is being done now
3. Question the present method
4. Determine actions to be taken
5. Chart proposed method
6. Get approval and apply
7. Solicit worker participation

L. Corrective Techniques of Job Improvement
Specific Problems
1. Size of workload
2. Inability to meet schedules
3. Strain and fatigue
4. Improper use of men and skills
5. Waste, poor quality, unsafe conditions
6. Bottleneck conditions that hinder output
7. Poor utilization of equipment and machine
8. Efficiency and productivity of labor

General Improvement
1. Departmental layout
2. Flow of work
3. Work plan layout
4. Utilization of manpower
5. Work methods
6. Materials handling
7. Utilization of equipment
8. Motion economy

Corrective Techniques
1. Study with scale model
2. Flow chart study
3. Motion analysis
4. Comparison of units produced to standard allowance
5. Methods analysis
6. Flow chart and equipment study
7. Down time vs. running time
8. Motion analysis

M. A Planning Checklist
1. Objectives
2. Controls
3. Delegations
4. Communications
5. Resources
6. Manpower

7. Equipment
8. Supplies and materials
9. Utilization of time
10. Safety
11. Money
12. Work
13. Timing of improvements

N. Five Characteristics of Good Directions
In order to get results, directions must be:
1. Possible of accomplishment
2. Agreeable with worker interests
3. Related to mission
4. Planned and complete
5. Unmistakably clear

O. Types of Directions
1. Demands or direct orders
2. Requests
3. Suggestion or implication
4. volunteering

P. Controls
A typical listing of the overall areas in which the supervisor should establish controls might be:
1. Manpower
2. Materials
3. Quality of work
4. Quantity of work
5. Time
6. Space
7. Money
8. Methods

Q. Orienting the New Employee
1. Prepare for him
2. Welcome the new employee
3. Orientation for the job
4. Follow-up

R. Checklist for Orienting New Employees   Yes   No
1. Do you appreciate the feelings of new employees
   when they first report for work?   ___   ___
2. Are you aware of the fact that the new employee must
   make a big adjustment to his job?   ___   ___
3. Have you given him good reasons for liking the job and
   the organization?   ___   ___
4. Have you prepared for his first day on the job?   ___   ___
5. Did you welcome him cordially and make him feel needed? ___   ___

	Yes	No

6. Did you establish rapport with him so that he feels free to talk and discuss matters with you? ___ ___
7. Did you explain his job to him and his relationship to you? ___ ___
8. Does he know that his work will be evaluated periodically on a basis that is fair and objective? ___ ___
9. Did you introduce him to his fellow workers in such a way that they are likely to accept him? ___ ___
10. Does he know what employee benefits he will receive? ___ ___
11. Does he understand the importance of being on the job and what to do if he must leave his duty station? ___ ___
12. Has he been impressed with the importance of accident prevention and safe practice? ___ ___
13. Does he generally know his way around the department? ___ ___
14. Is he under the guidance of a sponsor who will teach the right way of doing things? ___ ___
15. Do you plan to follow-up so that he will continue to adjust successfully to his job? ___ ___

S. Principles of Learning
   1. Motivation
   2. Demonstration or explanation
   3. Practice

T. Causes of Poor Performance
   1. Improper training for job
   2. Wrong tools
   3. Inadequate directions
   4. Lack of supervisory follow-up
   5. Poor communications
   6. Lack of standards of performance
   7. Wrong work habits
   8. Low morale
   9. Other

U. Four Major Steps in On-The-Job Instruction
   1. Prepare the worker
   2. Present the operation
   3. Tryout performance
   4. Follow-up

V. Employees Want Five Things
   1. Security
   2. Opportunity
   3. Recognition
   4. Inclusion
   5. Expression

W. Some Don'ts in Regard to Praise
1. Don't praise a person for something he hasn't done.
2. Don't praise a person unless you can be sincere.
3. Don't be sparing in praise just because your superior withholds it from you.
4. Don't let too much time elapse between good performance and recognition of it

X. How to Gain Your Workers' Confidence
Methods of developing confidence include such things as:
1. Knowing the interests, habits, hobbies of employees
2. Admitting your own inadequacies
3. Sharing and telling of confidence in others
4. Supporting people when they are in trouble
5. Delegating matters that can be well handled
6. Being frank and straightforward about problems and working conditions
7. Encouraging others to bring their problems to you
8. Taking action on problems which impede worker progress

Y. Sources of Employee Problems
On-the-job causes might be such things as:
1. A feeling that favoritism is exercised in assignments
2. Assignment of overtime
3. An undue amount of supervision
4. Changing methods or systems
5. Stealing of ideas or trade secrets
6. Lack of interest in job
7. Threat of reduction in force
8. Ignorance or lack of communications
9. Poor equipment
10. Lack of knowing how supervisor feels toward employee
11. Shift assignments

Off-the-job problems might have to do with:
1. Health
2. Finances
3. Housing
4. Family

Z. The Supervisor's Key to Discipline
There are several key points about discipline which the supervisor should keep in mind:
1. Job discipline is one of the disciplines of life and is directed by the supervisor.
2. It is more important to correct an employee fault than to fix blame for it.
3. Employee performance is affected by problems both on the job and off.
4. Sudden or abrupt changes in behavior can be indications of important employee problems.
5. Problems should be dealt with as soon as possible after they are identified.
6. The attitude of the supervisor may have more to do with solving problems than the techniques of problem solving.
7. Correction of employee behavior should be resorted to only after the supervisor is sure that training or counseling will not be helpful.

8. Be sure to document your disciplinary actions.
9. Make sure that you are disciplining on the basis of facts rather than personal feelings.
10. Take each disciplinary step in order, being careful not to make snap judgments, or decisions based on impatience.

AA. Five Important Processes of Management
1. Planning
2. Organizing
3. Scheduling
4. Controlling
5. Motivating

BB. When the Supervisor Fails to Plan
1. Supervisor creates impression of not knowing his job
2. May lead to excessive overtime
3. Job runs itself—supervisor lacks control
4. Deadlines and appointments missed
5. Parts of the work go undone
6. Work interrupted by emergencies
7. Sets a bad example
8. Uneven workload creates peaks and valleys
9. Too much time on minor details at expense of more important tasks

CC. Fourteen General Principles of Management
1. Division of work
2. Authority and responsibility
3. Discipline
4. Unity of command
5. Unity of direction
6. Subordination of individual interest to general interest
7. Remuneration of personnel
8. Centralization
9. Scalar chain
10. Order
11. Equity
12. Stability of tenure of personnel
13. Initiative
14. Esprit de corps

DD. Change

Bringing about change is perhaps attempted more often, and yet less well understood, than anything else the supervisor does. How do people generally react to change? (People tend to resist change that is imposed upon them by other individuals or circumstances.

Change is characteristic of every situation. It is a part of every real endeavor where the efforts of people are concerned.

1. Why do people resist change?
   People may resist change because of:
   a. Fear of the unknown
   b. Implied criticism
   c. Unpleasant experiences in the past
   d. Fear of loss of status
   e. Threat to the ego
   f. Fear of loss of economic stability

2. How can we best overcome the resistance to change?
   In initiating change, take these steps:
   a. Get ready to sell
   b. Identify sources of help
   c. Anticipate objections
   d. Sell benefits
   e. Listen in depth
   f. Follow up

II. Brief Topical Summaries

   A. Who/What is the Supervisor?
      1. The supervisor is often called the "highest level employee and the lowest level manager."
      2. A supervisor is a member of both management and the work group. He acts as a bridge between the two.
      3. Most problems in supervision are in the area of human relations, or people problems.
      4. Employees expect: Respect, opportunity to learn and to advance, and a sense of belonging, and so forth.
      5. Supervisors are responsible for directing people and organizing work. Planning is of paramount importance.
      6. A position description is a set of duties and responsibilities inherent to a given position.
      7. It is important to keep the position description up-to-date and to provide each employee with his own copy.

   B. The Sociology of Work
      1. People are alike in many ways; however, each individual is unique.
      2. The supervisor is challenged in getting to know employee differences. Acquiring skills in evaluating individuals is an asset.
      3. Maintaining meaningful working relationships in the organization is of great importance.
      4. The supervisor has an obligation to help individuals to develop to their fullest potential.
      5. Job rotation on a planned basis helps to build versatility and to maintain interest and enthusiasm in work groups.
      6. Cross training (job rotation) provides backup skills.

7. The supervisor can help reduce tension by maintaining a sense of humor, providing guidance to employees, and by making reasonable and timely decisions. Employees respond favorably to working under reasonably predictable circumstances.
8. Change is characteristic of all managerial behavior. The supervisor must adjust to changes in procedures, new methods, technological changes, and to a number of new and sometimes challenging situations.
9. To overcome the natural tendency for people to resist change, the supervisor should become more skillful in initiating change.

C. Principles and Practices of Supervision
1. Employees should be required to answer to only one superior.
2. A supervisor can effectively direct only a limited number of employees, depending upon the complexity, variety, and proximity of the jobs involved.
3. The organizational chart presents the organization in graphic form. It reflects lines of authority and responsibility as well as interrelationships of units within the organization.
4. Distribution of work can be improved through an analysis using the "Work Distribution Chart."
5. The "Work Distribution Chart" reflects the division of work within a unit in understandable form.
6. When related tasks are given to an employee, he has a better chance of increasing his skills through training.
7. The individual who is given the responsibility for tasks must also be given the appropriate authority to insure adequate results.
8. The supervisor should delegate repetitive, routine work. Preparation of recurring reports, maintaining leave and attendance records are some examples.
9. Good discipline is essential to good task performance. Discipline is reflected in the actions of employees on the job in the absence of supervision.
10. Disciplinary action may have to be taken when the positive aspects of discipline have failed. Reprimand, warning, and suspension are examples of disciplinary action.
11. If a situation calls for a reprimand, be sure it is deserved and remember it is to be done in private.

D. Dynamic Leadership
1. A style is a personal method or manner of exerting influence.
2. Authoritarian leaders often see themselves as the source of power and authority.
3. The democratic leader often perceives the group as the source of authority and power.
4. Supervisors tend to do better when using the pattern of leadership that is most natural for them.
5. Social scientists suggest that the effective supervisor use the leadership style that best fits the problem or circumstances involved.
6. All four styles—telling, selling, consulting, joining—have their place. Using one does not preclude using the other at another time.

7. The theory X point of view assumes that the average person dislikes work, will avoid it whenever possible, and must be coerced to achieve organizational objectives.
8. The theory Y point of view assumes that the average person considers work to be a natural as play, and, when the individual is committed, he requires little supervision or direction to accomplish desired objectives.
9. The leader's basic assumptions concerning human behavior and human nature affect his actions, decisions, and other managerial practices.
10. Dissatisfaction among employees is often present, but difficult to isolate. The supervisor should seek to weaken dissatisfaction by keeping promises, being sincere and considerate, keeping employees informed, and so forth.
11. Constructive suggestions should be encouraged during the natural progress of the work.

E. Processes for Solving Problems
1. People find their daily tasks more meaningful and satisfying when they can improve them.
2. The causes of problems, or the key factors, are often hidden in the background. Ability to solve problems often involves the ability to isolate them from their backgrounds. There is some substance to the cliché that some persons "can't see the forest for the trees."
3. New procedures are often developed from old ones. Problems should be broken down into manageable parts. New ideas can be adapted from old one.
4. People think differently in problem-solving situations. Using a logical, patterned approach is often useful. One approach found to be useful includes these steps:
   a. Define the problem
   b. Establish objectives
   c. Get the facts
   d. Weigh and decide
   e. Take action
   f. Evaluate action

F. Training for Results
1. Participants respond best when they feel training is important to them.
2. The supervisor has responsibility for the training and development of those who report to him.
3. When training is delegated to others, great care must be exercised to insure the trainer has knowledge, aptitude, and interest for his work as a trainer.
4. Training (learning) of some type goes on continually. The most successful supervisor makes certain the learning contributes in a productive manner to operational goals.
5. New employees are particularly susceptible to training. Older employees facing new job situations require specific training, as well as having need for development and growth opportunities.
6. Training needs require continuous monitoring.
7. The training officer of an agency is a professional with a responsibility to assist supervisors in solving training problems.

8. Many of the self-development steps important to the supervisor's own growth are equally important to the development of peers and subordinates. Knowledge of these is important when the supervisor consults with others on development and growth opportunities.

G. Health, Safety, and Accident Prevention
1. Management-minded supervisors take appropriate measures to assist employees in maintaining health and in assuring safe practices in the work environment.
2. Effective safety training and practices help to avoid injury and accidents.
3. Safety should be a management goal. All infractions of safety which are observed should be corrected without exception.
4. Employees' safety attitude, training and instruction, provision of safe tools and equipment, supervision, and leadership are considered highly important factors which contribute to safety and which can be influenced directly by supervisors.
5. When accidents do occur, they should be investigated promptly for very important reasons, including the fact that information which is gained can be used to prevent accidents in the future.

H. Equal Employment Opportunity
1. The supervisor should endeavor to treat all employees fairly, without regard to religion, race, sex, or national origin.
2. Groups tend to reflect the attitude of the leader. Prejudice can be detected even in very subtle form. Supervisors must strive to create a feeling of mutual respect and confidence in every employee.
3. Complete utilization of all human resources is a national goal. Equitable consideration should be accorded women in the work force, minority-group members, the physically and mentally handicapped, and the older employee. The important question is: "Who can do the job?"
4. Training opportunities, recognition for performance, overtime assignments, promotional opportunities, and all other personnel actions are to be handled on an equitable basis.

I. Improving Communications
1. Communications is achieving understanding between the sender and the receiver of a message. It also means sharing information—the creation of understanding.
2. Communication is basic to all human activity. Words are means of conveying meanings; however, real meanings are in people.
3. There are very practical differences in the effectiveness of one-way, impersonal, and two-way communications. Words spoken face-to-face are better understood. Telephone conversations are effective, but lack the rapport of person-to-person exchanges. The whole person communicates.
4. Cooperation and communication in an organization go hand in hand. When there is a mutual respect between people, spelling out rules and procedures for communicating is unnecessary.
5. There are several barriers to effective communications. These include failure to listen with respect and understanding, lack of skill in feedback, and misinterpreting the meanings of words used by the speaker. It is also common

practice to listen to what we want to hear, and tune out things we do not want to hear.
6. Communication is management's chief problem. The supervisor should accept the challenge to communicate more effectively and to improve interagency and intra-agency communications.
7. The supervisor may often plan for and conduct meetings. The planning phase is critical and may determine the success or the failure of a meeting.
8. Speaking before groups usually requires extra effort. Stage fright may never disappear completely, but it can be controlled.

J. Self-Development
1. Every employee is responsible for his own self-development.
2. Toastmaster and toastmistress clubs offer opportunities to improve skills in oral communications.
3. Planning for one's own self-development is of vital importance. Supervisors know their own strengths and limitations better than anyone else.
4. Many opportunities are open to aid the supervisor in his developmental efforts, including job assignments; training opportunities, both governmental and non-governmental—to include universities and professional conferences and seminars.
5. Programmed instruction offers a means of studying at one's own rate.
6. Where difficulties may arise from a supervisor's being away from his work for training, he may participate in televised home study or correspondence courses to meet his self-development needs.

K. Teaching and Training
1. The Teaching Process
Teaching is encouraging and guiding the learning activities of students toward established goals. In most cases this process consists of five steps: preparation, presentation, summarization, evaluation, and application.

   a. Preparation
   Preparation is two-fold in nature; that of the supervisor and the employee. Preparation by the supervisor is absolutely essential to success. He must know what, when, where, how, and whom he will teach. Some of the factors that should be considered are:
   1) The objectives
   2) The materials needed
   3) The methods to be used
   4) Employee participation
   5) Employee interest
   6) Training aids
   7) Evaluation
   8) Summarization

   Employee preparation consists in preparing the employee to receive the material. Probably the most important single factor in the preparation of the employee is arousing and maintaining his interest. He must know the objectives of the training, why he is there, how the material can be used, and its importance to him.

b. Presentation
In presentation, have a carefully designed plan and follow it. The plan should be accurate and complete, yet flexible enough to meet situations as they arise. The method of presentation will be determined by the particular situation and objectives.

c. Summary
A summary should be made at the end of every training unit and program. In addition, there may be internal summaries depending on the nature of the material being taught. The important thing is that the trainee must always be able to understand how each part of the new material relates to the whole.

d. Application
The supervisor must arrange work so the employee will be given a chance to apply new knowledge or skills while the material is still clear in his mind and interest is high. The trainee does not really know whether he has learned the material until he has been given a chance to apply it. If the material is not applied, it loses most of its value.

e. Evaluation
The purpose of all training is to promote learning. To determine whether the training has been a success or failure, the supervisor must evaluate this learning.
In the broadest sense, evaluation includes all the devices, methods, skills, and techniques used by the supervisor to keep himself and the employees informed as to their progress toward the objectives they are pursuing. The extent to which the employee has mastered the knowledge, skills, and abilities, or changed his attitudes, as determined by the program objectives, is the extent to which instruction has succeeded or failed.
Evaluation should not be confined to the end of the lesson, day, or program but should be used continuously. We shall note later the way this relates to the rest of the teaching process.

2. Teaching Methods
A teaching method is a pattern of identifiable student and instructor activity used in presenting training material.
All supervisors are faced with the problem of deciding which method should be used at a given time.

a. Lecture
The lecture is direct oral presentation of material by the supervisor. The present trend is to place less emphasis on the trainer's activity and more on that of the trainee.

b. Discussion
Teaching by discussion or conference involves using questions and other techniques to arouse interest and focus attention upon certain areas, and by doing so creating a learning situation. This can be one of the most

valuable methods because it gives the employees an opportunity to express their ideas and pool their knowledge.

c. Demonstration
The demonstration is used to teach how something works or how to do something. It can be used to show a principle or what the results of a series of actions will be. A well-staged demonstration is particularly effective because it shows proper methods of performance in a realistic manner.

d. Performance
Performance is one of the most fundamental of all learning techniques or teaching methods. The trainee may be able to tell how a specific operation should be performed but he cannot be sure he knows how to perform the operation until he has done so.
As with all methods, there are certain advantages and disadvantages to each method.

e. Which Method to Use
Moreover, there are other methods and techniques of teaching. It is difficult to use any method without other methods entering into it. In any learning situation, a combination of methods is usually more effective than any one method alone.

Finally, evaluation must be integrated into the other aspects of the teaching-learning process.

It must be used in the motivation of the trainees; it must be used to assist in developing understanding during the training; and it must be related to employee application of the results of training.

This is distinctly the role of the supervisor.

HOUSING AND COMMUNITY DEVELOPMENT GLOSSARY

ACRONYMS AND ABBREVIATED REFERENCES

ACC	Annual contributions contract.
AHOP	Areawide housing opportunity plan.
AHS	Annual housing survey.
AML	Adjustable mortgage loan.
APA	Administrative Procedure Act (5 U.S.C. 551 et seq.)
ARM	Adjustable rate mortgage.
BMIR	Below-market interest rate.
Budget Act	Congressional Budget and Impoundment Control Act of 1974.
Budget Res.	Concurrent resolution on the budget.
CBO	Congressional Budget Office.
CD	Community development.
CDBG	Community development block grant.
CFR	Code of Federal Regulations.
CIAP	Comprehensive improvement assistance program.
Continuing Res.	Joint resolution continuing appropriations for the next fiscal year.
CPI	Consumer Price Index.
DOE	Department of Energy.
EDA	Economic Development Administration.
EIS	Environmental impact statement.
ERTA	Economic Recovery Tax Act of 1981.
Fannie Mae	Federal National Mortgage Association.
FDIC	Federal Deposit Insurance Corporation.
FEMA	Federal Emergency Management Agency.
FFB	Federal Financing Bank.
FHA	Federal Housing Administration.
FHLBB	Federal Home Loan Bank Board.
FHLMC	Federal Home Loan Mortgage Corporation (Freddie Mac).
FmHA	Farmers Home Administration.
FMR	Fair market rent.
FNMA	Federal National Mortgage Association (Fannie Mae).
FR	Federal Register.
Freddie Mac	Federal Home Loan Mortgage Corporation.
FSLIC	Federal Savings and Loan Insurance Corporation.
GAO	Government Accounting Office.
Garn-St Germain	Garn-St Germain Depository Institutions Act of 1982.
GEM	Growing equity mortgage.
Ginnie Mae	Government National Mortgage Association.
GNMA	Government National Mortgage Association (Ginnie Mae).

GLOSSARY

GPM	Graduated payment mortgage.
Gramm-Latta	Omnibus Budget Reconciliation Act of 1981.
HAP	Housing assistance plan.
HFA	Housing finance agency.
HHS	Department of Health and Human Services.
HoDAG	Housing development grant.
HUD	Department of Housing and Urban Development.
HURRA	Housing and Urban-Rural Recovery Act of 1983.
IG	Inspector General.
IRS	Internal Revenue Service.
MBS	Mortgage-backed securities.
Mod Rehab	Moderate rehabilitation.
MPS	Minimum property standards.
MSA	Metropolitan statistical area.
NHP	National Housing Partnership.
NIBS	National Institute of Building Sciences.
NOFA	Notice of funding availability.
NSA	Neighborhood strategy area.
OBRA	Omnibus Budget Reconciliation Act of 1981.
OMB	Office of Management and Budget.
PAM	Pledged account mortgage.
PC	Participation certificate.
PFS	Performance funding system.
PHA	Public housing agency.
PLAM	Price-level adjusted mortgage.
PMI	Private mortgage insurance.
PUD	Planned unit development.
RAM	Reverse annuity mortgage.
RAP	Rental assistance payments.
REIT	Real estate investment trust.
RESPA	Real Estate Settlement Procedures Act of 1974.
SAM	Shared appreciation mortgage.
Solar Bank	Solar Energy and Energy Conservation Bank.
SRO	Single room occupancy housing.
Sub Rehab	Substantial rehabilitation.
TEFRA	Tax Equity and Fiscal Responsibility Act of 1982.
TMAP	Temporary mortgage assistance payments.
UDAG	Urban development action grant.
U.S.C	United States Code.
VA	Veterans' Administration.

ABBREVIATED STATUTORY CITATIONS

Sec. 5	United States Housing Act of 1937 (funding for public housing and section 8 housing).
Sec. 7(o)	Department of Housing and Urban Development Act (legislative review of HUD rules and regulations).

GLOSSARY

Sec. 8	United States Housing Act of 1937 (low-income rental housing assistance).
Sec. 9	United States Housing Act of 1937 (operating subsidies).
Sec. 14	United States Housing Act of 1937 (CLAP).
Sec. 17	United States Housing Act of 1937 (rental rehabilitation and development).
Sec. 101	Housing and Urban Development Act of 1965 (rent supplement).
Sec. 104	Housing and Community Development Act of 1974 (CDBG applications and review).
Sec. 105	Housing and Community Development Act of 1974 (CDBG eligible activities).
Sec. 106	Housing and Community Development Act of 1974 (CDBG allocation and distribution of funds).
Sec. 107	Housing and Community Development Act of 1974 (CD discretionary fund).
Sec. 108	Housing and Community Development Act of 1974 (CD loan guarantees).
Sec. 119	Housing and Community Development Act of 1974 (UDAG).
Sec. 201	Housing and Community Development Amendments of 1978 (troubled projects).
Sec. 202	Housing Act of 1959 (elderly and handicapped housing).
Sec. 203	Housing and Community Development Amendments of 1978 (management and preservation of HUD-owned projects). National Housing Act (single-family mortgage insurance).
Sec. 207	National Housing Act (multifamily mortgage insurance).
Sec. 213	Housing and Community Development Act of 1974 (allocation of funds for assisted housing). National Housing Act (cooperative housing mortgage insurance).
Sec. 221	National Housing Act (multifamily mortgage insurance).
Sec. 221(d)(3)	National Housing Act (BMIR rental housing mortgage insurance).
Sec. 231	National Housing Act (mortgage insurance for elderly and handicapped rental housing).
Sec. 235	National Housing Act (home mortgage interest reduction payments).
Sec. 236	National Housing Act (rental and cooperative housing interest reduction payments).
Sec. 302(b)(2)	Federal National Mortgage Association Charter Act (FNMA authority to deal in conventional mortgages).

GLOSSARY

Sec. 305(a)(2)	Federal Home Loan Mortgage Corporation Act (FHLMC authority to deal in conventional mortgages).
Sec. 312	Housing Act of 1964 (rehabilitation loans).
Sec. 502	Housing Act of 1949 (rural housing loans and loan guarantees).
Sec. 513	Housing Act of 1949 (rural housing authorization amounts).
Sec. 515	Housing Act of 1949 (elderly and handicapped rural housing).
Sec. 521	Housing Act of 1949 (rural housing loan interest credits and RAP).
Sec. 533	Housing Act of 1949 (housing preservation grants).
Title I	Housing and Community Development Act of 1974 (CDBG and UDAG). Housing Act of 1949 (urban renewal). National Housing Act (FHA property improvement loan insurance).
Title II	National Housing Act (FHA mortgage insurance).
Title V	Housing Act of 1949 (rural housing).

TERMS

Adjustable mortgage loan—See "adjustable rate mortgage".

Adjustable rate mortgage—A mortgage covering a loan the interest rate of which may vary periodically over the term of the loan, generally according to an established index. Also referred to as an adjustable mortgage loan.

Amortization—Gradual reduction of the principal of a loan, together with the payment of interest, according to a schedule of periodic payments so that the principal is fully paid by the end of the term of the loan.

Annual contributions contract—A contract under which HUD makes payments to a public housing agency equal to the amount of principal and interest owed by the PHA under obligations issued by it for the development, operation, or modernization of a public housing project.

Annual housing survey—An annual study by HUD and the Bureau of the Census regarding housing units, homeowners, and renters.

Appropriation—Constitutionally required legislation that grants Federal agencies the authority to make payments out of the Treasury for general or particular purposes. There are three general categories of appropriations legislation: general, supplemental, and continuing.

Areawide housing opportunity plan—A program to reduce the geographical concentration of lower income families by expanding housing opportunities throughout a wide area.

Assistance payments—Federal payments, made directly or through public housing agencies, to owners or prospective owners of rental housing to pay part of the rent of lower income tenants. See "interest-reduction payments".

Assumable mortgage—Mortgage in which the existing debt may be taken over by a third party without approval of the lender.

GLOSSARY

Authorization—Legislation granting authority for the congressional consideration of appropriations for general or particular purposes. Although unauthorized appropriations may be subject to points of order, they are legally valid if enacted.

Balloon mortgage—Mortgage under which the loan matures before the principal is fully repaid.

Below-market interest rate—HUD-insured mortgages financing homes for lower income families and displaced families bearing interest rates lower than the market rate, with the Federal Government bearing the cost of the difference in rates by purchase of the mortgages. See section 221(d)(3) of the National Housing Act.

Block grants—Grants by HUD on a noncategorical formula basis to assist community development and rehabilitation, including slum and blight elimination, conservation of housing, increased public services, improved use of land, and preservation of property. See title I of the Housing and Community Development Act of 1974.

Borrowing authority—Authority to incur indebtedness for which the Federal Government is liable, which authority is granted in advance of the provision of appropriations to repay such debts. Borrowing authority may take the form of authority to borrow from the Treasury or authority to borrow from the public by means of the sale of Federal agency obligations. Borrowing authority is not an appropriation since it provides a Federal agency only with the authority to incur a debt, and not the authority to make payments from the Treasury under the debt. Subsequent appropriations are required to liquidate the borrowing authority.

Budget authority—Legal authority to enter into obligations that will result in immediate or future outlays of Federal funds. Appropriations (unless liquidating borrowing authority or contract authority), contract authority, and borrowing authority are the three primary types of budget authority.

Coinsurance—HUD insurance of a mortgage, advance, or loan with the lender assuming a percentage of the loss on the insured obligation. See section 244 of the National Housing Act.

Commitment—An agreement to make or purchase a mortgage loan at a future date, or an agreement to insure a mortgage at a future date, if prescribed conditions are met by the mortgagee. Under HUD mortgage insurance, a traditional administration distinction exists between a special type of commitment known as a "conditional commitment" and other commitments known as "firm commitments". Under the former, a commitment is made to insure a mortgage (on a specific property for a definite loan amount) to be given by a future purchaser of the property involved if such a purchaser meets certain eligibility requirements. The term "standby commitment" is commonly used in the secondary market for residential mortgages to describe a commitment to purchase a mortgage loan or loans with specific terms, both parties understanding that the purchase is not likely to be completed unless particular circumstances make that advantageous to the seller of the mortgage. These commitments are typically used to enable the borrower to obtain construction financing at a lower cost on the assumption that permanent financing of the project will be available on more favorable terms than under the commitment when the project is completed and generating income.

Community development block grants—Block grants for community development made to States, urban counties, and metropolitan cities under section 106 of the Housing and Community Development Act of 1974.

GLOSSARY

Comprehensive improvement assistance—Assistance provided for the modernization of public housing projects under section 14 of the United States Housing Act of 1937.

Concurrent resolution on the budget—Concurrent resolution of the Congress establishing minimum revenues and maximum outlays for the congressional budget for the Federal Government.

Conditional commitment—See "commitment".

Condominiums—Multifamily housing projects with individual units owned by occupants, who also own an undivided interest in the common areas and facilities of the project.

Contract authority—Authority to enter into contracts obligating the Federal Government to make payments in the future, which authority is granted in advance of the provision of appropriations to make such payments. Contract authority is not an appropriation since it provides a Federal agency only with the authority to incur an obligation, and not the authority to make payments from the Treasury under the obligation. Subsequent appropriations are required to liquidate the contract authority.

Conventional mortgage—A mortgage covering a loan that is not insured by the HUD or guaranteed by the FmHA or VA.

Cooperatives—Multifamily housing projects owned by cooperative corporations with the stockholders of the corporations having the right to occupancy of the units.

Cost certification—A limitation, under HUD mortgage insurance for multifamily housing, on the amount of a mortgage eligible for insurance, which limitation is determined after completion of the project on the basis of the builder's certification as to the actual dollar amount of his costs for specific items of construction and prescribed related expenditures. Under this requirement, the insured mortgage is limited to a fixed percentage of that certified amount.

Deep subsidy program—Program of rental assistance payments under section 236(f)(2) of the National Housing Act.

Default—Failure to meet the terms of a mortgage or other loan agreement. Generally, a delinquency of more than 30 days under a mortgage is considered a default.

Delinquency—Failure to make any timely payment due under a mortgage or other loan agreement.

Direct endorsement—HUD program of delegated private mortgage processing of FHA loan applications under the single family mortgage insurance programs.

Discount point—An amount that may be payable to a lender by a borrower or seller in addition to principal and interest, equal to 1 percent of the principal amount of the loan.

Discretionary fund—Funds set aside for discretionary grants by HUD under section 107 of the Housing and Community Development Act of 1974.

Due-on-sale clause—A clause that may be included in a mortgage to authorize the mortgagee to require full repayment of the loan upon any transfer of the property.

Economic mix—Occupancy of rental housing by families of varying economic levels, including very low-income families, which is to be promoted by housing assistance payments. See section 8 of the United States Housing Act of 1937.

Elderly and handicapped housing—Generally refers to housing for elderly and handicapped persons developed by nonprofit sponsors with assistance provided by HUD under section 202 of the Housing Act of 1959.

GLOSSARY

Entitlement community—An urban county or metropolitan city eligible to receive a community development block grant directly from HUD.

Environmental impact statements—Statements required to be made under section 102(2)(C) of the National Environmental Policy Act of 1969 by Federal agencies in their recommendations or reports on proposals for legislation and other major Federal actions significantly affecting the quality of the human environment, as to the environmental impact of the proposed action; any adverse environmental effects that cannot be avoided should the proposal be implemented; relationship between local short-term use of man's environment and the maintenance and enhancement of long-term productivity; and any irreversible or irretrievable commitments of resources that would be involved in the proposed action should it be implemented. Applicants for block grants can assume responsibility for this statement under the community development program. See section 104(f) of the Housing and Community Development Act of 1974.

Estimated value—The basis of one of the limits on the amount of a mortgage that can be insured by HUD. For example, under certain programs the mortgage may not exceed 90 percent of the estimated value of the property when completed.

Fair market rent—An amount determined by HUD to be the cost of modest rental units in a particular market area.

Federal Home Loan Mortgage Corporation—A federally established and sponsored corporation, under the supervision of the Federal Home Loan Bank Board, that provides a secondary market primarily for conventional mortgages.

Federal Housing Administration—Part of HUD that has responsibility for carrying out the mortgage insurance programs of the National Housing Act.

Federal National Mortgage Association—A federally established and sponsored private corporation, under the general supervision of HUD, that provides a secondary market for mortgages.

Firm commitment——See "commitment".

Fiscal year—Annual accounting period of the Federal Government, beginning October 1 and ending September 30 of the subsequent calendar year. The fiscal year is designated by the calendar year in which it ends, so that fiscal year 2005 refers to the fiscal year beginning October 1, 2004 and ending September 30, 2005.

Flood insurance program—Program under which FEMA makes flood insurance available to participating communities under the National Flood Insurance Act of 1968.

Forebearance—The act of postponing or refraining from taking legal action against a mortgagor even though mortgage payments are in arrears.

Foreclosure—Legal procedure under which the property securing a loan is sold to pay the debt owed by a borrower who has defaulted.

Government National Mortgage Association—Federal corporation, and part of HUD, that provides a secondary market for federally guaranteed mortgages.

Graduated payment mortgage—A mortgage under which payments are comparatively low initially and then increase over a specified period before reaching a constant level.

Ground lease—Lease of land without improvements.

Growing equity mortgage—Mortgage under which payments increase over a specified period in order to accelerate the repayment of principal and thereby shorten the term of the loan.

Guaranteed loan—Loan in which a private lender is assured repayment by the Federal Government of part or all of the principal or interest, or both, in the event of a

GLOSSARY

default by the borrower. Unlike an insured loan, no insurance fund exists and no insurance premiums are paid.

Hold-harmless provision—Statutory provision ensuring the continued eligibility of a specified class for certain assistance for a limited period of time. The most commonly cited examples are contained in paragraphs (4) and (6) of section 102(a) of the Housing and Community Development Act of 1974.

Home equity conversion mortgage—A form of mortgage in which the lender makes periodic payments to the borrower using the borrower's equity in the home as security.

Housing allowance payments—Payments made by HUD under section 504 of the Housing Act of 1970 to assist families in meeting rental or homeownership expenses.

Housing assistance plan—A part of the CDBG application describing local housing conditions and sets quantitative goals for providing housing to low- and moderate-income residents.

Housing development grant—Grant made by HUD under section 17(d) of the United States Housing Act of 1937 for the new construction or substantial rehabilitation of rental housing.

Housing finance agency—State agency responsible for financing housing and administering assisted housing programs.

Housing preservation grant—Grant made by FmHA under section 533 of the Housing Act of 1949 for the rehabilitation of single-family housing, rental housing, or cooperatives for low- and very low-income families and persons.

Industrial revenue bond—A debt instrument issued by a municipality or development corporation to finance the development of revenue-producing projects. Project revenues are then used to pay the debt service on the bonds. Section 103(b) of the Internal Revenue Code of 1954 establishes certain limitations.

Installment land contract—See "land contract".

Insured loan—Loan in which a private lender is assured repayment by the Federal Government of part or all of the principal or interest, or both, and for which the borrower pays insurance premiums.

Interest rate credits—Generally refers to the FmHA program of subsidized interest rate loans for single-family and multifamily housing for low or moderate income families under section 521(a)(1)(B) of the Housing Act of 1949. The subsidy may reduce the interest rate to as low as 1 percent.

Interest reduction payments—Periodic assistance payments by HUD to mortgagees to permit lower interest rate payments by lower income families (varying with fluctuations in incomes) on HUD insured mortgages financing homes, rental housing, or cooperative housing. See sections 235 and 236 of the National Housing Act.

Land contract—An agreement to transfer title to a property upon fulfillment of the contract conditions. Under an "installment land contract", the purchaser assumes possession immediately and makes periodic payments to the vendor (the owner of the property); title is transferred only when all payments have been made.

Leased housing—Low-rent housing provided by public housing agencies in housing leased from private owners.

Leveraging—The maximization of the effect of Federal assistance for a project by obtaining additional project funding from non-Federal sources. See section 119 of the Housing and Community Development Act of 1974.

Lien—Any legal claim on a property for payment of a debt. A mortgage is one example.

GLOSSARY

Loan-to-value ratio—The relationship between the amount of the mortgage loan and the appraised value of the property involved, expressed as a percentage of the appraised value. It is one of the traditional limitations on a mortgage eligible for mortgage insurance.

Lower income family—Generally, a family whose income does not exceed 80 percent of the median family income of the area involved.

Manufactured home—Housing, including a mobile home, that is factory-built or prefabricated.

Market rent—Rental that would be charged by the owner of a HUD-insured multifamily dwelling unit if the owner were paying interest on the loan at the HUD-approved market interest rate.

Metropolitan city—For purposes of the CDBG program, a city that is the central city of a metropolitan area or that has a population of not less than 50,000.

Metropolitan statistical area—Metropolitan area defined by the Office of Management and Budget. Previously referred to as standard metropolitan statistical area.

Minimum property standards—HUD regulations establishing minimum acceptable standards for properties to be purchased with HUD-insured mortgage loans.

Moderate income family—For purposes of the CDBG program, a family whose income exceeds 50 percent of the median family income of the area involved, but does not exceed 80 percent of the median family income of the area.

Moderate rehabilitation—Rehabilitation that is less comprehensive than substantial rehabilitation, such as repair or replacement of the heating or electrical system of a project.

Modernization—See "comprehensive improvement assistance".

Mortgage—Conveyance of an interest in real property as security for repayment of a loan, including a loan made for the purchase or improvement of the real property.

Mortgage-backed securities—Obligations issued by an organization that has held and set aside mortgages as security for payment of the obligations. FNMA, GNMA, and FHLMC, as well as private organizations, issue such obligations.

Mortgage insurance programs—Generally refers to the insured loan programs carried out by HUD, through the FHA, under the National Housing Act.

Mortgage revenue bonds—Tax-exempt bonds issued by State and local governments and agencies to finance the sale or repair of single-family housing. The bonds are payable from revenues derived from repayments of interest on the mortgage loans financed from the proceeds of the bonds. Section 103A of the Internal Revenue Code of 1954 establishes certain limitations. Referred to as mortgage subsidy bonds in the Internal Revenue Code of 1954.

Mortgagee—A lender who is conveyed an interest in real property under a mortgage.

Mortgagor—A borrower who conveys an interest in real property under a mortgage.

Multifamily housingGenerally a project containing dwelling units for more than 4 families.

National Housing Partnership—A private limited partnership established under title IX of the Housing and Urban Development Act of 1969 for the purpose of carrying out the building, maintenance, or rehabilitation of housing and related facilities for lower or moderate income families. It can enter into partnerships or joint ventures, conduct research, provide technical assistance, and make loans or grants to accomplish its purpose.

GLOSSARY

National Institute of Building Sciences—A nonprofit nongovernmental organization established under section 809 of the Housing and Community Development Act of 1974 to make findings and to advise public and private sectors of the economy with respect to the use of building science and technology in achieving nationally acceptable standards for use in housing and building regulations.

Negative amortization—A loan prepayment schedule under which payments do not cover the full amount of interest due. The unpaid interest is added to the principal and, as a result, the outstanding principal balance increases rather than decreases.

Neighborhood development grant—A grant made by HUD to an eligible neighborhood nonprofit organization under section 123 of the Housing and Urban-Rural Recovery Act of 1983 to assist the organization in carrying out certain neighborhood development activities.

Neighborhood strategy area—Area in which concentrated housing rehabilitation and community development block grant activities are being undertaken.

Nonentitlement area—For purposes of the CDBG program, an area that is neither a metropolitan city nor urban county, and is therefore generally ineligible for direct grants from HUD.

Nonprofit sponsor—A group organized to undertake a housing project for reasons other than making a profit.

Notice of funding availability—A notice by HUD to inform potential project sponsors that contract authority is available.

Off-budget program—Federal program the transactions of which are not included in the Budget of the United States Government as a result of statutory requirement.

Operating subsidies—HUD payments to public housing agencies to assist the payment of operating expenses of public housing, or to the owners of certain multifamily projects for low income families. See section 9 of the United States Housing Act of 1937.

Participation loan—Loans made by the FmHA or others when another lender makes part of the loan.

Pass through—Principal and interest receipts on housing mortgages are "passed through" by GNMA, FNMA, FHLMC, or other organizations to the purchasers of their securities or obligations that have been sold and secured by the mortgages set aside as security for the obligations.

Planned unit development—Development and construction of a residential community as a unit in accordance with a plan for the entire development.

Pledged account mortgage—A graduated payment mortgage in which part of the buyer's down payment is deposited in a savings account. Funds are drawn from the account to supplement the buyer's monthly payments during the early years of the loan.

Pocket of poverty—For purposes of the UDAG program, a contiguous area of particularly severe poverty in a city or urban county. A city or urban county that fails to meet the general eligibility standards for UDAG assistance may be eligible if it contains such an area.

Prepayment penalty—A penalty that may be levied for repayment of a loan before it falls due.

Price-level adjusted mortgage—Mortgage under which the outstanding balance is adjusted according to an established price index, while the interest rate remains fixed.

Principal—The amount of debt, exclusive of accrued interest, remaining on a loan. Before any principal has been repaid, the total loaned amount is the principal.

GLOSSARY

Private mortgage insurance—Insurance by private companies of lenders against losses on mortgage loans.

Program reservation—HUD action reserving funds for a specific approved public housing project. This reservation is subject to PHA fulfillment of all HUD requirements.

Public housing—Lower income housing owned and operated by a public housing agency and assisted under the United States Housing Act of 1937 (other than under section 8 or 17).

Public housing agency—Public agency established by a State or local government to finance or operate low-income housing assisted under the United States Housing Act of 1937.

Real estate investment trust—A trust established by real estate investors primarily for the management and control of investments in mortgages and to sell obligations secured by mortgages and property held by the trust.

Recapture—Requiring repayment of assistance provided, either because the assistance has not been used within a certain period of time or a specified event (such as the sale of assisted property) occurs that permits repayment of all or a part of the assistance. See section 235(c)(2) of the National Housing Act.

Refinancing—Payment of a loan with amounts borrowed under a new loan.

Rehabilitation—The improvement or repair of property. Such term includes substantial and moderate rehabilitation, but excludes new construction.

Rehabilitation loans—Loans made by HUD under section 312 of the Housing Act of 1964 for the rehabilitation of property.

Reinsurance—Program under section 249 of the National Housing Act to demonstrate possible advantages of having private mortgage insurance companies enter into reinsurance contracts with HUD, under which such private insurers would assume a percentage of the risk on certain single-family mortgages insured by HUD.

Rent control—Limitation of annual rent increases by municipal ordinance, State, or Federal law.

Rent supplements—Annual Federal payments to owners of housing built with certain HUD mortgage insurance on behalf of prescribed types of lower income families.

Rental assistance payments—Generally refers to the FmHA program of rental assistance for low income families in rural areas under section 521(a)(2)(A) of the Housing Act of 1949.

Replacement cost—The basis of one of the limits placed on the amount of a mortgage that can be insured by HUD under certain programs, such as the mortgage may not exceed 90 percent of replacement cost of the housing when completed.

Reverse annuity mortgage—See "home equity conversion mortgage".

Rural area—A non-urban area meeting the requirements of section 520 of the Housing Act of 1949 and eligible assistance under the FmHA housing programs.

Second mortgage—A mortgage that grants rights subordinate to the rights granted by the initial mortgage. A second mortgage generally bears a higher rate of interest than the initial mortgage to reflect the greater risk of the lender.

Secondary mortgage market—Nationwide market for the purchase and sale of mortgages. FHLMC, FNMA, and GNMA are the 3 federally established entities that purchase mortgages in the secondary mortgage market, thereby increasing the availabilty of funds to financial institutions for additional residential loans.

Seed money—Advances, loans, or grants to cover preliminary expenses of constructing housing projects, such as the cost of planning and obtaining financing.

GLOSSARY

Shared appreciation mortgage—Mortgage under which the borrower receives financial assistance in purchasing a property and agrees in return to give the lender a portion of the future increase in the value of the property.

Shared housing—Generally refers to arrangements under which elderly and handicapped persons share the facilities of a dwelling with others in order to meet their housing needs and reduce the costs of housing. See section 8(p) of the United States Housing Act of 1937.

Single-family housing—Generally a structure containing dwelling units for 1 to 4 families.

Single room occupancy housing—Residential properties in which some or all dwelling units do not contain bathroom or kitchen facilities. See section 8(n) of the United States Housing Act of 1937.

Small city—A city that does not qualify as a metropolitan city for purposes of receiving a community development block grant under section 106 of the Housing and Community Development Act of 1974.

Standby commitment—See "commitment".

Substantial rehabilitationImprovements of a property from substandard to safe and sanitary conditions. It can vary from gutting and reconstruction to accumulated deferred maintenance. It may also involve conversion of nonresidential property to residential use.

Supplemental loans—HUD-insured loans under section 241 of the National Housing Act for improvements or additions to multifam-ily housing, nursing homes, group practice facilities, or hospitals.

Tandem plan purchases—The purchase by GNMA of certain housing mortgages at higher prices than would be paid by FNMA, FHLMC or other mortgage purchasers, with subsequent resale by GNMA at the best price obtainable, or as back-up of GNMA's mortgage-backed securities. The term derives from the original practice of FNMA purchasing from GNMA "in tandem" with the GNMA purchase.

Temporary mortgage assistance payments—Mortgage assistance payments authorized to be made under section 230(a) of the National Housing Act to a mortgagor of a single-family residence who defaults on the mortgage due to circumstances beyond the mortgagor's control. Constitutes an alternative to acquisition of the mortgage by HUD under section 230(b) of the National Housing Act.

Tenant contribution—The monthly amount of rent required to be paid by a tenant receiving rental assistance under a Federal housing program. Currently is 30 percent of monthly adjusted family income. See section 3(a) of the United States Housing Act of 1937.

Total development costs—The sum of all HUD-approved costs for planning, administration, site acquisition, relocation, demolition, construction and equipment, interest and carrying charges, on-site streets and utilities, nondwelling facilities, a contingency allowance, insurance premiums, off-site facilities, any initial operating deficit, and all other costs necessary to develop the project.

Troubled housing—Rental or cooperative housing project receiving assistance from HUD under section 201 of the Housing and Community Development Amendments of 1978 to restore financial soundness, improve management, and maintain the low and moderate income character of the project.

GLOSSARY

Turnkey housing—Housing initially financed and built by private sponsors and purchased upon completion by public housing agencies for use by lower income families under the public housing program.

Unit of general local government—A general purpose political subdivision of a State, such as a county, city, township, town, or village.

Urban county—For purposes of the CDBG and UDAG programs, generally refers to a county in a metropolitan area that has a combined population of not less than 200,000.

Urban development action grant—A grant made to an urban county, city, or unincorporated portion of an urban county under section 119 of the Housing and Community Development Act of 1974.

Urban homesteading—Program of HUD transfers of unoccupied residences under section 810 of the Housing and Community Development Act of 1974 to individuals or families without any substantial consideration where the individuals or families agree to occupy the residences not less than 5 years and to make repairs and improvements required to meet health and safety standards within certain time limits. Under a demonstration multifamily homestead-ing program, HUD transfers properties to local governments for conversion or rehabilitation to use primarily as housing for lower income families.

Urban renewal—Elimination and prevention of the development or spread of slums and blight, including slum clearance and redevelopment, or rehabilitation and conservation, assisted by HUD advances, loans, and grants under title I of the Housing Act of 1949. Program is being terminated under the provisions of title I of the Housing and Community Development Act of 1974.

Usury laws—Laws limiting the maximum rate of interest that may be charged on a loan.

Vacancy rate—In reference to dwelling units, the percentage of the total dwelling units in an area that are vacant and available for residence.

Variable interest rate—A means by which a lender is permitted to adjust the interest rate on a loan to reflect changes in the prime rateusually within a prescribed range and with advanced notice.

Very low-income family—Generally, a family whose income does not exceed 50 percent of the median family income of the area involved.

Voucher demonstration—Demonstration program of rental assistance under section 8(o) of the United States Housing Act of 1937. Assistance payments are provided for an eligible family based on the difference between the payment standard established by the Secretary for the area involved and 30 percent of the family's monthly adjusted income. The tenant contribution is the difference between the rent negotiated by the family and the amount of the monthly assistance payment.

www.ingramcontent.com/pod-product-compliance
Lightning Source LLC
Chambersburg PA
CBHW081812300426
44116CB00014B/2331